MIXING & MASTERING
2ND EDITION
Bill Gibson

HAL LEONARD RECORDING METHOD, BOOK 6

Hal Leonard Books

An Imprint of Hal Leonard Corporation

180414

Copyright © 2007, 2012 by William A. Gibson
All rights reserved. No part of this book may be reproduced in any form, without written permission, except by a newspaper or magazine reviewer who wishes to quote brief passages in connection with a review.

Second edition published in 2012 by
Hal Leonard Books
An Imprint of Hal Leonard Corporation
7777 West Bluemound Road
Milwaukee, WI 53213

Trade Book Division Editorial Offices
33 Plymouth St., Montclair, NJ 07042

First edition published in 2007 by Hal Leonard Books

Printed in the United States of America

Book design, illustrations, and DVD audio and video production by Bill Gibson
Front cover photo courtesy of Steve Burdick/Westlake Recording Studios & Technical Services
Library of Congress Cataloging-in-Publication Data is available upon request.
ISBN 978-1-4584-0297-4
www.halleonardbooks.com

Acknowledgments

To all the folks who have helped support the development and integrity of these books. Thank you for your continued support and interest in providing great tools for us all to use.

- Acoustic Sciences, Inc.
- AKG
- Antares
- Apple Computer
- Audio-Technica
- Avid
- Jamie Dieveney: Vocals, songwriting, friendship
- Eugene Bien: Piano
- Doug Gould: Worship MD
- Faith Ecklund: Vocals, songwriting, inspiration
- Gibson Guitars
- IK Multimedia
- JBL Pro: Peter Chaikin, Joseph Wagoner, and Alfred Reinprecht
- Mike Kay: Ted Brown Music
- London Bridge Studios: Geoff Ott, Jonathan Plum, Stephen Michael Hogan
- Monster Cable
- John Morton: Guitar and stories
- Native Instruments
- Ben O'Brien: Production Assistant
- Primacoustic Studio Acoustics
- PreSonus
- Radial Engineering
- Robbie Ott
- Roger Wood
- Royer Labs
- Sabian Cymbals
- Shure
- Spectrasonics
- T.C. Electronic
- TC Helicon
- Taye Drums
- Universal Audio
- Waves
- Yamaha

Contents

Audio and Video Examples xi

Preface xvii

Chapter 1: Getting Ready 1
Conceptualizing the Mix 1
Documenting the Mix 3
    Track Sheet 3
    Mix Sheets 4
    Lyric Sheet 5
Virtual Track Sheets and Metadata 6
Basic Setup Procedure 10
Bounce to Hard Drive 10
    Digital Recording Hardware 12
Sync Devices 13

Chapter 2: Analog and Digital Considerations 17
Analog Tape Recorders 18
    Analog Tape 20
    Analog Tape Speed 22
Connecting the Digital Mixer and the Mix Recorder 22
    Digital Format 22
    Cables 23
Connecting the Analog Mixer and Mix Recorder 24
    Connecting the Mixer and Recorder 24
    Matching Levels and Impedance 26
Getting the Recorder Ready: Cleaning and Demagnetizing 26
    Demagnetizing the Analog Tape Machine 27
    Cleaning the Analog Recorder 29
    Tones on the Analog Recorder 30
    Tones on the Digital Recorder 32
Playback and Record Alignment and Equalization 32
    Record EQ 33
    Calibration Tones 33
    Reference Tone 35
Media Selection: CD, DVD, and Magnetic Tape 36
    Magnetic Tape 36
    CD and DVD Media 36
    Comparison of Reflective Surfaces 37
    Storing Magnetic Tape 37
Time Code 39
    Striping SMPTE 40
    Getting the Sequencer to Follow SMPTE 41
Starting the Mix: Zeroing the Board 42
Outboard Gear to Have on Hand 42

Chapter 3: Monitoring 47

Characteristics of an Excellent Studio Monitor 47
- Balanced Frequency Response 47
- Monitor Proximity 48
- Excellent Transient Response 48
- Low Distortion 48
- Efficient Power 50
- Durability and Efficiency 50
- The Right Monitor for You 52
- Multiple Sets of Monitors 52

The Mixing Environment 57
- The Room 57
- Dimensions and Angles 58
- Absorption 58
- Portable Acoustic Solutions 59

Setting Up Your Monitor System 60
- Monitoring Configurations 60
- The Real-Time Analyzer (RTA) 67

Tracking and the Mixdown 68
Comparison to Other Projects 68

Chapter 4: Mixing Theories 73

Mix Approach 73
The Arrangement 74
Signs of an Amateur Musical Recording 76
- Lack of Consistent Focal Point 77
- No Contrast 77
- Excessively Wide Dynamic Range 77
- Low Levels 77
- Noisy, Dull, and Lifeless Mixes 79
- Level-Dominating Outbursts 79
- Distant, Sterile Mixes That Lack Intimacy 80
- Dull and Uninteresting Sounds 80
- Unsatisfactory Instrumental Solo Levels 80

Characteristics of a Good Mix 81
- Strong, Solid, Yet Controlled Lows 81
- Mids Distributed Evenly Among Various Instruments 81
- Strong, Smooth Highs That Are Easy To Listen To 81
- Balance 82
- Depth 82
- Width 82
- Momentum 82
- Consistent Playback Quality 83
- Sounds Good in Stereo, Surround, and Mono 83
- Consistent Focal Point throughout the Song 83
- Controlled and Appropriate Use of Effects 83

Motion	83
Inclusion of Acoustic Information	84
Simplicity	84
Mixing Styles	84
East Coast (New York)	86
West Coast (Los Angeles)	86
Southern (Nashville)	86
European (London)	87
Mix-Building Concepts	87
Ineffective Approaches to Mixing	87
Using Dynamics Processors to Create a Blend	88
Arranging during Mixdown	90
Multiple Mixes	90
Mix Versions	91
Stems	94
Different Mixes	95

Chapter 5: Imaging 99

The Spherical Approach to Panning and Positioning	100
Speaker Position and Choice	103
Mic Techniques	103
Panning	110
Reverberation	114
Space in a Space	117
Combining Wet and Dry	119
Delay	120
Panning	123
Chorus, Flanger, and Phase Shifter Effects	125
Monitors and Your Stereo Image	126

Chapter 6: Mixing 129

Equalization: The Cumulative Effect	130
Combining EQ	130
Allocating EQ across the Audible Spectrum	132
Fitting the Puzzle Together	132
Practicing	132
Sweeping a Peak to Find a Problem	132
Basic Procedures for Building the Mix	133
Drums	134
Combining an Excellent Drum Kit and an Excellent Drummer	134
Kick Drum	135
Snare Drum	136
Live Toms	136
Drum Set Overheads (Live)	137
Drum Machines, Sound Modules, and Sample Libraries	137

Bass Guitar 140
Mixing Guitars 141
    Acoustic Guitar 141
    Dynamic Control 142
    Electric Guitar 143
    Keyboards 145
Lead Vocal 147
    Intonation 149
    Compression 152
    Expander 152
    Vocal EQ 153
    Exciter 153
    Simple Delay 153
    Add Backing Vocals 154
Rhythmic Keyboards and Rhythm Guitars 156
    Filling in the Holes with the Guitar or Keys 156
Lead Lines and Solo Parts 157

Chapter 7: Automation 163

Analog Mixer Automation Systems 163
    VCA-Based Automation 164
    Automation Data Time Reference 164
Digital Mixer Automation Systems 165
Basic Automation Types 166
    Snapshot Automation 166
    Dynamic Automation 166
Automation Parameters 167
    Mutes 169
    Pan 169
    Function of Fader Motors in the Digital Domain 170
    Graphic Automation 170
    Snapshot Automation 171
Operational Procedures 172
    Saving 173
    Undo and Redo 174
    Building Automation 176
Software Plug-Ins 178
Mix Procedure Using Automation 179
    Inserts 179
    Write Mutes 180
Documenting the Mix 180
    Outboard Gear Without Patch-Storage Capabilities 181
    Locate Points and Markers 181
Copy Moves and Settings 182
Digital/Plug-In Equalization 182
Dynamic Control and Special Effects 183
Automation Data Storage Format 184
Audio Storage Formats 184

  Hard Disk 184
  DAT 185
  CD or DVD Recorder 186
VU Mix Levels 186
Peak Level 187
Fades 187
Summary 189

Chapter 8: Pulling It Together 193

Predetermine the Mix Density 193
Develop Your Own Sonic Signature 195
Blending the Drums and Bass 196
Blending Electric Guitars 197
Blending Acoustic Guitars 197
  Simple Acoustic Production 198
  Acoustic Guitar with the Band 198
Creating the Lead Vocal Sound 199
  Intelligibility 199
  Clarity 199
  Consistent Audibility 200
  Dominance of the Appropriate Mix Space 200
Perfectly Controlling Ambience 200
Appropriate Vocal Balance with the Instrumentation 201
Procedures for Creating a Good Lead Vocal Sound 202
  Compression 202
  Equalization 203
  Effects 204
Blending Backing Vocals 205
  Level Control 205
  Equalization 206
  Find the Melody 206
  Watch Out for the High Parts 207
  Thin the Thick and Thicken the Thin 207
  Don't Over-Bass the Bass 207
  Panning 208
  Compression/Limiting 209
Emphasize the Important Ingredients 209
Eliminate Unimportant Ingredients 210
Include High, Mid, and Low Frequencies 210
  High Frequencies in the Mix 210
  Midrange Frequencies in the Mix 211
  Low Frequencies in the Mix 211
Classic Recordings: How'd They Do That? 211
Surround Mixing 216
  Layout 218
  Mixdown Formats 219
  Surround Master Track Assignments 221
  Stereo Compatibility 222

Chapter 9: Getting Ready to Master 225

Preparing the Analog Master 227
    Tools for Razorblade Editing..228
    Procedure for Razorblade Editing..230
Preparing the Digital Master 235
    Selecting the Edit Point...235
    Shortening, Lengthening, and Replacing...236
Sequencing the Album/Song Order 236
    Spacing between Songs...237
    Save It for the Mastering Engineer...237
Timing Issues for Tape and Vinyl 238
Stereo Master Preparation Considerations 239
    Technical Notes 240
    Reference Tones..242
Surround Considerations..242
    Lossy Versus Lossless...243

Chapter 10: Mastering 247

To Master or Not to Master 248
    Should You Do Your Own Mastering? 249
    What's the Advantage to Doing Your Own Mastering at Home? 249
    The Advantage to Hiring an Experienced Mastering Engineer 250
Acoustic Considerations...250
Monitoring 252
    Speakers..252
    Volume 253
Digital Versus Analog...253
    Should You Use a Digital or an Analog Source for Mastering?............................253
Mastering to Error-Correcting Recorders 254
    Errors 255
    Data Protection 255
Digital Modeling..256
Cabling Considerations..256
    Some Cable Theory..256
    Do Cables Really Sound Different?...258
    Digital-Interconnect Cables..260
Assembling the Album..262
Equalizing 263
    Air...263
    Highs 264
    Mids 264
    De-Essing..264
    Lows 264
    Software Versus Hardware Equalizers 265
Noise Reduction 265
Real-Time Analyzer (RTA)...266

- Acoustical RTA Measurements ... 267
- Electronic Evaluation of Frequency Content ... 268

Levels ... 269
- Normalize ... 269
- Real Versus Apparent Levels ... 269
- The Highpass Filter ... 272

Image Enhancement and Reverberation ... 272

Limiting: How to Sound Loud ... 274
- How Hot Is Hot Enough? ... 275
- Software Versus Hardware Limiting ... 276

De-Essing ... 276

The CD-Mastering Environment ... 278
- Write Modes ... 278
- Red Book ... 278
- Scarlet Book ... 279
- Yellow Book ... 280
- Green Book ... 280
- Orange Book, Parts I and II ... 280
- White Book ... 281
- Blue Book/CD-Extra ... 281
- PQ Subcodes ... 281
- ISRC Code ... 281
- Emphasis ... 282
- SCMS ... 282
- Track Number ... 282
- Indexes ... 283
- Noise Shaping ... 283
- Image Files ... 283
- Dither ... 284

A Systematic Approach to the Mastering Process ... 286

Summary ... 286

Index ... 291

Test Answers ... 298

Audio and Video Examples

Video Example 2-1	30
Cleaning and Demagnetizing the Analog Tape Path	
Audio Example 2-1	31
Oscillator-Generated Sine Waves	
Audio Example 2-2	31
1,000-Hz Tone	
Audio Example 2-3	41
SMPTE Time Code	
Video Example 3-1	68
RTA Studio	
Audio Example 4-1	95
Complete Mix	
Audio Example 4-2	95
Minimalist Mix	
Audio Example 4-3	95
Band Stem	
Audio Example 4-4	95
Vocal Stem	
Video Example 5-1	104
Reamping Electric Guitar	
Video Example 5-2	104
Reamping Acoustic Drums	
Audio Example 5-1	105
X-Y Configuration	
Audio Example 5-2	106
Spaced Omni Pair	
Audio Example 5-3	107
Spaced Omni Pair with a Baffle	
Audio Example 5-4	107
The Crossed Bidirectional Configuration	
Audio Example 5-5	108
Mid-Side Configuration	
Audio Example 5-6	110
Mono Mix	
Audio Example 5-7	110
Guitar Right, Keyboard Left	

Audio Example 5-8 Splitting the Bass	112
Audio Example 5-9 Distracting Pan Position	113
Audio Example 5-10 Panning the Triangle	113
Audio Example 5-11 Adding the Cowbell	113
Audio Example 5-12 Snare Reverberation	114
Audio Example 5-13 Mono Reverberation	114
Audio Example 5-14 Moving the Drum Around the Room	116
Audio Example 5-15 Moving the Drum Around a Smaller Room	116
Audio Example 5-16 Marimba with Tight Room Reverb	118
Audio Example 5-17 Marimba with Large Hall Reverb	118
Audio Example 5-18 Marimba Next to the Concert Hall Door	118
Audio Example 5-19 Stereo Images	118
Audio Example 5-20 The Roaming Guitar	119
Audio Example 5-21 Low Pad, High Strings	120
Audio Example 5-22 Reverb on the Low Pad	120
Audio Example 5-23 Reverb on the High Strings	120
Audio Example 5-24 Creating a Stereo Guitar Sound	120
Audio Example 5-25 Short Delays from Mono to Stereo	121

Audio Example 5-26	123
Fine-Tuning the 25-ms Delay for Mono	
Audio Example 5-27	123
Fine-Tuning the 50-ms Delay for Mono	
Audio Example 5-28	124
Equalizing the Stereo Split	
Audio Example 5-29	124
17-ms Delay	
Audio Example 5-30	124
15-ms Delay	
Audio Example 5-31	124
11-ms Delay	
Audio Example 5-32	124
7-ms Delay	
Audio Example 5-33	125
3-ms Delay	
Video Example 6-1	133
Equalization Techniques	
Video Example 6-2	137
Building the Drum Set Sound	
Video Example 6-3	143
Building the Acoustic Guitar Sound	
Video Example 6-4	145
Building the Electric Guitar Sound	
Video Example 6-5	154
Building the Lead Vocal Sound	
Video Example 6-6	156
Building the Backing Vocal Sound	
Audio Example 7-1	189
Seven-Second Fade	
Audio Example 7-2	189
Ten-Second Fade	
Audio Example 7-3	189
Fifteen-Second Fade	
Audio Example 7-4	189
Five-Second Fade	

Audio Example 8-1 Build the Drum Sound	196
Audio Example 8-2 Kick Tone	196
Audio Example 8-3 Building the Drum and Bass Mix	196
Video Example 8-1 Building the Drum and Bass Mix	196
Audio Example 8-4 Several Amps Combined to One Sound	197
Audio Example 8-5 One Guitar Track Blended into the Mix	197
Audio Example 8-6 Simple Acoustic Production	198
Audio Example 8-7 Acoustic Guitar Blended with the Band	199
Video Example 8-2 Mixing the Lead Vocal	204
Video Example 8-3 Adding the Vocals to the Mix	209
Video Example 9-1 Performing Edits	236
Audio Example 10-1 Comparison of First- to Sixth-Generation DAT	254
Audio Example 10-2 Mic on Acoustic Guitar Using Common Mic Cable and then Monster Studio Pro 1000 Cable	259
Audio Example 10-3 Vocal Using Common Mic Cable and then Monster Studio Pro 1000 Cable	259
Audio Example 10-4 AES/EBU to DAT Using Common Cable and then SP1000 AES Silver Digital Monster Cable	260
Audio Example 10-5 S/P DIF to DAT Using Common RCA Cables and then M1000 D Silver Digital Monster Cable	260
Audio Example 10-6 Analog Out to DAT Using Common XLR Cables and then Prolink Studio Pro 1000 XLR Monster Cables	260
Audio Example 10-7 ADAT Light Pipe into Digital Performer Using Common Optical Cable, Bounced to Disk	260

Audio Example 10-8 — 261
ADAT Light Pipe into Digital Performer Using Monster Cable's Interlink Digital Light Speed 100 Optical Cable, Bounced to Disk

Audio Example 10-9 — 264
Reference Mix (No EQ)

Audio Example 10-10 — 264
Air Increased and then Decreased at 18 kHz

Audio Example 10-11 — 265
Highs Increased and then Decreased at 5 kHz

Audio Example 10-12 — 265
Mids Increased and then Decreased at 400 Hz

Audio Example 10-13 — 265
Lows Increased and then Decreased at 60 Hz

Video Example 10-1 — 267
Noise Reduction, Metering, and the RTA

Video Example 10-2 — 273
Widening the Stereo Image

Audio Example 10-14 — 275
Normal Mix

Audio Example 10-15 — 275
3-dB Louder Waves L3 Multimaximizer

Audio Example 10-16 — 275
6-dB Louder Waves L3 Multimaximizer

Audio Example 10-17 — 275
9-dB Louder Waves L3 Multimaximizer

Video Example 10-3 — 277
Using the De-Esser

Preface

Welcome to the sixth book in the *Hal Leonard Recording Method by Bill Gibson*. This edition is packed with information you need to know about developing a professional-sounding mix that compares favorably to the recordings you hear on your favorite CDs, DVDs, and media presentations. Learn some tested techniques for creating high-quality music using modern technology.

If you enjoy great music and appreciate creativity, emotion, and passion, you must develop formidable mixing skills. Additionally, it is very important that you understand the mastering process. Mastering is to music as polishing is to a gemstone. If you hold an attractive rock in your hand, it's probably obvious that it has a unique and appealing character. Once that rock is polished, much of the beauty that resided in the natural formation shines through the roughness, revealing the depth and beauty that were there all along—even though they were hidden by natural roughness. It's also important to note that mixing and mastering are subjective activities. Like any art, one man's masterpiece can easily be another man's trash. There are, though, certain points of agreement in the mixing and mastering process:

- It's good to have an even tonal balance of low, mid, and high frequencies.
- There should be an evenly balanced feel between the left and right channels.
- Changes in texture help create an interesting mix that can better hold a listener's interest.
- It's best when a mix sounds good on many different sound systems and at all volume levels.
- Mastering can help bring more life into the mix and it can help an album of songs feel like they belong together; however, the mix engineer shouldn't rely on the mastering engineer to fix his or her work.

The topics covered in this book are very important in music production today. If the music you produce in your studio doesn't sound professional and impressive, there is very little chance that it will receive the attention and recognition that it should. There is absolutely no reason to start a musical project if you don't intend to do the very best job possible all the way through the process. A great mixdown can dramatically increase the power and impact of any musical work. A poorly executed mixdown can easily destroy the power and impact of any musical work.

Expend a lot of creative and technical energy in the pursuit of recording excellent audio tracks—it will make your mixing job easier. However, if you must budget and precisely allocate time reserves throughout a production, leave ample time for mixdown. There is nothing that crushes creative potential more effectively than a shabby attempt at an amateurish mixdown.

The techniques and procedures described in this book provide time-tested tools to help you create mixes that compete well in the musical marketplace. Carefully implement the information presented herein. Constantly evaluate your work. Listen to your mixing and mastering efforts on every system you have. Make minute changes to the mix after you've evaluated them, and then evaluate them again.

The explanations and examples in this book will help you, whether you're operating in your home studio or in a professional recording facility. There is a lot involved with music production both technologically and artistically. And, the more types of technologies you incorporate in your productions, the more you should gain a greater understanding of those technologies. You must know enough about your tools to get the most out of them in the pursuit of high-quality musical productions. In this age, technological advances are commonplace—often, they seem to happen on a daily basis. The information in this book will help you optimize your current setup, and it just might reveal some tools that you can add to your system in order to increase your productivity. In addition, the topics covered in this book hold great potential for supporting the artistic and creative vision that is yours alone.

It's exciting that our tools are getting better and better. The good news is that almost anyone can develop a system capable of producing hit-quality audio—that's also the bad news. If you're going to have an edge in an increasingly competitive industry like music and audio, you must get both your technical and artistic acts together. It's imperative. In the professional music and recording world, we all need to continually increase our skills and knowledge—the process of repeatedly taking what we're capable of to the next level is both mandatory and exhilarating.

THE ACCOMPANYING DVD-ROM

All media examples can be found on the accompanying DVD-ROM and online at www.hlrmonline.com. Stream the examples online for super-easy access or, if you prefer, import all of the full-resolution media from the DVD-ROM directly into iTunes or any other full-featured media player for easy playback. This is especially convenient when you're on the go with your laptop, tablet device, or smartphone and unable to connect to the Internet.

All Audio and Video Examples are produced specifically to support the concepts and principles presented in the printed text, with the examples clearly marked in each chapter. The Audio Examples demonstrate many of the concepts that are explained in the text and accompanying illustrations. The Video Examples show you specifically how to build your skills. They are very powerful and they're produced with your education in mind. You won't find a lot of rapid-motion, highly stylized shots; you will find easy-to-understand instructional video that is edited for optimal instruction and learning.

·· **Audio Examples**

Audio Examples are indicated like this.

·· **Video Examples**

Video Examples are indicated like this.

QR CODES

Throughout this book, you'll see an occasional QR code. These codes are actually digital links to supporting websites; they're designed to be read by a QR code reader on a smartphone or a tablet computer. Simply download a free QR code reader app, show the code to the smart device's camera, and the supporting link will automatically show up in its browser.

QR codes are a convenient way to quickly delve deeper into the supporting material used to help create this work. Once you have your QR code reader, let your smart device scan this QR code to be taken directly to the support site for the *Hal Leonard Recording Method*.

CHAPTER TESTS

Each chapter ends with a 20-question test. These tests are designed to help reinforce the information you've learned. Retake the tests until you're sure that you understand the concepts presented in each chapter. The knowledge presented throughout this method is cumulative. If you understand each chapter, you will be able to function well in the world of high-quality audio.

SUMMARY

I'm excited to share this information with you. Mixing and mastering are a huge part of the recording world. Take advantage of the vast array of tools available—build productions that express your creativity and emotional passion. Use technology to serve your musical and emotional soul. Provide a production that other like-minded folks can identify with and support.

Above all, have fun producing great music!

Getting Ready

CHAPTER 1

CHAPTER AT A GLANCE

Conceptualizing the Mix 1
Documenting the Mix 3
Track Sheet 3
Mix Sheets 4
Lyric Sheet 5
Virtual Track Sheets and Metadata 6
Basic Setup Procedure 10
Bounce to Hard Drive 10
Digital Recording Hardware 12
Sync Devices 13

There are hundreds of details to consider during mixdown. At first these factors are a bit overwhelming; however, if you develop an organized and fundamental routine for documenting and constructing your mix, you'll soon find yourself in control and fully functional.

Follow the creative path deliberately from conceptualization to implementation. It's important that you develop a preconceived notion of what the mix will be like at the end of the process. It's also important that you construct a plan for achieving the concept and that you follow it closely while remaining open to new creative directions when they present themselves.

CONCEPTUALIZING THE MIX

Even though each song is built during the tracking process and the creative vision is largely formed already, mixdown provides an opportunity to select the best mix ingredients and to fine-tune the balance, blend, and effects so the music sounds professional and polished. Rarely do you actually incorporate every ingredient that was tracked into the final mix. Many creative decisions are made during the mixdown process about which tracks to eliminate during the mixdown process. However, the more experience you gain in the recording and producing processes, the better you'll be at predicting what will be in the final mix.

It helps to make notes about your vision for the final mix. Compare the sound you envision to that of other artists. If you keep in mind that your goal is to create a mix that resembles a Beatles song, you'll find greater focus and a more decisive mix direction. A Steely Dan sound would lead you in a completely different direction, and an Incubus sound in yet another direction. Settling on a foundational sound will help provide you with direction during mixdown. In addition, if others are involved in the mix process, this simple comparison quickly gets everyone on the same creative page.

Planning Chart

Use this chart to help plan the number of tracks you'll need to get the desired final sound. Your song might have totally unique requirements. Try to anticipate as many of the features of your particular piece of music as possible.

This type of preplanning will help calculate what it'll take to get the sound you want. Even if tracks are unlimited, preparing for the entire arrangement and production helps provide an intelligent use of your existing resources.

If you're working in an environment with a finite number of available tracks, this type of preparation could be the only way to achieve the sound your music deserves.

Ingredients	Sounds Required		Track Count
Type of sound for final product	❏ Pop rock ❏ Orchestral ❏ Brass band ❏ Grunge	❏ Country ❏ R & B ❏ Jazz ❏ Other	
Lead vocal	❏ Solo ❏ Solo with overlapping lines	❏ Duet	
Guitar sound	❏ Acoustic ❏ Dist. rhythm ❏ Stereo ❏ Nylon string	❏ Clean electric ❏ Dist. lead ❏ Mono ❏ Other	
Piano	❏ Acoustic ❏ Rhodes-type ❏ Mono	❏ Electric grand ❏ Stereo ❏ Other	
Synth	❏ Strings ❏ Bells ❏ Stereo ❏ Special effects	❏ Brass ❏ Analog synth ❏ Mono ❏ Other	
Drums	❏ Kick ❏ Toms ❏ Crash ❏ Special effects	❏ Snare ❏ Ride ❏ Hi-hat ❏ Other	
Percussion	❏ Triangle ❏ Conga ❏ Bongos ❏ Special effects	❏ Claves ❏ Tambourine ❏ Shaker ❏ Other	
Backing vocals	❏ Single Part ❏ Sm. group mono ❏ Sm. group stereo ❏ Massive live	❏ Sm. group stereo ❏ Lg. group stereo ❏ Layered ❏ Other	
Solos	❏ Guitar ❏ Sax ❏ Flute	❏ Keyboard ❏ Trumpet ❏ Other	
Hand claps	❏ Large stereo	❏ Small mono	
Sound effects	❏ Stereo	❏ Mono	
Time code	❏ SMPTE	❏ Sync pulse	
Sequenced parts running from time code	❏ Keys ❏ Guitars ❏ Percussion ❏ Sound effects	❏ Synth ❏ Drums ❏ Solos ❏ Other	

Once the vision is set and agreed upon, follow the procedures outlined in this book to build an excellent mix. This should be a starting point for your personal creative style. The routines I mention are time-tested and commonly used in the recording industry; however, your style will develop over time. Be open to these ideas and always look for better ways to develop your own music. Primarily, eliminate randomness from your mixing regimen while increasing focused musical creativity.

DOCUMENTING THE MIX

Keep good records. There is typically a point during the mix where the sheer volume of details becomes overwhelming. Even if you are perfectly in control throughout the mixing process, there is a strong likelihood that the song you work on today could be shelved for days, weeks, months, or years. If you take great notes today, in the future you'll be able to quickly pick up right where you left off. As you stick with the recording industry, such scenarios will confront you. If you've been conscientious in documenting the recordings, you will look like a genius.

Track Sheet

It's important to start with a good track sheet or track list. During tracking you should have taken great notes, so there should not be any questions about which ingredients are on each track. In many situations, there might be multiple instruments or voices on a single track. Your track sheet should indicate exactly which ingredient has been recorded and where. Always reference tracking combinations to an accurate recorder counter or, preferably, to time code.

If the track sheet is sketchy or inaccurate, spend the time to listen through each track. Note any combinations of instruments, voices, or effects along with noises such as pops, clicks, or buzzes. Reference these instances relative to the recorder counter or time code.

Even in the digital domain, a paper track sheet is very useful. Most software-based digital recorders allow for comments on each track, and many provide actual track sheet utilities. Print out the track sheet or start a new paper track sheet—just be sure to leave plenty of room for notes.

Mixing & Mastering .... by BILL GIBSON

Traditional Studio Track Sheets

If you exclusively use a DAW, your need for physical track sheets might be limited. However, the organizational system within the software functions to keep a record of each track and its pertinent information. There is typically a field for comments, which serves as a perfect area to store specific information that will be necessary if the mix needs to be restored.

If you are using an analog or digital tape-based multitrack recorder, the use of track sheets is a necessity. Keep meticulous records of track contents. If various ingredients share a track, mark the entrance time for each ingredient.

The traditional studio track sheet was developed to fill the needs of a 24-track professional studio. Many studios print these on 11 × 17–inch paper to maximize the space available for record keeping.

This track sheet can be downloaded as a PDF file from *The Hal Leonard Recording Method* Support area of www.billgibsonmusic.com.

Mix Sheets

Sometimes all of the mix details will fit neatly on the track sheet. But most of the time it's most efficient to create a mix sheet with all of the most important tracking information and plenty of room for keeping track of mix data.

Digital recording consoles and high-powered DAWs remember and recall all of the internally configured mix patching, routing, and effects settings. Even in such a system, there are variables that should be noted. If you expect to recreate any mixdown for minor changes and touch-ups, you must make precise notes on all externally patched processors, sound module settings, auxiliary effects, and so on. Take note of all pertinent settings. Indicate:

- Input and output levels of outboard gear.
- Input trim settings on channels with external devices connected.
- Any parameter settings and adjustments during the mixdown.
- Effects settings and parameters.

- Pan positions,
- Sub master assignments and level settings.
- Specific fader, pan, aux level, EQ, or routing changes that are physically performed during the mixdown.
- Automation information, such as effects selected, subgroups, input trim levels, or any other information that might not be recalled in a snapshot or real-time automation.

Lyric Sheet

A lyric sheet is very useful. Mark your moves with the tape counter number by the lyric. It's easier for most musically inclined engineers to follow lyrics than just

Non-Traditional Studio Track Sheets

The track sheet in this illustration is a diversion from the traditional track sheet. It serves to optimize the amount of information that can be logged when a project uses several tracks and a combination of recording formats.

There is nothing wrong with keeping too many notes about a recording process; however when it's time to reconstruct a mix, just to fix a couple problems, insufficient session notes pose a cumbersome difficulty.

Track sheets that are in list format are very conducive to use on a computer. If your production utilizes a DAW in combination with a hardware multitrack, these track sheets are a perfect choice. Keep them easily accessible on your studio computer and use them to maintain an excellent record of your project.

This track sheet and others are available for download in the Hal Leonard Recording Method Support area of www.billgibsonmusic.com.

Track Sheet · page 1

Track	Instrument	Playback Source	FX 1	FX 2	Notes
1	Kick insde	Studer analog			
2	Kick outside	Studer analog			
3	Snare top	Studer analog	TC		P#123
4	Snare bottom	Studer analog	Lex		P#04
5	Hi tom	Studer analog			
6	Mid tom	Studer analog			
7	Low tom	Studer analog			
8	OH hat side	Studer analog			
9	OH ride side	Studer analog			
10	Hat	Studer analog			
11	Room hat side	Studer analog			
12	Room ride side	Studer analog			
13	Bass Guitar Radial J48	Pro Tools			
14	Strat: Marshall close 421	Pro Tools	Delay		P#34 (289 ms)
15	Strat: Marshall distant M49	Pro Tools			
16	PRS: Matchless close Beta 57	Pro Tools			
17	Acoustic Guitar hole	Pro Tools			
18	Acoustic Guitar neck	Pro Tools			
19	Conga L	Pro Tools			
20	Conga R	Pro Tools			
21	Wind Chimes, Tambourine	Pro Tools			
22	Shaker	Pro Tools			
23	Triangle	Pro Tools			
24	Lead Vocal take 1	Pro Tools			
25	Lead Vocal take 2	Pro Tools			
26	BGV	Pro Tools			
27	BGV	Pro Tools			
28	BGV	Pro Tools			

Mixing & Mastering .... by BILL GIBSON

Mix Sheet

Modern technology makes great use of computer-assisted automation during mixdown; however, there are many instances where an analog mixer is used without automation. The mix sheet provides a way to log fader moves over the timeline.

This mix sheet provides a grid that can be marked for specific mix changes, including fader moves, EQ changes, aux adjustments, changes of outboard equipment settings, an so on. In relation to an automated digital mixdown, this process seems archaic, but it does a good job of providing assistance when performing a manual mixdown.

Many experienced and very successful mix engineers prefer to perform manual mixes because they believe the intuitive process of mixing on the fly produces more energetic and powerful mixes.

Other mix sheets should be used for other necessary mix moves and settings, such as effects settings, aux sends, pan positions, and so on.

Song Title:			Mixmeister:			Date:	
Time	Fader Move	EQ Change	Aux	Aux	Aux	Outboard	Other
:32	14 to -7						
:45		-2 @ 3k					
1:10			up to -5				

numbers. For some, a simple list of counter numbers with specific notes in the order they occur is the ideal approach.

If a fader or any other control is constantly moving from one position to another, mark the two or three positions on the board with a grease pencil. These marks are easily removed and provide instant visual cues. If a fader moves between two positions, it's also efficient to place tape below the lower fader position and above the upper position to use as bumpers. Everyone develops a preference for how he or she works best. Try several approaches and use the one that works best for you. Organization is the key.

VIRTUAL TRACK SHEETS AND METADATA

Though paper track sheets, lyric sheets, and mix sheets are valuable, they have become most valuable as a backup to stored data. The modern DAW somewhat

Lyric Sheet

Use up and down arrows to indicate instrumental or vocal level changes. Circle the lyrics where the changes should occur. It is also very convenient to use numbers to indicate specific fader positions and channel numbers.

Lyric sheets are extremely important in the producing and engineering workflow, whether tracking or mixing. They provide an excellent point of reference when discussing takes and tracks. Mark the timeline location of each musical section on the lyric sheet and also make markers for each musical section in your digital file. A lyric sheet is a fundamental tool in an efficient musical or media production.

forgoes the basic need for a track sheet because the tracks are probably labelled while working through the tracking and mixing process. But don't get lazy just because it seems easy in the moment. As I mentioned before, it is very common for a project to take longer than expected. There might be a call for a remix, or for stems to be built for a game—the list goes on and on. If the track information has been well-documented and properly labelled, there is little problem in ramping right back up to speed , even years later. On the other hand, many engineers, in the moment, figure they'll remember where everything is and don't bother to even label the track names. It is a real time-waster to open a session and find 48 tracks labelled from "Audio 01" to "Audio 48!" Take the time during tracking and mixing to enter precise track names and to enter notes that tell the name of the performer, the piece of equipment, microphone used, and so on.

One of the problems that has arisen out the digital revolution in the recording world is the apparent disappearance of good session documentation. At the highest level, adequate notes and documentation are frequently acquired because many of the participants have grown accustomed to their importance. In the world of digital audio, notes like these are called metadata. Metadata that documents sessions and their participants has become an extremely important consideration. There needs to be a way to identify the participants in a project. Because the revenue model in the music world is changing so rapidly, this metadata might be the only hope that a musician or other contributor can share the revenue stream that's generated by a work.

The Recording Academy Producers and Engineers Wing has worked tirelessly along with the Library of Congress, Sony Music Group, Universal Music Group, BMS Chase, and others to build a solid and reputable system for cataloging this important session data. It is planned that this metadata gathering system will eventually be incorporated directly into the DAW for the easiest possible integration into the creative workflow. This new data collection application is currently called the Content Creator Data Collection Tool (CCD). From the CCD website:

> "The free, cross platform, CCD Collection Tool is designed to make it as easy as possible to gather master media and creative participant metadata in the recording studio, whether a professional facility or a home studio. The Collection Tool also stores metadata about recording locations, dates, times, and recording equipment. Exported metadata populates the relevant fields of the CCD schema as deployed by users."

The data that is gathered must be entered by someone in the creative stream, such as the engineer, producer, assistant, or record label. It includes data about a project, such as:

- Session dates and times
- Artist name/band name
- Song titles
- Lyrics
- Vocalists
- Instrumentalists
- Producers
- Engineers
- Songwriters
- Studio
- Recording format
- Converters

Chapter 1 .... GETTING READY

- DAW program
- Clocking info
- Operating system and version
- Equipment information
- Number of tracks
- Storage media or type of tape
- Take and version numbers
- Percentage splits on applicable fields
- Assistants
- Publishers
- Participants' contact info for proper crediting and payment (email address)

Metadata Collection Tool

The collection of session metadata could be one of the most important current issues in music and media production and recording. The Recording Academy, BMS/Chase, and the Library of Congress have worked closely together to create a metadata collection tool to help those involved in modern recording and media production receive credit and payment for their work.

The entry of metadata is a relatively simple process that promises to become integrated into the modern DAW for seamless integration into the creative workflow.

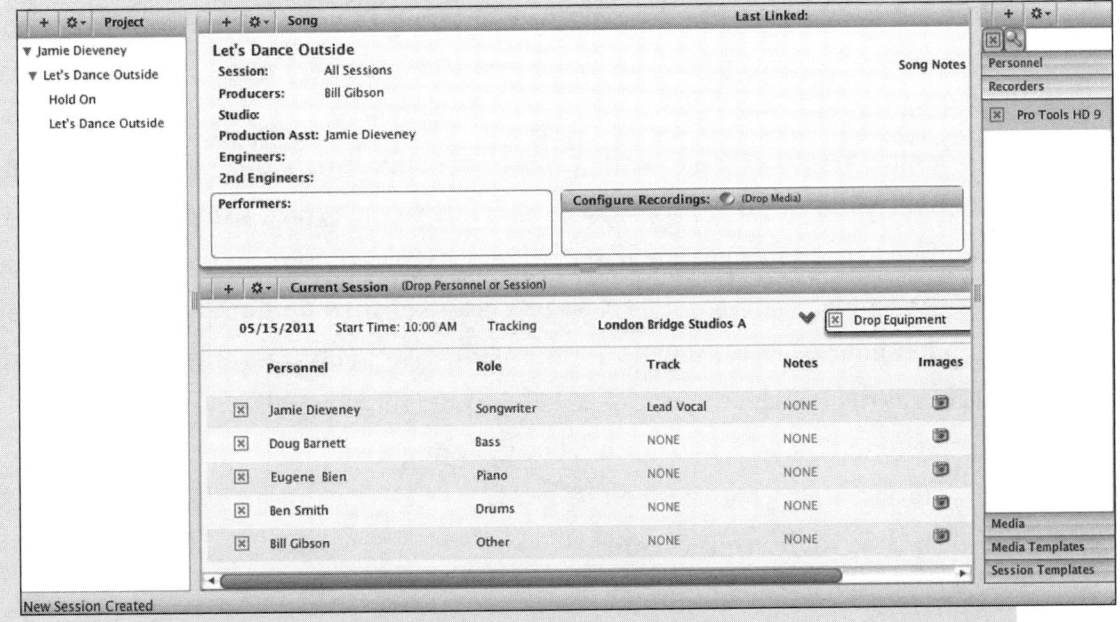

BASIC SETUP PROCEDURE

Modern systems are much more efficient, especially during mixdown. Computer-assisted automation often remembers and replays every possible move made during mixdown. Internal effects and MIDI-controlled devices are also capable of complete automation. However, many engineers still prefer to work with vintage analog equipment and work more by feel than by technology. There is a certain charm and musicality that comes from real people making calculated (although imprecise) changes during mixdown that are performed in relation to a handwritten mix sheet. I've mixed many songs in both automated and manual modes, and although it's a bigger adrenaline rush to be under the wire, actually executing mix changes as the mix runs to the mix recorder, I also appreciate computer-assisted automation, which allows me to go get a cup of coffee while the completed mix is printed to tape, hard drive, or some other storage medium.

BOUNCE TO HARD DRIVE

Digital recording software and hardware DAWs provide the ability to mix the recorded tracks within the computer domain, commonly referred to as "mixing in the box." In other words, mixing, balancing, panning, blending, and applying effects occurs without ever leaving the computer domain. This is a very efficient and accurate way to print your mixes for storage and transfer to the playback medium.

Simply assign all tracks and effects to the appropriate outputs, and the computer will combine all appropriate ingredients to each track using your specifications. For a stereo mix, assign all ingredients to the same stereo pair of outputs or, for a surround mix, assign the tracks to a group of surround outputs and have the computer bounce everything down internally. Stereo outputs are configured with Track 1 as the left channel and Track 2 as the right channel.

Surround outputs in 5.1 are typically configured:
- Track 1: Left front channel
- Track 2: Right front channel
- Track 3: Center channel
- Track 4: Left rear channel

- Track 5: Right rear channel
- Track 6: LFE (sub)

The bounce-to-disk procedure eliminates the need for a dedicated mixdown recorder. It is standard to expect your DAW to provide the ability to insert a limiter or other processing at the end of the mixdown signal path. This way, mastering procedures such as limiting and global equalization can be easily applied during the bouncing process.

Bouncing the Final Mix

If the mix is performed completely within the DAW, bouncing to a connected hard drive provides a means of rendering a high-definition or surround mix without purchasing an expensive mixdown recorder.

In addition, the insertion of high-quality effects, dynamics, and analysis plug-ins vastly extends your sound-shaping capabilities while maintaining ultra-high fidelity. This example inserts a multiband limiter followed by a frequency analyzer. This combination works particularly well on an entire mix or other broadband audio group where it's important to verify an even balance across the frequency spectrum.

Mixing & Mastering .... by BILL GIBSON

Digital Recording Hardware

Digital recording hardware has become inexpensive and very good. CD and DVD recorders are capable of excellent recordings. Purchase a recorder that is capable of recording 24-bit samples and has the ability to sync to an external word clock. If your recorder can sync to high-definition audio formats, you can be somewhat

The Digital Word Clock Master

If you use several digital devices in your recording setup, consider using a high-quality master word clock source. Connect all devices to the master word clock generator so that each device steps through the sample timeline in perfect unity. Erratic or unreliable word clock sync connections result in unwanted pops and clicks as well as system lockups and crashes.

Master sync source provides word clock to all digital devices.

reassured that you'll be satisfied with it throughout the growth and development of digital audio technology.

If you're serious about music and recording, do everything you can to buy for the future: purchase technology that promises to grow with your needs and requirements. At least be informed and keep your purchase decisions in perspective. If you buy for today, your gear could be out of date by mid-afternoon. If you are educated about your technical options, you'll be ahead of the curve. You'll be aware of purchases that are a short-term fulfillment of an immediate need and you'll also be equipped to purchase with future growth in mind. One of the advantages provided by computer-based recording systems is their ability to grow as software manufacturers release updates and revisions.

SYNC DEVICES

If your system includes multiple digital devices, such as a mixer, recorder, audio interface, effects, and other devices, consider using a master word clock interface. Apogee provides a popular digital clock source called Big Ben. This device provides a rock-solid, jitter-free clock source. All digital devices connect to master source, ensuring that they all receive identical, dependable clock information.

In these types of systems it is generally understood that all digital word clock sync cables should be the same length. In practicality, your system will function with multiple sync cables of differing lengths; however, it is ideal and logical that the best communications across the digital network occur when the sync master is at the center of the system, connected to all devices with the highest-quality digital sync cables of the same length.

14

Mixing & Mastering .... by BILL GIBSON

CHAPTER TEST

1. Once the production is prepared for mixdown, virtually all of the creative decisions have already been made.
   a. True
   b. False

2. Using other recordings as a benchmark for the sound you're trying to achieve:
   a. is a creative copout
   b. is not advisable because it detracts from the uniqueness of the artist's musical personality
   c. helps get everyone on the same creative page
   d. Both a and b

3. Over the course of a project, you'll be perceived as a very intelligent person:
   a. if you've acted like you were smarter than everyone else throughout the recording
   b. by other intelligent people
   c. if you've been conscientious about documenting the recording process
   d. once everyone gets to know that you're polite and kind
   e. All of the above

4. A _____ is used to keep track of the contents of hardware recorder tracks.
   a. spreadsheet
   b. hardware report
   c. track record
   d. track sheet

5. If you're working in an environment with a finite number of available tracks, _____ could be the only way to achieve the sound your music deserves.
   a. preplanning
   b. adding more tracks
   c. building a bigger studio
   d. layering

6. _____ are extremely important in the producing and engineering workflow, whether tracking or mixing, because they provide an excellent point of reference when discussing takes and tracks.
   a. Streamers
   b. Lyric sheets
   d. Metadatas
   e. All of the above

7. Track sheets have no purpose in the modern digital workflow.
   a. True
   b. False

8. Mix sheets:
   a. are an indispensable part of the digital creative workflow
   b. are most valuable in analog mixdown sessions
   c. are the scripts that drive the automation in a modern DAW
   d. provide a grid that can be marked for specific mix changes, including fader moves, EQ changes, aux adjustments, and changes of outboard equipment settings
   e. Both b and d

9. One of the problems that has arisen out the digital revolution in the recording world is the apparent disappearance of good session documentation.
   a. True
   b. False

10. When beginning a mixdown it's important that you:
    a. develop a preconceived notion of what the mix will be like at the end of the process
    b. construct a plan for achieving the concept
    c. follow a plan closely while remaining open to new creative directions when they present themselves
    d. All of the above

Chapter 1 .... GETTING READY

11. Since digital files are so quick and easy to access, there is no need to waste time labelling the DAW tracks—they'll be easy to identify if there's ever a need to remix or provide stems.
    a. True
    b. False

12. Because the revenue model in the music world is changing so rapidly, _____ might be the only hope that a musician or other contributor can share in the revenue stream that's generated by a work.
    a. sync rights
    b. metadata
    c. stream tags
    d. All of the above

13. If the mix is performed completely within the DAW, bouncing to a connected hard drive provides a means of _____.
    a. instantly getting your work on the web
    b. getting into the analog domain
    c. rendering a high-definition or surround mix without purchasing an expensive mixdown recorder
    d. All of the above

14. Even with all of the advances in digital technology, many engineers still prefer to work with vintage analog equipment and work more by feel than by technology.
    a. True
    b. False

15. Surround outputs in 5.1 are typically configured:
    a. Track 1: Left front channel, Track 2: Right front channel, Track 3: Center channel, Track 4: Left rear channel, Track 5: Right rear channel, Track 6: LFE (sub)
    b. Track 1: Center channel, Track 2: Left front channel, Track 3: Right front channel, Track 4: Left rear channel, Track 5: Right rear channel, Track 6: LFE (sub)
    c. Track 1: LFE (sub), Track 2: Center channel, Track 3: Left front channel, Track 4: Right front channel, Track 5: Left rear channel, Track 6: Right rear channel
    d. Track 1: Right front channel, Track 2: Left front channel, Track 3: Center channel, Track 4: Right rear channel, Track 5: Left rear channel, Track 6: LFE (sub)

16. The _____ eliminates the need for a dedicated mixdown recorder.
    a. digital sampler
    b. timecode synchronizer
    c. mix-based x-coder
    d. bounce-to-disk procedure

17. Connect all devices to the _____ so that each device steps through the sample timeline in perfect unity.
    a. AC outlet
    b. master word clock generator
    c. MIDI interface
    d. All of the above

18. The best communications across the digital network occur when the sync master is at the center of the system, connected to all devices with the highest-quality digital sync cables of the same length.
    a. True
    b. False

19. Most engineers agree that if you spent the time to track something, it needs to be incorporated in the mix somehow, no matter what.
    a. True
    b. False

20. The data that is gathered must be entered by someone in the creative stream, such as the engineer, producer, assistant, or record label. It includes data about a project, such as:
    a. session dates and times, artist name/band name, studio, recording format, assistants, publishers
    b. song titles, lyrics, vocalists, songwriters, instrumentalists, producers, engineers, percentage splits
    c. converters, DAW program, clocking info, operating system and version
    d. equipment information, number of tracks, storage media or type of tape, take and version numbers
    e. All of the above

Test answers are on page 298

Analog and Digital Considerations

CHAPTER 2

Some engineers prefer to include analog tape recorders in the creative workflow at some point, whether in the beginning during basic tracks or at the end during mixdown. But, it has become extremely rare to find an engineer working exclusively in the analog domain. Editing and tracking overdubs is so efficient and easy inside a DAW that it's difficult to justify the time investment required by a purely analog production chain. When basic tracks are recorded to analog tape, they are almost always bounced immediately into a DAW and sometimes when mixes are completed they're printed onto analog tape. Third-millennium mixdown sessions almost always center around a computer but, more and more, analog tape is a rarity. Analog tape has gotten more and more difficult to find and the price has increased. With the cost of digital media being negligible, it's difficult, on a modern-day recording budget, to justify the cost of multiple multitrack and two-track tapes. The tape cost for a purely analog project can easily approach or surpass $2000!

Whether you choose to print an analog or digital mixdown, it is fundamentally important that you build a mix that is musical, blended, balanced, and emotionally compelling and powerful. However, analog tape and recorders are important enough in the scope of modern recording that they're covered in this book. In the coming years, we'll discover just how long analog tape recording can hang on.

CHAPTER AT A GLANCE

Analog Tape Recorders.....................18
Analog Tape 20
Analog Tape Speed 22
Connecting the Digital Mixer and
  the Mix Recorder 22
Digital Format...................................22
Cables 23
Connecting the Analog Mixer and
  Mix Recorder................................24
Connecting the Mixer and Recorder ..24
Matching Levels and Impedance........26
Getting the Recorder Ready: Cleaning
  and Demagnetizing 26
Demagnetizing the Analog Tape
  Machine 27
Cleaning the Analog Recorder...........29
Tones on the Analog Recorder...........30
Tones on the Digital Recorder 32
Playback and Record Alignment
  and Equalization 32
Record EQ 33
Calibration Tones..............................33
Reference Tone 35
Media Selection: CD, DVD, and
  Magnetic Tape 36
Magnetic Tape 36
CD and DVD Media..........................36
Comparison of Reflective Surfaces 37
Storing Magnetic Tape......................37
Time Code..39
Striping SMPTE 40
Getting the Sequencer to Follow
  SMPTE...41
Starting the Mix: Zeroing the Board...42
Outboard Gear to Have on Hand......42

ANALOG TAPE RECORDERS

As digital technology has built its dominance in the audio world, analog tape recorders are rapidly decreasing in availability. Excellent analog recorders are still at a premium in certain circles, but there is a price to pay for those who still prefer to use them. They are prohibitively expensive for most home recordists and small studios and they require a lot of maintenance. Setting them up demands that a meticulously technical routine be performed on a regular basis—this isn't optional.

The modern recordist has been sheltered, in most instances, from any thoughts about calibration and recorder maintenance, but in order for an analog tape machine to function at an acceptable level of accuracy and reliability it must frequently be aligned and electronically adjusted. Depending on the amount of use the recorder is getting, the heads should be checked for wear and positioning accuracy at least every couple of months. Also, the electronic record and playback levels, equalization settings, and bias adjustments should be checked frequently, but every time a new type of tape is used, all of the adjustments on every track must be checked and reset according to the tape manufacturer's specifications.

The constant movement of the tape—rust-coated plastic—across the heads wears them down, so they eventually need to be lapped. Lapping involves precision machining the head surface so the portion that touches the tape is smooth, even, and consistent across all of the tracks. When heads are lapped, they are sent away for a week or two or three, depending on how willing you are to pay rush charges and overnight shipping fees, so the recorder is out of action until they return. And along with all of the rest of the inconveniences, the tape rubs off on the heads and everything else it touches in the tape path, so those surfaces get dirty and need to be cleaned thoroughly on a daily basis. And, still more fun and games, the magnetism from the tape is transferred to the heads, which eventually affects the recording quality in a bad way—an increase in noise and decrease in accuracy—so the heads must be demagnetized every eight hours of use or so. However, when everything is set properly and all is said and done, even though they're big, noisy, heat-producing, money-sucking, temperamental beasts, there's nothing digitally recorded that quite matches the warm smooth sonic quality and feel of an analog recording. With all of that in mind, this book includes analog recording concepts

The Elusive Analog Tape Recorder

Finding a good analog tape recorder that's capable of capturing professional-quality audio is not always an easy process. If you know exactly what machine you want, eBay or Craigslist might be an option, but that route often has potholes because you can't be sure that you're getting is in serviceable condition and there is usually no warranty or customer service.

If you live in or near a major city that has an active recording industry, considering renting a recorder for a specific project. This is a great way to find out if an analog machine really fits comfortably into your normal workflow. Rental machines are usually in good shape and are regularly serviced, so they provide a good point of entry for many who are unfamiliar with what to expect from these classic devices.

Recommended Tape Machines and Common Price Ranges

Two-track mixdown recorders provide an incredible way to infuse an analog component into your mixes. Even if everything up to mixdown is digital, simply printing the final mix to a 2-track analog mixdown recorder can add a smooth, warm, analog component to your mixes. The following machines are excellent choices and, depending on their condition, can typically be purchased for about 600 to 3,000 USD.

- Ampex ATR 100/101/102, half- and quarter-inch.
- Studer A-80
- Studer A-819
- Sony APR
- Otari 5050 BII

Recording basic tracks onto a high-quality analog 16- or 24-track recorder establishes the analog sonic personality immediately. However, it's important to transfer the analog track into a DAW or other digital recorder directly after the tracking session. Tape almost immediately starts to lose high frequency content and increase in noise level! The following multitrack recorders are excellent and can usually be purchased used for about 2,000 to 8,000 USD.

- Ampex MM 1000, 1100, 1200
- Otari MTR 90, MX 80
- Studer A 820, A 827
- Sony/MCI APR 24, JH-24

and considerations because they are still important, interesting, and in the big picture, enlightening and possibly revelational.

Unfortunately, purchasing an analog tape recorder is not as easy as running up to the local music store or pro audio supplier. No one manufactures them anymore, so it takes a little more legwork to find something that's available. And, it's hit or miss whether or not the machine will be functional.

Finding the best deal on a tape machine is more complicated than discovering a Studer that belonged to someone's uncle that they'd pay you to haul away. A "deal" is only a value if it doesn't require completely outfitting the recorder with all new components. If the machine runs, records, plays back, rewinds, fast forwards, and sounds good without an abundance of snaps, crackles, and pops blended in with the recording, it's probably a good find. The best deal on a tape recorder is often the more expensive unit that has relatively new or recently reconditioned head, is documented as operational and satisfactorily performing according to the manufacturer's original specifications, and has a documented history of professional maintenance. Machines like this demand a premium price, but one way or another you'll want to bring recorder up to par. New heads could cost a few thousand dollars! So it is often well worth the cost to buy the most expensive machine if you can tell that it is truly functional and ready to go.

If you buy a machine that needs a little work, be prepared to spend as much or more than you paid for the recorder to bring it up to a functional specification. It's not easy to find an excellent technician to fix the ailments of a classic (uh … vintage, old, worn out, put out to pasture) analog machine. However, once you have purchased a relatively solid machine, it can be restored to its original specifications or maybe even a little better. With a few exceptions, these are not overly complicated electronic designs and most of the components are still available.

Analog Tape

Using the newest tape formulations and possibly Dolby or dbx noise reduction, an analog recorder can approach the dynamic range and signal-to-noise ratio provided by a digital recorder. Many world-class engineers who can afford the very best of everything still prefer the sound of analog recordings over the sound of digital recordings. It has even become fairly common to print tracks or mixes to a good analog recorder to get the analog sound, and then immediately dump the mix or tracks to a digital recorder for long-term storage and/or manipulation. Some engineers even record basic tracks by recording at the record head, with the

Chapter 2 ....ANALOG AND DIGITAL CONSIDERATIONS

machine set to playback from the play head, which is connected directly to the DAW. The tracks are transferred within milliseconds of when they're recorded!

I prefer to mix music to a 2-track Ampex, Studer, or Otari analog tape recorder running at 30 ips, using half-inch tape and no noise reduction. Even though I always take multiple digital formats into a mastering session along with the analog half-inch masters, the consensus consistently favors sound delivered by the analog tape.

Analog tape, itself, isn't always easy to come by. It is typically available only in the large-city recording hubs around the country, such as New York, Los Angeles, Nashville, and so on. It is usually available online and a lot of people have begun to buy used tape and reuse it as long as they can.

Finding Analog Tape

Analog tape is no longer readily available in every area. Large recording centers around the country are likely to have a supplier or at least representation from the few remaining tape manufacturers. Tape can be purchased online, but beware: it is heavy (expensive to ship) and pricey.

In the last years of the analog heyday, Quantegy GP 9 was the standard for high-output tape. Even though it is still occasionally possible to find new reels of GP 9 that are part of remaining stock on hand, Quantegy has discontinued manufacturing it.

Two companies are now manufacturing analog tape: ATR and RMG.

Here are a few URLs for tape manufacturers or suppliers:

- http://reeldealpa.com/shop/
- http://www.atrtape.com/
- http://www.rmgi.eu/
- http://www.ntspromedia.com

RMG QR Code

ATR QR Code

Analog Tape Speed

Analog tape speed is measured in inches per second, sometimes just called ips. Standard music recording speeds are 7-1/2 ips, 15 ips, and 30 ips.

Faster tape speeds result in better signal-to-noise ratio, less wow and flutter, and better high-frequency response. If your tape recorder has two tape speeds, use the faster of the speeds for recording music. If you're recording dialogue, the slower of the tape speeds can work well enough and will conserve tape.

The exception to this rule of thumb comes when choosing between 15 ips and 30 ips. Faster tape speeds also change the low-frequency response, and many engineers prefer to record at 15 ips using good-quality noise reduction because they like the extra punchy low end at 15 ips. Other engineers prefer 30 ips because of the more accurate high frequencies at the higher tape speed.

CONNECTING THE DIGITAL MIXER AND THE MIX RECORDER

If you choose to bounce your mixes to your computer hard drive, you eliminate several considerations that are very important in the digital recording process. The simple data transfer is easily stored on the hard drive or other storage media—it can be played back on the computer or stored to CD, DVD, or other digital playback format.

When digital recorders and playback devices are digitally connected together, they must operate in perfect sample-accurate sync to transfer accurate, glitch-free digital audio data. Therefore, one device must act as the master word-clock source and all other connected devices must be set to successfully slave to the master—they must follow it sample by sample.

Digital Format

Connections between digital devices must be compatible. Typically, S/PDIF, AES/EBU, T-DIF, and optical formats must connect with like formats for successful communication and accurate data transfer—S/PDIF connects to S/PDIF, optical connects to optical, and so on. However, if you find a situation that demands two different formats connect together, simply include a real-time digital format converter.

Chapter 2 .... ANALOG AND DIGITAL CONSIDERATIONS

What Makes Analog Tape Sound So Good?

Previously in the *Hal Leonard Recording Method*, we've seen how digital technology represents the smooth increases and decreases in amplitude by discrete stair steps, which occur at a specified rate per second. These steps sharply shift to the next amplitude level in an attempt to provide a building-block picture of a linear event.

The analog recording process converts continuously variable acoustic amplitude into continuously variable changes in magnetism. This continuous variation in magnetism is imprinted onto the magnetic analog tape and later converted by the playback head into a continuously varying electrical flow. A high-quality analog recording retains the nuance and smooth energy variation of the original sound wave. In addition, the digital recording process filters all frequencies above a specific point (20 kHz in the case of CD-quality audio). There is a valid argument that even though the filtered frequencies are above the audible frequency spectrum, their effect on the sound quality is important. Analog recordings use no such electronic filtering systems.

When this analog system is efficient, the resulting sound is dramatically smooth, pleasing, and true to the original sound source.

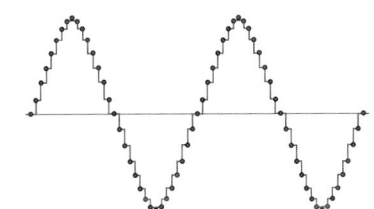

Digital stair steps approximate the audio wave.

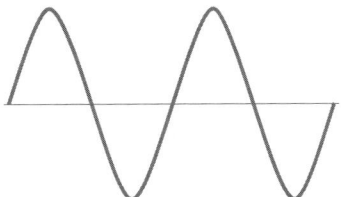

The analog recording process captures the wave's continuously varying amplitude.

Format converters receive various digital formats at the input and simultaneously deliver other digital formats at the converter output. Digital data is consistent throughout the formats, but clock data and proprietary information create specific variations.

The digital audio purist prefers to avoid format conversion; however, in listening tests a high-quality format converter is virtually sonically transparent.

Cables

As we discussed previously in this series, use high-quality cables specifically designed for digital audio connections. Even though S/PDIF uses RCA connections, do not simply use a hi-fi audio cable even though it has the right type of connector. The impedance of an audio cable is incorrect for digital data transfer.

If you try to use an audio cable for a digital connection, you'll probably find that it seems to work okay; however, the data will be prone to errors and other digital anomalies.

Your music deserves to be accurately transferred at the mixdown stage. It is well worth the cost to use excellent cable with high-quality connectors to ensure the best possible digital audio quality.

It is often necessary to connect word-clock sync cables between the master and slave devices to ensure proper sample-accurate sync in a complex digital audio network. When connecting two digital devices, the digital data flow from the output of the master device provides the proper clock information for sample-accurate sync with the slave device.

CONNECTING THE ANALOG MIXER AND MIX RECORDER

Digital devices are currently the norm in home studios and many small commercial facilities; however, analog technology offers excellent sonic quality and is used frequently by most world-class studios and increasingly by home studios and small commercial facilities.

Connecting the Mixer and Recorder

Plug the outputs of the multitrack into the line inputs of your mixer. If you're using an analog multitrack, be sure you're in playback mode (sometimes called repro or tape). If you're in sync, simul-sync, sel-sync, or overdub mode, the playback sound quality could be dramatically diminished. Some tape machines don't offer any of these options.

- Be sure you've selected the proper type of input for each of the multitrack channels on the mixer.
- Assign all channels of the mixer channels to the correct stereo or surround mixdown bus. Some mixers have a dedicated stereo bus that's fed by the main faders, and some mixers require the use of multitrack bus assignments to send your mix to the mixdown recorder.
- Connect the outputs of your mix bus to the inputs of your mixdown recorder. Use the highest-quality cables for all analog or digital connections.

Chapter 2 ....ANALOG AND DIGITAL CONSIDERATIONS

- If you're mixing to an analog multitrack recorder, be sure the correct head is selected for best playback reproduction.
- If your multitrack master was recorded using noise reduction, make sure that you're either playing back on the same machine on which you recorded with the noise reduction, or you're playing back on a machine equipped with exactly the same kind of noise reduction. Dolby A, Dolby B, Dolby C, Dolby

Basic Mix Setup

Connecting equipment for a basic mixdown is relatively simple, especially in the analog domain.

- Connect the multitrack line outputs to the mixer line inputs.

- Assign all mixer channels to a stereo bus, such as buses 1 and 2. Most mixers let you pan between odd- and even-numbered buses—typically, odd is left and even is right.

- Connect the stereo mixer bus to the left and right inputs of the mixdown recorder. In the case of surround mixes, simply connect each output to a corresponding mixdown recorder input.

- Since the connections between the mixer and mix recorder are minimal, invest in the best possible cable and connectors.

Multitrack outputs connect to mixer inputs.

Stereo or surround bus connects to the mix recorder inputs.

SR, and dbx noise reduction are not cross-compatible. If your tape has been encoded using one method, it must be decoded using the same method.
- Build a list of fader, mute, and other moves for the duration of your song, referenced to the tape counter or time code. Digital mixer and analog automation systems will keep track of many of the moves and changes and perform them at the perfect time, but definitely note any move or change that must be performed by a human.

Matching Levels and Impedance

Be sure that each connected analog device functions at the same operating level, while exhibiting matching impedance. Many recorders and mixers have a +4/-10 switch—be sure each device is set to the same value. Professional operating level is +4 dBm and is desirable; however, equipment operating at -10 dBV is sonically identical to equipment operating at +4 dBm as long as it is used with other equipment operating at -10 dBV—and as long as it is used within its limitations.

Equipment with an operating level of -10 dBV is often unbalanced, which could result in increased radio frequency interference (RFI) and other noises if long cable runs are necessary. Equipment operating at +4 dBm is typically balanced, eliminating most noise and RFI concerns.

GETTING THE RECORDER READY: CLEANING AND DEMAGNETIZING

Digital and analog recorders differ in their maintenance needs. Many digital machines use a rotating head, video recorder–type mechanism, or hard drive. These transports are relatively easy to clean on a periodic basis. Use a CD/DVD, VHS, or 8 mm video-cleaning tape or disc to keep things operating well. Don't overuse cleaning tapes, though; they are abrasive, and too-frequent use damages the head.

It's best to occasionally have your recording devices cleaned and serviced by a factory-authorized service agent. They'll take the device apart, do a thorough cleaning of all serviceable areas, and verify functionality. Check the manufacturer's specifications for maintenance and adhere to them; it will pay off in the long run.

If you're using a computer-based recorder, you'll mostly need to worry about maintaining plenty of available space on your hard drives, removable media drives, and backup systems. Oh yeah, back up regularly. If you really care about the project you're working on, back up your backups regularly.

Demagnetizing the Analog Tape Machine

Although digital recorders are the norm for many setups, analog machines offer warmth and smoothness that surpasses the music created using the current state of digital recording. Analog recorders also require the most regular maintenance. To function optimally, certain adjustments and routines must be regularly performed and verified.

As a rule, you should clean analog tape recorder heads about every four to eight hours and demagnetize them every eight to 16 hours, depending on the activity of your sessions. You can't hurt anything by doing this too often, so if you have a question about whether it's time to perform these routine duties, go ahead and do it.

1. Turn the tape recorder off.
2. Take any tape off the recorder.
3. Plug the demagnetizer in at least three feet away from the tape recorder and any tapes. If the demagnetizer has an on/off switch, be sure that you're holding the demagnetizer at least three feet from the recorder when you switch on the demagnetizer.
4. Once the demagnetizer is on, start moving slowly toward the recorder (the accepted speed is about one inch per second).
5. Move slowly through the entire tape path. Start at the supply reel—on the left—and then move slowly along the tape path. Most demagnetizers have rubber or plastic tips, so feel free to touch metal parts with the demagnetizer; be most careful with the heads. If you touch the heads with the demagnetizer, make contact away from the center of the head, where the gap is. When you develop the right touch with the demagnetizer, you can usually get very close to the head without actually touching it. Never touch the heads with a metal-tipped demagnetizer that's not covered with rubber or plastic.
6. When you encounter tape guides, idlers, or heads, move slowly up and down the guide, idler, or head a couple of times.
7. Continue along the tape path until you've reached the take-up reel (on the right).

8. Once you've covered everything, draw the demagnetizer slowly away to a distance of at least three feet.
9. Switch off the demagnetizer.
10. Turn on the tape recorder.

Be certain that the demagnetizer isn't turned off while it's close to the heads. The demagnetizer is actually a magnet that dominates the magnetic field around the heads and constantly changes polarity back and forth from north to south in response to the 60-cycle alternating current that comes from the wall outlet. As the demagnetizer is pulled slowly from the head, the head is subjected to equal strengths of north and south magnetism; hence, the resulting net magnetism is zero. If, however, the demagnetizer is turned off when it's very close to—or touch-

Demagnetizer/Degausser

Demagnetizing the analog recorder is one of the simplest and most important preparatory procedures in analog recording. In the digital era, recorder maintenance has become a non-issue for most recordists. Whereas new digital gear typically requires little to no care and tweaking, analog recorders require constant cleaning and setup to operate at their peak efficiency. Demagnetizing the tape path is only part of the complete maintenance routine.

Follow the demagnetizing procedure contained in this text. Be sure to move slowly with the active head demagnetizer and never unplug it when it's close to the heads—it will quickly magnetize the heads if you do. The demagnetizer functions by emitting continuously varying north and south magnetism in response to 60-cycle AC current. When the device is moved slowly toward the head, it creates an increasing magnetic field around the head, which eventually dominates any stored polarity. As the demagnetizer moves slowly away, the head is neutralized as the strong north/south oscillation fades to a state of zero magnetism. This is a true case of fighting fire with fire.

Keep the demagnetizer moving at all times.

ing—the head, the heads see a strong north or south impulse. The result is a very magnetized head that will require three or four cycles of demagnetizing to be free from magnetism.

Cleaning the Analog Recorder

Machine alignment and EQ settings are tedious and often confusing at first, but if you expect to progress in a positive way in engineering, you'll need to eventually master these more technical procedures. If you're feeling totally inept in this regard, pay the price to hire a very good technician to set up your recorder properly. Ask if you can be present during the procedure. You'll pick it up pretty quickly once you see someone go through the steps. You'll at least pick up some of the basic maintenance routines that are easy to perform and will keep your recorder in reasonably good shape.

Even experienced engineers occasionally hire a top-notch maintenance technician to make sure that the recorder is performing to its optimum specifications. It isn't always practical to own some of the high-end equipment capable of ensuring that everything is just right.

Most recorder manuals spell out the manufacturer's alignment and EQ procedures. Rather than trying to combine all manufacturers' procedures into one generic list, I recommend that you read your owner's manual thoroughly and practice the procedures recommended in it.

By the way, these procedures apply to analog recorders, such as reel-to-reel and cassette. Digital recorders are much more stable media and aren't limited in their basic operation by the same constraints as analog magnetic tape recorders. Maintenance is minimal on a digital machine, and any adjustments or repairs are best left to factory-qualified service technicians.

Once the tape path has been demagnetized, clean all tape path surfaces with the solutions suggested in your equipment manuals. Heads can be cleaned with isopropyl alcohol, but be sure it's at least 90-percent pure. Most drug stores carry 99-percent pure isopropyl alcohol, which works very well for heads and other metal parts. Denatured alcohol is also commonly used. Rubbing alcohol is only 70-percent pure and contains too many impurities to act as a good cleaner.

Dip a cotton swab, such as a Q-tip, in the cleaning solution, and then swab the parts in the tape path. Be sure to move up and down the recorder heads in the same direction as the gap; this increases the cleaning action and decreases the

Cleaning the Analog Tape Head

Use a cotton swab soaked in denatured or 99-percent pure isopropyl alcohol to clean the recorder heads. Use up and down movements that follow the direction of the head gap.

Cleaning is one of the most important procedures whenever using an analog tape machine. Clean the heads before each session. If the session lasts longer than six hours, clean the heads again.

If old tape is being used, the heads might need to be cleaned much more often. If a swab soaked in alcohol is discolored after cleaning the heads, they needed to be cleaned. Dirty heads cause increased noise and less than optimal sonic performance.

chance of damaging the head gap. It is very important that the swab is completely wet. Rubbing a dry swab on a metal head will create a static charge, diminishing the effect of the demagnetization.

··· Video Example 2-1
Cleaning and Demagnetizing the Analog Tape Path

Tones on the Analog Recorder

If the technical stability of your tape recorder is suspect, have it checked out by a capable technician. The owner's manual will usually have a procedure for setting the EQ and alignment of the machine. This is very important, and you should become comfortable with performing these kinds of adjustments. However, I recommend that the first time or two you try this kind of setup procedure, you have your work checked out by a technician, just to make sure you're on the right track.

When you're sure the tape recorder is going to do the best job it can, you can be sure you're on the right track to getting the best recordings possible.

Many mixers have a built-in tool called a tone oscillator or tone generator. This has real value as you get deeper into the recording process. The oscillator produces test tones (simple sine waves) you can use as reference tones for EQ and level adjustments.

................................Audio Example 2-1
Oscillator-Generated Sine Waves

If your mixer doesn't have an oscillator, pick one up at your local electronics supply store. They can be purchased at a fairly low cost, and you can easily plug them into your mixer.

The simplest and most fundamental use of the tone generator involves setting the oscillator to produce a 1,000-Hz (or 1-kHz) tone. Audio Example 2-2 demonstrates a 1,000-Hz tone.

................................Audio Example 2-2
1,000-Hz Tone

A 1,000-Hz tone is considered an average reference. If a normal musical source is peaking around 0 VU, the average of all the energies at all frequencies is typically 0 VU.

A 1-kHz tone should be simultaneously sent to all of the output buses of the mixer. Adjust all of the output bus levels to read 0 VU from the same oscillator send, and then adjust all the tape recorder inputs to read 0 VU while the mixer output buses read 0 VU. Only when this scenario has been completed can you trust that the meters on the mixer accurately represent the levels the recorder needs to receive.

When the adjustments are set and the recorder has been cleaned and demagnetized, record about 30 to 45 seconds of the 1-kHz tone on all tape tracks. If your recorder is set up correctly, you should be able to record 1 kHz at 0 VU on all tracks and then play the tape back with the meters reading 0 VU.

The reason you record this tone is twofold:
+ You can see whether the tape recorder output levels are set properly on playback.
+ When it's time for mixdown, you can adjust the levels of the tape recorder outputs to read 0 VU from this tone, optimizing the capabilities of the tape recorder. Without this procedure, it's very difficult to optimally play back your tape on different machines. For each machine your tape is played on, you can adjust the output levels to read 0 VU for each channel; this will

ensure that you get the most accurate representation of the impact of your music.

Along with a 1-kHz tone, record about 30 seconds of a 10-kHz tone and a 100-Hz tone. Record these tones at 0 VU. Their purpose is to verify the accuracy and consistency of the high and low frequencies. If your recorder is set up properly, any frequency recorded at 0 VU will play back at 0 VU.

Tones on the Digital Recorder

Tones on the digital recorder are used primarily for reference levels. Typically, 30 seconds of a 1-kHz tone is adequate for overall level adjustments. Digital recorders have an accurate and steady enough frequency response that it isn't necessary to record 10-kHz or 100-Hz tones for high- and low-frequency adjustments.

PLAYBACK AND RECORD ALIGNMENT AND EQUALIZATION

The purpose of playback alignment is to set your recorder playback levels in relation to an accepted standard in the recording industry and ensure that basic head positioning is correct. This procedure should be followed for your analog multitrack and analog two-track mixdown machines.

One of the fundamental tools in this process is a professionally manufactured reproducer calibration tape. These tapes are available in all analog formats. They contain several different frequencies (sine waves) recorded at very specific magnetic strengths, measured in a unit called a Weber—in particular, a billionth of a Weber, called a nanoWeber. The actual magnetic impulse applied to the magnetic tape by the record head is called flux. The magnetic strength, measured in nano-Webers, is called the reference fluxivity.

All frequencies on the reproducer calibration tape are recorded at the same reference fluxivity. The goal of the playback alignment procedure is to get the same reading on your tape recorder output meters for each frequency on the calibration tape.

Reproducer calibration tapes are available from Magnetic Reference Library in Mountain View, California. Their URL is www.mrltapes.com.

Record EQ

The purpose of the record alignment procedure is to adjust input, record levels, and record equalization. Once the record alignment is finished, you should be able to record any frequency at 0 VU into the recorder and get 0 VU out of the recorder on playback.

The alignment and EQ procedure can also include adjusting head position and bias levels. (See your tape recorder manuals for procedures.)

If your tape recorder has been adjusted properly in relation to a standard reproducer calibration tape, you're on the road to producing recordings that are compatible with any other conscientious engineer's equipment in the world.

Calibration Tones

Adjusting the tape recorder outputs to the mixer inputs is an important step. If your mixer doesn't have input level controls for each channel, you should at least set up your multitrack recorder so its VU meters read 0 from the output of the reproducer calibration tape reference tones. You can do this with the internal calibration level adjustments or the main output levels on the machine.

If you're serious about high-quality recordings, you should have your equipment calibrated by a technical specialist, or you should make it your goal to learn how to calibrate your gear yourself.

One vital step in setting up for a mix is adjusting the output of the stereo mix bus to match the input of your two-track recorder.

If your board has a tone oscillator, send a 1-kHz tone to the stereo bus output VU meters and adjust the oscillator level for a 0-VU reading. The tones produced by the oscillator are simple sine waves.

If your mixer doesn't have a built-in oscillator, purchase one at the local electronics supply store. Prices and features vary, but for this purpose, a simple and inexpensive oscillator will do fine. Simply patch the oscillator into any mixer channel and assign the channel to the stereo bus. Be sure the pan control is centered and, assuming the stereo bus output fader is up to normal operating range, adjust the input fader for a 0-VU reading on the stereo bus output VU meters.

If the output of the stereo bus is patched to the input of your mixdown recorder, and if the recorder is in record/pause or input mode, a reading should register on the mixdown recorder input meters.

If you're using an analog mixdown machine, adjust the input level of the recorder to read 0 VU from the same 1-kHz tone that's coming from the mixer output.

If you're using a digital mixdown recorder, such as a DAT recorder, the 0 VU that's coming from the board VU meter should read -18 to -12 on the digital recorder meter. The key with any digital recorder is to get as close as possible to zero on the digital meter at some point in the song. If you reference 0 VU to -18 on the DAT meter, you'll always have plenty of headroom, but you might not be using the full resolution of the digital recording system.

If you only reach half the maximum level on a digital recorder, it's almost as if you are only using half the system bits—instead of 16-bit digital recording, you might be realizing only eight bits. That's not good; fill up the digital meters to

Three-Head Tape Recorders

The three-head tape recorder has one erase head, one head optimized for playback, and one head optimized for recording—professional-quality machines use this configuration. The heads are always arranged in the same order: erase, record, playback.

The record head can also play back, but it usually doesn't sound as good as the playback head. The electronics of the machine have been adjusted for optimum sound from the playback head.

The theory of multitrack recording demands that we listen to playback of the previously recorded tracks from the record head in order to eliminate the time delay between the record and playback heads. Selecting Sync, Sel-Sync, Simul-Sync, Auto, or Overdub lets us monitor the previously recorded tracks from the record head while recording new tracks. This ensures that the old and new tracks are in sync. Once the overdubs are completed, switch to monitor from the playback head for mixdown.

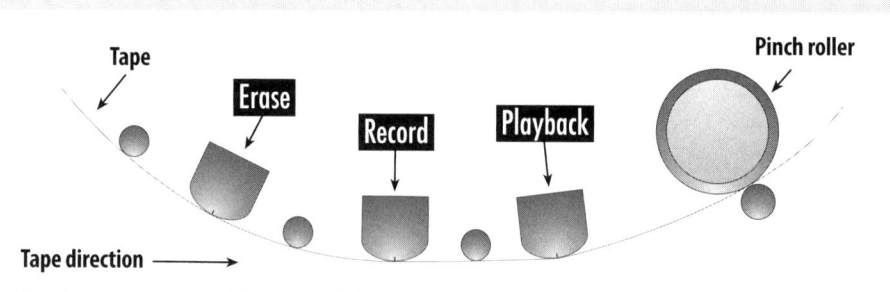

ensure ultimate digital audio clarity. I often reference 0 VU to -12 on the digital meter.

Once this is done, you can be sure that what you see on your mixer's stereo meters will be what the inputs of the mixdown machine sees.

Reference Tone

Since you have the oscillator on and working, now is the time to print reference tones. This involves recording three tones onto your stereo master: 1 kHz, 10 kHz, and 100 Hz.

A 1-kHz tone is recorded as a standard reference tone. 1 kHz at 0 VU is used as a benchmark level for the average level of a mix that has been printed with its levels around 0 VU. You can use this 1-kHz tone as a reference in making dubs of your master mixes. Setting the record level on the dubbing machine is usually as simple as playing the 1-kHz tone from the master into the dubbing machine, and then adjusting the dub machine record level to read 0 VU. This process is much quicker than trying to play through the entire song to accurately set the levels. The primary requirement for this procedure is that you've recorded the mixed master without allowing the mix level to go past +1 or +2 VU.

1 kHz is also used by the duplication/product manufacturing facility for this general level setting. They'll also use the 10-kHz and 100-Hz reference tones to adjust their equipment for accurate high-frequency and low-frequency content. In this process, they can match their playback EQ more closely to the playback EQ of your tape recorder. If your mixdown recorder is inaccurate in the highs and/or lows, this will show up when the duplication engineer plays the tones you've recorded back on his or her playback machine. Even if the duplicator needs to artificially boost or cut certain frequencies to match your reference tones, you'll end up with a much more satisfying final product simply by nature of the fact that you sent a reference of what you thought 0 VU of highs, mids, and lows should be.

I almost always print 0 VU of 1 kHz at the beginning of each song's group of mixes. This is a convenient way to verify levels when assembling all the mixes into an album.

When the edited master is finished—and all the songs are in their proper order and spaced correctly—the reference tones are included, but only at the beginning of the album master. The reference tones should be separated from the first song by 10 to 15 seconds.

MEDIA SELECTION: CD, DVD, AND MAGNETIC TAPE

The choices you make in media selection and the quality standards you adhere to are important today. However, a few years from now they'll seem even more important. Don't skimp on media. Buy the best and store it in a safe, dry place.

Magnetic Tape

The tape you use makes a big difference. If you're using any magnetic tape–based recording system, always use the current industry-standard tape. Don't try to save money on tape! If you're going to spend hours of your time recording a piece of music that's coming straight from your heart and soul, don't risk messing it up by buying tape that's second best.

All major professional tape manufacturers have excellent formulations and continue to upgrade their products. Ask a knowledgeable salesperson at a store that specializes in professional audio needs which tape is currently best for your situation. Try the two or three most highly recommended tape formulations, read about them, and form your own opinion about what works best with your setup.

CD and DVD Media

My experience has been consistent with all types of storage media for audio. Cutting costs by sacrificing quality is the most expensive route to follow. If you buy the cheapest discs you can find, you run a higher risk of disc errors and manufacturing defects. Many discount media are simply rejects from reputable manufacturers. All media have a failure rate; any disc holds a chance for defect. When it comes to data loss, keep your exposure low; always back up your data and always use premium-quality media.

Especially for long-term data archival, use high-quality, well-respected digital storage media. Inexpensive CD and DVD recordable media sometimes have a tendency to deteriorate over a period of several years. High-quality media seem to retain their form and shape for a longer period of time than very inexpensive media. Although inexpensive media might tend to exhibit a slightly higher error rate than expensive media, it is still very acceptable in most short-term reference applications.

I keep both inexpensive generic media and higher-priced media on hand. For daily references, inexpensive media makes sense. When it comes time to make a master for duplication or replication, use the most respected and highly touted media you can find.

Brands such as TDK, Taiyo Yuden, and Kodak have good reputations. Note that each manufacturer might make levels of media that vary in quality, and they may recommend various levels for specific applications.

Inexpensive, generic store brands are risky—they might be okay but they also might be very questionable in terms of their ability to hold data accurately over time. Some inexpensive media begin to deteriorate within the first couple months of use.

High-quality CD-RW media are expected to last up to 25 years under ideal storage conditions and aren't recommended for long-term storage.

The life-expectancy of CD-R media depends on:
- The material used to construct the reflective surface
- The manufacturing process
- Whether or not data has been written to the disc

Comparison of Reflective Surfaces

There is a substantial difference in expectations regarding disc longevity, depending on the composition of the reflective surface.
- Manufacturers claim a 75-year life expectancy from green discs, which use cyanine dye.
- Manufacturers claim a 100-year life expectancy from gold discs, which use phthalocyanine dye.
- Manufacturers claim a 200-year life expectancy from platinum discs, which use advanced phthalocyanine dye.

The shelf life of an unrecorded disc is estimated at between five and 10 years. In general, CD±Rs and DVD±Rs are less tolerant of adverse environmental conditions than pressed CDs and DVDs, and they should be treated with more care.

Pressed CD-ROMs might last for just 10 to 25 years due to corrosion of the aluminum reflective surface.

Storing Magnetic Tape

If you follow these tape storage recommendations, your tape should be safe:
- Keep your tapes away from speakers. The speaker's magnet could destroy all your hard work by erasing your tape.

- Don't store your tapes in extreme heat or cold. If the temperature is uncomfortable for you, it's probably not good for your tape.
- Control the humidity of the area where you keep your tapes. A lack of humidity is fine; but if you store your tape in a humid area, it can destroy your recorded tracks.
- Keep tapes away from doors that lead outside. The constant temperature and humidity changes are very damaging.
- Don't place or leave your tapes in the trunk of your car. This might seem obvious, but I've seen some pretty bad-looking tapes as a result of this kind of treatment.
- Don't leave tapes in exposed sunlight (for instance, in your car on a sunny day). It doesn't even have to be hot to cause damage. The sun can ruin your tapes in the car even on a chilly sunny day.
- Once you understand that tape doesn't respond in a positive way to heat, cold, and humidity, use common sense and good judgment to keep your tapes out of these conditions.

Analog tape must be stored in a cool, arid environment. If you live in an area that is warm and humid, you should consider building a climate-controlled storage area that maintains a constant temperature of between 65 and 69 degrees Fahrenheit and between 30- and 45-percent relative humidity. For long-term archival, store tapes in a controlled environment around 50 degrees Fahrenheit with a relative humidity between 20 and 30 percent.

Substantial temperature or humidity changes are very hard on magnetic tape—large changes result in moisture condensation, which is very damaging. Humidity or temperature should not change by more than 10 percent in a 24-hour period.

Store tape "tails out." It is best for the tape if you play the reel all the way through in real time before storing, leaving the tail end of the tape exposed. This packs the tape evenly and minimizes the likelihood of damaged edges that can result from uneven tape winds created by fast-forward and fast-rewind tape shuttling.

Store tape vertically. Stand the tape reels on end for storage. Laying the reels flat increases the chance that tape edges, which might be exposed from fast winding before storing, will be bent or flattened. This type of tape damage could cause transport problems or decrease overall audio playback performance.

Keep tape away from magnets. Although it is very convenient to lay tapes on top of or near your monitor speakers, this could be the worst place in your studio for them. The woofers in your studio monitors contain large magnets which, although they probably won't erase your tapes, could decrease high frequencies or increase noise.

TIME CODE

As you're planning your session, you need to decide whether the music and facilities available to you demand all live performances or whether you'll want to include MIDI-sequenced instruments. Strive to include every technological advantage at your disposal in a musically supportive way. Musicians often turn up their noses at certain tools that are provided by some technological breakthrough because they question the tools' musical authenticity. Although the musicians' skepticism might have merit, there's also a lot to be said for the added texture and refinement facilitated by these newer tools.

One particularly useful tool is the MIDI sequencer, locked to time code. With the current flexibility of a computer with good software, MIDI parts can be added to almost any song, either sequenced ahead of time or played against a live track. In effect, you are adding more live tracks to your tape recorder.

If you take the traditional approach of a total live recording with no sequencer assistance on the song you're working through, you are immediately limited to eight tracks. You can bounce parts down from a group of tracks to one or two tracks, but every time you bounce down, you lose quality. Plus, you typically end up with all mono tracks because in the four- and eight-track worlds, stereo mixdown is a luxury that's rarely justifiable. The preceding illustrations compare the capabilities of recording with and without the aid of a sequencer locked to time code.

If you use time code and have a mixer with some extra channels, you can dramatically increase the dimension of any recording. The MIDI sequence never needs to be printed to tape; it can simply follow along in reference to time code. In mixdown, the ability to use sounds directly from the synth and drum machine—instead of having to print to tape first—dramatically increases the potential number of tracks and has a definite effect on overall sound of the final mix. Combining some of the stereo sounds from your sound modules with tracks recorded to the multitrack produces a much more impressive and dimensional sound than would be possible without this technique.

I've seen many situations in which this approach has helped create recordings that were far more impressive than they would have been without it. The beauty of this kind of recording is that you don't have to commit to level settings, pan adjustments, instrument tuning, or any other MIDI-controllable parameter until the final mixdown. Only in mixdown do you have the proper perspective to make these adjustments. Using the sequencer to support your analog or digital hardware-based recordings can dramatically increase your ability to create a mix that will sound sonically impressive and musically powerful.

Striping SMPTE

If you're using an analog multitrack, print the SMPTE track at the beginning of the session. It's best to record the code throughout the entire length of the tape rather than trying to stop and print code at the beginning of every song on the reel. This process of recording time code is called striping.

In the digital domain, clock and timing information typically reside within the digital data stream.

To stripe SMPTE time code, all you need is a SMPTE generator. Many MIDI interfaces come complete with a SMPTE reader/generator, but generators can also be purchased separately. SMPTE is almost always recorded on the tape track with the highest number.

SMPTE readers and generators typically suggest recording levels ranging from -10 VU to 0 VU. Follow the procedure outlined by the manual for your particular piece of equipment and experiment to see what really works with your recorder.

The problem with recording time code too cold is that it's more likely to drop out or be disrupted if the tape wears on the edge, although time code that has been recorded colder won't tend to bleed into the next track as much. Sometimes when code is recorded too hot, it becomes audible in the final mix. That's not good because SMPTE code sounds like Audio Example 2-3. The advantage to recording the code a little hotter is that it tends to be more durable over time and more reliable. I've found that recording time code at -3 VU is a pretty good compromise for my setup. A few test runs will show you what's best for yours.

Chapter 2 ....ANALOG AND DIGITAL CONSIDERATIONS

....Audio Example 2-3

SMPTE Time Code

Getting the Sequencer to Follow SMPTE

Once the tape is striped, it's time to get the sequencer to follow the code. Plug the output of the time-code tape track into your SMPTE reader. In the case of our example, the reader is part of my MIDI interface. If the patch is correct, you'll be able to see the time code displayed on the reader as the tape plays back. The reader will stop when the tape stops.

Even though the majority of the recording we do in the third millennium is in the digital domain, analog recorders are still important. They are frequently used for multitrack and mixdown recording, even at the highest and most professional levels. I've included this section on setting up an analog tape recorder to provide depth and for your reference purposes.

Sync Screen and SMPTE Reader

Connect the line output from the tape track containing SMPTE time code to the input of the SMPTE reader. When the tape is played back, be sure the SMPTE reader is set to accept and respond to the time code that's been striped.

When the reader receives valid code it triggers the sequence to start at the measure and beat number referenced to the specific SMPTE time. Notice that this sequencer is set to chase time code and that the SMPTE reader window is visible to verify a constant time-code progression.

STARTING THE MIX: ZEROING THE BOARD

It's important that you develop a routine to start each mixdown—start from a clean slate each time. This process is called "zeroing." If you're using an analog mixer, that means you must physically reset each control to a unity, off, or centered position. If you're using a digital mixer, set all of the controls to your preferred starting position and then save the settings as a snapshot. This way, each time you begin a new mix you simply recall the "New Mix" snapshot. Consider these points when zeroing your console for mixdown.

- Make sure you start each mix with your mixer in a neutral state. Switch all EQs to bypass or, if there aren't bypass switches, set all EQs to flat.
- Match 0 VU out of the multitrack to 0 VU on the mixer.
- Match the stereo outputs of the board to the stereo inputs of the mixdown machines.
- Print 30 to 45 seconds of a 1-kHz tone, a 10-kHz tone, and a 100-Hz tone at the beginning of your master reel, at 0 VU. This is necessary on the final mixed master for use by the duplication facility, and it will help you in making dubs for your own use.

Some of these basic technical and mechanical adjustments might seem unnecessary or too much of a bother, but attention to these details will make your recordings sound better.

The importance of adjusting your recording equipment to perform to its optimum specifications equates exactly to the importance of tuning any other musical instrument. As I've mentioned before, if you can make several small points better in your recordings, the result will be a substantially and noticeably better recording.

OUTBOARD GEAR TO HAVE ON HAND

Any or all of these choices for outboard equipment are valuable in most mixing situations. Most people build their arsenal of effects and processors a little at a time.

If you're building your setup a piece at a time, one good multi-effects processor will go a long way. As you've seen, with one processor you might need to print some of your sounds to tape with effects, but try to save the main reverb or effect for the mixdown. The more effects you accumulate, the more you can save for mixdown.

A second multi-effects processor can really boost the power of your setup. A simple delay or dedicated reverb is also a good choice for an addition to your setup. Basically, the more involved and advanced your recordings become, the greater your chances of extravagant equipment needs.

But remember, if you overuse effects and processing, you run the risk of producing a confusing and vague-sounding mix. Too much reverb is detrimental to the punch and impact of a mix, and too much delay confuses a mix in much the same way. Too much compression can produce a mix that sounds thin and lacks the punch of a mix that has strong dynamic range.

Other effects that are useful to have available in a mix are a digital delay; more reverb; a compressor, stereo compressor, or EQ-specific compressor/enhancer, such as the Aphex Dominator; and gates.

Depending on your setup and the amount of noise coming from your tape recorder and instruments, multiple gates might be a valuable addition to a clean, noise-free, punchy sound. Many high-end, world-class boards have a gate built into every channel. I've done several mixes where I've used up to 16 or so gates on a 24-track mix. Some tracks just aren't suited to gating, but many are.

Parametric and graphic EQs are sometimes the only solution to many sound-shaping problems. Having these tools available, even though they're not always essential, can save the day.

Exciters can also be useful in many situations, but I've done an awful lot of mixes without using them, even when there have been a handful of them available.

Another valuable tool is the real-time spectrum analyzer. This tool uses a calibrated microphone to visually show you the frequency content of your music. One version of a spectrum analyzer shows a series of 31 LED meters. Each meter responds to a specific frequency. These LEDs typically respond to the frequencies available on a 31-band graphic EQ. If there's too much or too little of a frequency or frequencies, you can see it on the LEDs. Other analyzers register these frequencies using onscreen computer graphics. Some even show a graphic representation of decay over a period of time.

Spectrum analyzers can be very useful. Prices vary from about four hundred dollars to several thousand, but even the simplest and least expensive can still indicate some inherent problems with your mixes or your sound system.

Chapter 2 ....ANALOG AND DIGITAL CONSIDERATIONS

CHAPTER TEST

1. Depending on the amount of use the recorder is getting, the heads should be checked for wear and positioning accuracy at least:
   a. every couple of months
   b. once a year
   c. daily
   d. at the beginning of each new project

2. _____ involves precision machining the head surface so the portion that touches the tape is smooth, even, and consistent across all of the tracks.
   a. Setting the azimuth
   b. Milling
   c. Slimming
   d. Lapping

3. Recording basic tracks onto a high-quality analog 16- or 24-track recorder establishes the analog sonic personality immediately, but it's important to:
   a. transfer the analog track into a DAW or other digital recorder directly after the tracking session
   b. demagnetize the tape as soon as possible after the session
   c. play the tape a few times to let the oxide settle in and then transfer to a digital format
   d. Both a and b

4. Tape almost immediately starts to lose high frequency content and increase in noise level.
   a. True
   b. False

5. Analog tape speed is measured in inches per second, sometimes just called ips. Standard music recording speeds are 1-7/8 ips and 3-3/4 ips.
   a. True
   b. False

6. _____ are typically capable of powerful computer-assisted mix automation.
   a. DAWs
   b. Modern analog consoles
   c. MIDI devices
   d. All of the above
   e. Both a and b

7. In this modern digital era, there really isn't much need for analog equipment anymore.
   a. True
   b. False

8. The easiest, cleanest, and most flexible way to record your mixes in stereo or surround:
   a. is internally within the DAW via a bounce to the hard drive
   b. utilizes an analog multitrack
   c. utilizes an ADAT or DA-88
   d. is direct to vinyl disk

9. Excellent analog recorders:
   a. are at a premium in certain circles
   b. are prohibitively expensive for most home recordists
   c. can still provide audio quality that rivals or exceeds digital audio quality
   d. require a complex maintenance routine
   e. All of the above

10. The _____ captures the sound wave's continuously varying amplitude.
    a. 192-kHz, 24-bit sample
    b. DVD-Audio format
    c. analog recording process
    d. RAM buffer

11. When digital recorders and playback devices are digitally connected together:
    a. they must operate in perfect sample-accurate sync to transfer accurate, glitch-free digital audio data
    b. there must be one master clock source for all connected devices
    c. digital audio data can be transmitted through the analog outputs
    d. All of the above
    e. Both a and b

12. An optimal digital connection between two devices using S/PDIF format with RCA connectors can be made using any decent cable that has an RCA connector on each end.
    a. True
    b. False

13. A mixed analog master tape that is ready for the mastering process must include:
    a. reference tones
    b. a 1-kHz tone
    c. a 100-Hz tone
    d. a 10-kHz tone
    e. All of the above

14. Inexpensive CD and DVD recordable media:
    a. have a tendency to deteriorate quicker than higher-priced CDs and DVDs over a period of several years
    b. are about the same as higher-priced media
    c. work well because of the advantages of digital storage
    d. All of the above

15. Manufacturers claim a _____ life expectancy from platinum discs that use advanced phthalocyanine dye.
    a. 200-year
    b. 100-year
    c. 50-year
    d. 15-year

16. To keep recording tape safe, be sure to keep it away from _____.
    a. telephones
    b. magnets
    c. radios
    d. iPods

17. The process of recording time code to a track of a tape-based recorder is called _____.
    a. SMPTE-ing
    b. striping
    c. burning
    d. layback

18. The process of setting the console to a neutral status for mixdown is called _____.
    a. striping
    b. a snapshot
    c. zeroing
    d. recalling

19. The importance of adjusting your recording equipment to perform to its optimum specifications equates to the importance of tuning any other musical instrument.
    a. True
    b. False

20. When using an analog tape recorder, 30 ips always sounds better than 15 ips.
    a. True
    b. False

Test answers are on page 298

Monitoring

CHAPTER 3

The mix environment, the monitor speakers, and the way they interact play integral parts in the quality of your mixes. This chapter provides several important considerations that will help you get the most out of whatever you have for a mixing space and monitoring system.

CHARACTERISTICS OF AN EXCELLENT STUDIO MONITOR

The importance of using an accurate and reliable set of monitors cannot be overstated. Use reference monitors designed for recording studio applications. In the recording world, monitor choice depends on accuracy in a mixdown application—unlike in the hi-fi audio world, where monitor choice depends completely on how well the user likes the final sound in the listening space.

Balanced Frequency Response

A good studio monitor should reproduce a balanced frequency response. Speakers that are more efficient in the high- and low-frequency ranges might sound better to you next to an accurate studio monitor, but that doesn't mean they will provide what you need to create a great mix.

CHAPTER AT A GLANCE

Characteristics of an Excellent
  Studio Monitor 47
Balanced Frequency Response 47
Monitor Proximity 48
Excellent Transient Response 48
Low Distortion 48
Efficient Power 50
Durability and Efficiency 50
The Right Monitor for You 52
Multiple Sets of Monitors 52
The Mixing Environment 57
The Room 57
Dimensions and Angles 58
Absorption 58
Portable Acoustic Solutions 59
Setting Up Your Monitor System 60
Monitoring Configurations 60
The Real-Time Analyzer (RTA) 67
Tracking and the Mixdown 68
Comparison to Other Projects 68

If you purchase a monitor that reproduces exaggerated highs, you'll probably respond by reducing the high-frequency content of your mix; therefore, your mix likely will sound dull and lifeless on any system without a similar boost in highs. The same concept is equally likely for any frequency range that reproduces in excess. If the monitor produces exaggerated bass tones, you'll respond by creating a mix with decreased low-frequency content; therefore, your mixes will sound weaker than they should in the low end when they are heard on many systems.

Monitor Proximity

Near-field, mid-field, and far-field monitors are designed for specific placement in relation to the mixing position (where the mix engineer sits for hours on end). Only use studio monitors within their suggested proximity ranges. These monitors are designed to project a balanced frequency response that is focused at the mix position.

Using far-field monitors in a near-field proximity provides an inaccurate frequency balance. Typically in this setting, the low frequencies aren't developed at the near-field position, so you will create a mix with accentuated lows in an effort to compensate.

Using near-field monitors at a far-field proximity or any other positioning outside of the designed proximity placement is unreliable and produces mixes that are likely to sound bad on more systems than they sound good on.

Excellent Transient Response

Studio monitors must provide excellent reproduction of transient content. Transient information is often confused with high-frequency content because most transient information resides in the upper frequencies. Typically, in an effort to hear the fine detail of tracks that contain transients, most engineers boost high frequencies.

If your monitors are incapable of reproducing transient detail, you'll probably create mixes that sound harsh in the upper-frequency range.

Low Distortion

For mixdown applications, use monitors and amplifiers that exhibit minimal distortion. If you mix for long periods of time, keep in mind that distortion is the major cause of ear fatigue. Even if the distortion levels are imperceptible, the ear

Monitor Proximity

Near-field monitors are typically designed to be positioned one meter apart, about 10 degrees above and one meter from the listener's head, aimed down at the ears.

still gets overly fatigued in its effort to follow the jagged and distorted sound wave. If you work on music for hours at a time, use monitor components that are very low in distortion. A total harmonic distortion specification below 0.05 percent at 1 kHz at full output is typically acceptable—lower is better.

Sometimes it's appropriate to monitor a strong volume—mostly when the band is in the room and they want to turn it up. Normally you should attempt to control your monitor levels, especially during the bulk of the mixing process—your ears will thank you. Mixing at a low volume decreases the damaging effects of distortion and could increase the length of your career.

Maintain the best possible signal integrity at each point in the signal path. If you allow distortion at any input, it is just as bad as if you use inexpensive monitors with an unacceptable amount of distortion. Mixing with excessive distortion, even at moderate levels, fatigues the ear.

Distortion specifications are easy for manufacturers to skew. Ratings depend on input level, output level, and the specific frequency used during testing. Major manufacturers are usually proud of their distortion specifications, and their tests are realistic. Even though the distortion specifications are sometimes confusing, make this an important consideration in your studio monitor purchase. Avoid generic and unrealistically inexpensive monitors—they are often inefficient and exhibit excessive distortion.

Efficient Power

There was a day when an ideal studio monitor system consisted of the very best power amplifier, interfaced with expensive electronic crossovers and the best-loved speaker enclosure. In many commercial applications, this is still the recipe for an outstanding monitor system. However, many engineers at all home and professional levels have to grown to appreciate the simplicity and predictability of a high-quality powered monitor.

Non-powered monitor speakers with built-in passive crossovers possess one primary disadvantage: The signal that enters the speaker comes from the powered amplifier outputs. When used for long periods of time, these powered connections build substantial heat in the crossover circuitry, causing a change in response characteristic. In other words, a system that utilizes a power amp connected to monitors that use internal passive crossovers sounds different at the beginning than it does at the end of the workday.

Self-powered studio monitors receive a line-level signal from the mixer output, which is divided into two or more frequency bands prior to reaching the amplifying circuitry. In addition, the amplifier circuits are designed and optimized specifically for the included components. Because the crossover inputs are line-level, there is less likelihood that the circuitry will overheat to the point of signal degradation.

Durability and Efficiency

If you're serious about the music and the other audio you record, invest in a high-quality set of studio monitors that suit your application perfectly. Although cost is an issue for nearly everyone, invest heavily in the fundamental tools. Without decent microphones, an excellent signal path, and dependable monitors, you'll be working with a seriously debilitating handicap.

Chapter 3 .... MONITORING

Powered Monitor Compared to Component-Based Monitors

The systems below represent two common monitor systems as used in the recording studio environment. One system uses a mixer and powered monitors. The other uses separate components combined into a complete system. It is very important that your system is accurate and durable.

The system on the left utilizes powered studio monitors. It is a very simple and efficient system—it's easy to connect and electronically designed to optimize each gain stage. Connect the mixer line outputs to the speaker line inputs and you're ready to go.

The system on the right represents an equivalent system to the powered monitor system. Since the powered monitor operates at line level into the specially designed internal electronic crossovers, the system using non-powered monitors requires a line-level electronic crossover for a lateral comparison. In the more complex component-based system, the left and right line outputs connect to the crossover, which divides the signal into two, three, or four bands. Each band is connected to the line inputs of a power amplifier—or at least one side of a power amplifier—and then the speaker outputs are connected from the amplifiers to the available speaker components. High-quality non-powered monitors typically divide the speaker components into accessible groups optimized to receive specific frequency ranges.

For many applications, powered monitors are the perfect choice. On the other hand, if you're willing to invest heavily in an impressive and wonderful system, purchase the best component for each stage, and combine them all with the best cables and connectors, both systems are very functional and impressive.

The Right Monitor for You

The perfect monitor for is you is the one that causes you to create an excellent mix that sounds great on any type of system. A set of monitors isn't necessarily good or bad for you just because a particular famous engineer uses it. The equipment in your signal path, the acoustic impact of the recording environment, and your personal musical taste are all factors for determining the specific monitor that's right for you.

Test-drive a few different sets of monitors in your studio—this is where a good relationship with your local music merchandiser has great value. Evaluate studio monitors in three primary areas:

- Verify that the specifications meet your needs and requirements. Demand low-distortion specifications and high-quality components.
- Determine that the monitors provide a good balance of frequencies. Play some of your favorite mixes through the system and evaluate the sound of the highs, lows, and mids, along with the clarity of transient information.
- Mix some music through the monitors and check the mixes everywhere possible. If the mix sounds good in your car, your buddy's car, your family room, through the sound system at the gig, and anywhere else you can find to reference it, it's worth considering.

Don't let the cost of the monitor influence your decision. You need to pay a certain price to get the quality of components necessary to function well in the long-term studio application. However, once you attain the basic quality level, choose the monitor based on its functionality in your studio. I've used extremely expensive monitor systems that were useless for my monitoring needs, and I've heard several systems well under $1,000 that I thought could be very valuable during mixdown. On the other hand, my favorite systems so far have been costly, to say the least. Use your ears and your brain to evaluate your needs and to choose the monitor that is best for you.

Multiple Sets of Monitors

It's best to monitor your mixes on several types of systems. As you develop your mixing skills, there is a fairly high probability that you'll be able to adjust your mixes to sound just the way you want on your monitoring system. However, the main objective of any experienced mix engineer is to develop a mix that sounds great on all systems.

There's a good chance that your favorite recordings sound good whether you listen to them on your laptop computer or on a ridiculously expensive home theater system. An experienced mix engineer builds a mix that is full enough to sound impressive on a small system, yet not so full that it sounds boomy and dull on a large system.

The mix engineer also spreads the frequency content of a complete mix across the musical components. He or she also positions the ingredients specifically in the stereo or surround-sound field so that they are sonically visible. These ingredients must also be balanced in a way that they are still visible and appropriately mixed when down-mixed to mono or stereo.

Near-Field Monitors

As I've discussed before, it's best to mix using a good set of near-field reference monitors. Near-field monitors are designed for the recording studio and are optimized for monitoring from a distance of about one meter. Choose a neutral monitor that forces you to produce a good mix—a mix that sounds good on a wide variety of systems.

Reference monitors must provide accurate reproductions of delicate and aggressive transient information without accentuating or hyping the high-frequency range. Low frequencies should be tight and smooth.

Mixdown engineers strive to produce mixes that sound good on any system they're played on. The mixes don't need to sound exactly the same on every system, but they should sound good. In addition to the near-field monitor system, check your mixes on far-field monitors as well as very small radio-like speakers. Verify that your mix sounds good on a variety of sound systems.

There is one primary advantage to mixing on near-field monitors, especially in a small studio. Because near-field monitors are close to the mix engineer and they focus the accurate image at a relatively small sweet spot, acoustic interaction from the control room design is minimized. If you monitor on an excellent set of near-field reference speakers at reduced volumes, you'll hear a mix image that is as accurate as if you used the same speakers in the most lauded commercial recording studio. Near-field monitors are great tools. They help the home recordist in a small studio approach the accurate mixdown environment of high-priced professional studios.

Far-Field Monitors

Far-field monitors are typically hung on, or built into, the wall behind the mixer. They're usually between 10 and 20 feet from the mix position. Because they're farther from the mix engineer, they are influenced heavily by the acoustic design of the control room. If your control room isn't well designed, don't bother with far-field monitors. If you have a control room that has excellent acoustic integrity, far-field monitors are very valuable.

Far-field monitors offer a few distinct advantages:

- By the nature of their position and integration with the acoustic environment, far-field monitors are typically large systems, capable of dominating the control room airspace. The components in the far-field system are typically larger than the near-field monitors, and the system is likely to include a subwoofer. An excellent far-field system offers a perspective that is very valuable. The increased low-frequency response of the system offers a means to evaluate sub-bass frequencies that might not be audible on smaller systems.
- Far-field systems typically provide a wider sweet spot for mixing. If you regularly mix with others in attendance, a far-field system could be the only way to provide an accurate mix image to all concerned.
- Another advantage of the far-field system is the cosmetic and emotional appeal provided by an impressive look. Although this factor doesn't have much to do with mix accuracy, it has a lot to do with getting business. Part of the appeal of any studio is the look. A great-looking studio will help get clients in the front door. However, to keep clients coming back you need to provide an excellent product.

Auratones, Avantones, and Other Small Speakers

For better or worse, it's important that your mixes sound good on small speakers. Many listeners spend most of their music-listening time in front of their computers or in their cars. To predict how your mixes will sound on these small systems, include a set of small speakers in your mixing bag of tricks.

Auratone is a brand of speaker that has provided the standard small-speaker reference for many years in their Model 5C. They don't necessarily sound good, but they provide a way to guess what a mix will sound like outside the control room. Many of the best classic mixes have been mixed primarily on one Auratone positioned in the center, on top of the mixer's meter bridge. Mixing for the best

Auratone Versus Avantone and Behritone

Auratone speakers, which have been out of production for a number of years, have become a classic mixing tool. They require an external power amplifier and have been a key component of professional monitoring systems since their introduction 30+ years ago. They were never touted as hi-fi devices. In fact, they were touted as lo-fi devices because their sole purpose was to give the mix engineer and producer an idea of what the listener would hear over the radio or on television. Many studios set one lone Auratone in the center position, usually on top of the meter bridge, and fed it a mono-summed mix because the majority of programs were broadcast in mono. Mixes were built for the Auratone and cross-referenced to the near-, mid-, and far-field monitors just to make sure they'd sound okay on larger systems. But at the time, radio was king, so these single 5-inch monitor speakers ruled the mixing moment.

The original Auratone 5C can still be found used on eBay or other used equipment outlets.

Typical price: 150–250 USD per pair.

The Avantone MixCube is a more robust version of the Auratone 5C and is available in passive and active configurations.

Typical price: 450–500 USD per pair.

Behringer has also reverse-engineered the Auratone 5C—surprise! It's called the "Behritone."

Typical price: 240 USD per pair.

mono sound from this small speaker and constantly cross-referencing in stereo or surround provides a mix that is likely to sound good on a greater number of systems.

Avantone provides a bit more robust and self-powered small monitor, called the MixCube, in the vein of the original Auratone. It fulfills the same function as the Auratone, with the added convenience and reliability provided by the built-in amplifier. They also manufacture a passive, non-powered version of the same speaker.

I also like to set up a small set of computer speakers. These simply provide another perspective by which to judge the mix. Because nearly everyone uses a personal computer, it's important that your mixes sound good on these types of systems. The sound design for video games industry takes this so seriously that it has become a commonplace routine to adapt a normal laptop so the internal speakers can receive a line-level send from the mix. The mix engineer can easily select the laptop from the monitor switcher in the same way he or she would select any other available monitor.

Subwoofers

Including a subwoofer in your monitor system has value, but only when incorporated in an intelligent way. Be sure the system is designed for the inclusion of a subwoofer. If you're augmenting the response range of existing systems, be sure the frequencies provided by the sub are filtered out of the other components. If you're using a good set of near-field monitors, there's a good chance that they already provide a full-bandwidth mix at the mix position. If you simply add a subwoofer to these monitors, you'll confuse the low-frequency range, possibly creating more problems than you're eliminating.

If you filter the low frequencies from the rest of the system, a sub can provide greater accuracy throughout an extended frequency range. The advantage to including a subwoofer in any monitor system is that it provides accurate information in a range that, though unimportant on radio or other small-speaker listening environments, is very important when listening on home theater and other high-fidelity home systems. Even though most high-quality near-field reference monitors tout accuracy throughout the audible spectrum, a subwoofer offers greater accuracy when you are mixing for other systems that include a sub.

The Car

After they complete a mixdown, engineers around the world do one thing before anything else—they walk straight to their cars to see what the mix sounds like in a real-life setting. The undeniable fact is that most people spend the majority of their music-listening time in their cars, with the engine running and angry motorists honking. This creates a situation in which the sound of the mix in the car is as important as the sound of the mix in the living room—besides, the mix engineer will probably listen to the mix on the way home in the car.

Headphones

It has always been important to listen to your mix on headphones, primarily to uncover awkward pan positions that tend to make the mix sound lopsided and to identify noises and other problems that seem to hide in an acoustic environment.

With the popularity of iPods and other personal-listening systems that utilize ear buds and other headphone systems, evaluating your mix through headphones has become mandatory. In fact, it is important that you convert your mix to a standard-resolution MP3, AAC, or other data compression scheme of the day to hear what your mix sounds like to the average music consumer.

THE MIXING ENVIRONMENT

The acoustic environment is just as important as the monitor speakers. If your control room has multiple standing waves and poor absorption and diffusion characteristics, you will have a difficult time creating a dependable mix. That doesn't mean it will be impossible; it means that you won't be able to depend on the room to tell you the truth.

Most engineers are intelligent enough to quickly learn how to compensate for a substandard and inaccurate mixing space—that's not the real problem. As you produce and engineer music for more and more different artists, you'll soon tire of making excuses for your control room. Strive for the ideal. Strive to develop a monitor system that lets you mix from what you hear rather than from what you've learned to do to compensate for what you hear. This way, you'll learn to depend on what you hear, and the comments from the artists you produce will hold greater value.

The Room

Most home recordists work within a pre-existing space simply because it is convenient and inexpensive. The inherent problem in this process is that the mixing console and outboard gear end up in a room designed for someone to sleep in. The dimensions of a typical bedroom are not well suited to acoustic accuracy and integrity. However, there are several useful techniques that can quickly help transform a poor mixing space into an acceptable one. For more useful tips on controlling your acoustic mixing space, refer to Chapter 1 of *Instrumental & Vocal Recording* from *The Hal Leonard Recording Method*.

Dimensions and Angles

If you are building your own mixing space, keep in mind that the overall dimensions are crucial to the resulting acoustic response characteristics. The ratios between dimensions are critical, and the angle between each opposing surface controls the reflection characteristic within the mixing space. A studio with interesting angles around the room and well-designed acoustical safeguards has a good chance of providing a dependable mixing environment.

The science of acoustics is very involved—obviously, theoretical concepts and common practices don't always coincide. Acoustic interactions between sound and studio surfaces depend on obvious placements of walls and other structural designs. In addition, material density and structural rigidity also influence acoustical response. Therefore, even if your basic dimensional ratios fit the ratios previously outlined in this series and other acoustic science references, the resulting space and its interactions with sound are still in question in many ways. As soon as you include ever-changing equipment setups and variable numbers of musicians in the equation, you change the overall response of the room.

Within reason, large rooms tend to maintain their basic tonal response when filled with people and equipment simply because of the ratio of open airspace to variable acoustic components, such as people and gear.

Absorption

Absorptive surfaces, such as foam, curtains, sofas, and egg cartons, control high frequencies. However, they don't do much to affect the inherent problems that reside in a poorly designed mixing and recording space. In fact, too much absorption might do more to reveal problem axial standing modes in a room than it would do to control high-frequency reflections. With that said, absorption is still very useful in the control of flutter echoes and high-frequency ringing that frequently exists in many generically designed rooms, but if you need to control low and low-mid frequencies, you must create structural changes.

Chapter 3 .... MONITORING

Portable Acoustic Solutions

A few manufacturers create excellent portable acoustic control solutions for studio and home use. These products help turn a substandard acoustic space into a workable and quite functional recording and mixing space.

Portable Acoustic Solutions

The simple realization that acoustic considerations are a very important part of the recorded sound provides motivation to control negative acoustic interactions with your intended source. It is best to record in a room that is brilliantly designed by a team with experience and an excellent track record. However, when you're not in that type of environment, use your ears to assess the sound you hear on the recorded track, and use portable acoustic treatments to control ambient influences.

There are several commercially available products, such as the Studio Traps pictured below from Acoustic Sciences, Inc. and the pictured foam products from Primacoustic. They do an excellent job of helping control unwanted ambience and acoustic anomalies; however, you can also control unwanted reflections with blankets suspended from mic stands, cardboard boxes placed strategically in the room, or even a sheet of plywood strategically positioned to redirect an axial standing wave around the room instead of allowing it to continue bouncing back and forth between two opposing parallel surfaces.

Acoustic Sciences Corporation offers several products that control reflections and ambience through diffusion and absorption. One notable tool is the Tube Trap. This column is reflective on one side and absorptive on the other. When several are placed around an instrument, vocalist, or mix position, the resulting sound can be molded and shaped by varying the number and proximity of the devices. In a home studio created in existing space, these can change your recordings from amateurish to professional. Tube Traps are used in all settings, from the home studio to the world-class commercial complex—they help shape and fine-tune any recording space.

Primacoustic, another excellent company, offers several effective and affordable foam products to help control room acoustics. Many of the on-wall products control various specific frequency ranges—some control specific reflective problems, such as flutter echo and acoustic accumulations in corners. They also offer small portable absorbers that can be positioned much like the ASC Tube Traps to fine-tune almost any space into a usable recording environment.

SETTING UP YOUR MONITOR SYSTEM

If your control room has not been designed and acoustically treated to optimize the mixing environment, it's usually best to take the room out of play by using near-field monitors at a minimal volume. If you intend to mix at a louder volume, you'll need to evaluate the frequency balance of your system as it interacts with the room. This can create the need for a very involved process if you intend to adjust dimensions and add diffusion and absorption to compensate for acoustic problems. If this is your intent, hire a professional to at least develop the plans for the perfect version of your control room. Even if you enjoy carpentry and building, invest in someone who can provide a realistic plan for excellence. Then, break out the hammer, glue, and nails and get to work.

Monitoring Configurations

In a stereo mixdown environment, it's important to choose speakers that take advantage of acoustic strengths or minimize acoustical weaknesses of the room. Realistically, most people work in spaces that are less than ideal for a number of reasons. The room dimensions might not be conducive to a trustworthy sound quality; there might be too many reflective surfaces in the listening sweet spot, which cause colorations and other phase anomalies; or there might just be a radical difference in the number of people in attendance at the session, which also changes to the sound in the room. With this in mind, near-field reference monitors are usually the most reliable choice.

Even large commercial studios, designed by world-class designers, keep a set of near-field monitors within about a meter or so of the engineer's ears, as an option to their far-field or mid-field monitors. In a surround mixing environment, there are additional considerations.

Stereo Configuration

When using near-field monitors, a stereo listening environment can be ideally set up for a single engineer. There is only one real sweet spot in the mixing field where everything is perfectly balanced. But music is frequently a team activity, so it's nice if two people can share in the audio sweet spot during a mix. In small studios, there is a a constant compromise during a mix session. An advantage provided by a large commercial studio is the inclusion of mid- and/or far-field monitors. The farther the speakers from the mix position, the larger the audio sweet spot, so more people can effectively collaborate in this essential and creative process.

Whether using near-, mid-, or far-field monitors, keep the monitors and the mix position at the three points of an equilateral triangle. Include a subwoofer for accurate mix decisions regarding the low-frequency band.

Stereo

A stereo pair of near-field reference monitors should be placed at two points of an equilateral triangle, with the speakers pointed at the engineer, who is at the third point of the same triangle. The speakers should be about 10 degrees above—and pointed down at—the engineer's ears.

A subwoofer is frequently combined with a stereo pair of monitors, although it is not usually fed a separate signal. Instead, a crossover isolates the low frequencies from the entire mix and routes them to the sub, and then routes the remaining bandwidth to the main stereo monitors. A subwoofer is a valuable monitoring tool because it lets the mix engineer hear the low band that would otherwise be invisible on many near-field monitors—problems often exist in these sub bass frequencies that are only audible on large systems with a subwoofer. However, there are two potential problems that commonly result from the use of a stereo system with a subwoofer:

1. It's fun to hear the sub bass frequencies, so it's tempting for the mix engineer to rely on them to fill out the mix. Since the low frequencies produce the most energy, which boosts the playback level, excess lows often result in an artificially strong playback level. So the master mixes might be excessively noisy or they might feel clouded or muffled in comparison to better balanced mixes.
2. Because the low frequencies produced by the sub are not audible on smaller speakers, such as near-field monitors, television sets, radios, computers, and so on, a mix that is extremely powerful in the studio might be extremely weak when played back on another system.

Recommendation: Use a subwoofer combined with the main monitors in the studio to accurately balance the lowest frequencies, but always cross-reference to normal full-range, near-field monitors as well as small monitors like Auratones or inexpensive computer speakers. Also, note that sub bass frequencies are not directional, so the exact position of the subwoofer in the room is not specified.

Mono

Although AM radio seems to be our last existing mono broadcast format, is is still a good idea to have some way to monitor your mixes in mono. When mono radio and television broadcasts were the norm, a single Auratone was usually right in front of the mix engineer at all times. If the mix didn't sound good through that single five-inch speaker, it wasn't complete.

Monitoring in mono on small speakers is still important today in order to test for playback on a computer's built-in speakers and to verify playback integrity over a mono live sound system. Many mixers, monitor controllers, and control surfaces provide a "mono" button that sums the left and right channels and sends the identical signal to both speakers. Check your mixes in mono whenever possible. It usually only takes a couple of small changes to achieve excellence in both mono and stereo.

Surround

Although surround sound for movies has been popular since the mid '90s, the soundtrack to Walt Disney's *Fantasia* was played back in an extremely similar configuration to 5.1 surround. That was in 1938! It has always been a powerful presentation tool, but it's not always easy for the consumer to establish a perfect

5.1 and 7.1 Surround

These two surround formats are currently most common. Both of these configurations specify the Universal Telecommunications Union (ITU) standard.

More Surround Configurations

Quadraphonic Sound: Four full-range monitors surround the listener. This was a pretty exciting development, experimented with in the '50s and '60s and released commercially by JVC in 1970. It didn't catch on.

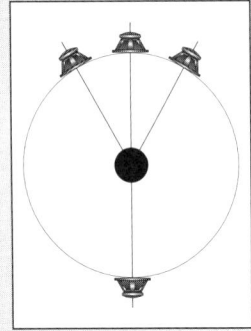

LCRS: Originally the Dolby Pro Logic format, this four-channel layout uses left, center, right, and surround channels. The surround channel is positioned directly behind the listener and a lowpass filter is applied to reduce its high-frequency content.

6.1 Digital Dolby EX or DTS ES Surround: Like 5.1 with an added rear speaker in the back center position.

7.1 (SDDS-Sony Dynamic Digital Sound) Surround Format: Commonly used in large theaters equipped with Sony decoding and playback hardware.

playback environment and it equally difficult for the home recordist to establish an excellent mixing environment.

The nomenclature is consistent when discussing surround configurations ($n1.n2$), where $n1$ represents the discrete number of surround speakers and n2 represents the number of subwoofers. Therefore, 5.1 surround indicates five surround speakers combined with one subwoofer; 7.2 surround indicates seven surround speakers combined with two subwoofers; or, this might be a few years down the road, 64.8 would indicate 64 surround speakers combined with eight subwoofers! Surround formats such as Quadraphonic sound or LCRS surround don't indicate the use of a a subwoofer.

Though we might know how many channels should be in a 5.1 or 7.1 surround setup, we need to place those speakers according to a standard, or else we're not listening in a reliable environment and our mixes can't be trusted to play back consistently well on a broad range of systems. The International Telecommunications Union (ITU) established a standard for surround speaker placement in 1994. It places speakers equidistant from the listener at unique points on a circle. Configuring the monitors in accordance with this standard will help establish a reliable mixing environment.

A 5.1 surround system utilizes six discrete audio channels feeding five identical monitors and one subwoofer. In many cases, space restrictions make near-field monitors the only speaker option—and they can provide an acceptable mixing

Surround Downmix to Stereo

A surround mix is often easier to perform than a stereo mix. As the mix ingredients and ambience spread around the system, the sound is powerful—it is relatively easy to create a mix in which the ingredients are visible and impressive.

Part of the surround protocol involves automatic downmix of the surround mix to stereo. Although this is a simple way to be sure that the stereo mix is available to the consumer, it is not optimal. If you want to include a stereo mix on a surround release, create a separate stereo mix and include it in place of the automatic downmix.

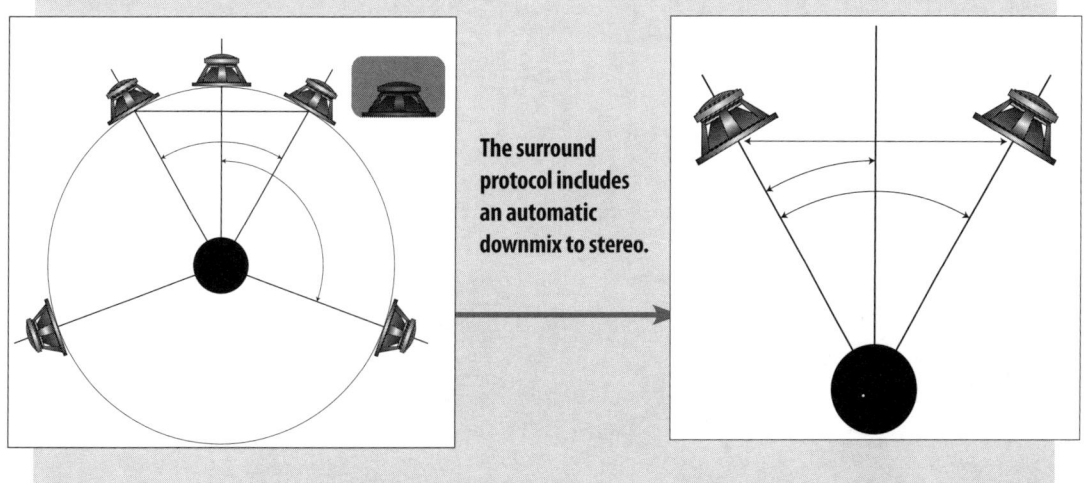

The surround protocol includes an automatic downmix to stereo.

experience—but the use of mid-field monitors helps simulate the way home and theater listeners hear the surround audio. For 5.1 surround mixing, notice that the sub channel is fed its own information, which is filtered to provide only the low band to the target subwoofer. This is very unlike the stereo system that simply sends the low-frequency component of the complete stereo mix to the sub because it lets the mix engineers fill the low frequencies with specific information. And, it can be expected that the mixes will be heard on a surround system, which, by design, includes a subwoofer to play back the specific low-frequency content.

The RTA and the 31-Band Equalizer

Typically, when a real-time analyzer is used to set up the frequency response characteristic of a reference monitor system, the mixer outputs are each routed through a 31-band graphic equalizer.

A calibrated, flat-response microphone is plugged into the RTA input and, while pink noise is generated through the speakers, the RTA display indicates the energy reading of 31 specific frequency bands. These bands correspond to the frequency center points of each control on the 31-band graphic equalizer.

To create a flat frequency response, simply adjust the graphic equalizer faders in response to the amplitude readings on the RTA display.

Although the ultimate goal for any system is a flat frequency response across the audible spectrum, it is common for the actual response to decrease below about 50 Hz and above 15 kHz or so.

The most common surround configurations are 5.1 and 7.1, but there are other surround options.

The 5.1 surround configuration for the DAW outputs are standardized as:
- Channel 1: Left front
- Channel 2: Center
- Channel 3: Right front
- Channel 4: Left rear (Also called "left surround")
- Channel 5: Right rear (Also called "right surround")
- Channel 6: Subwoofer (Also called "Low Frequency Effect" or "LFE")

For 7.1 surround mixing, DAW outputs are standardized as:
- Channel 1: Left front
- Channel 2: Center
- Channel 3: Right front
- Channel 4: Left surround side (LSS)
- Channel 5: Right surround side (RSS)
- Channel 6: Left rear
- Channel 7: Right rear
- Channel 8: LFE

The Real-Time Analyzer (RTA)

One simple and inexpensive way to quantify the response of your system in the mixing environment is to use a real-time analyzer (RTA) and a 31-band graphic equalizer. The RTA includes a pink-noise generator (all frequencies at an equal level), a calibrated microphone, and 31 meters that respond to the level of each frequency band correlating to the bands on a 31-band graphic equalizer.

With this system, follow these steps:
- Patch the output of the mixer's monitor bus through the equalizer (stereo or surround) and into the monitor speakers.
- The pink noise is connected to a mixer input and played through the equalizer into the monitors.
- The calibrated microphone is placed at the mix position and the pink noise is turned up to a normal mix volume (typically 85–95 dB SPL).
- With the pink noise up and the calibrated mic in place, the RTA senses and displays the level of each frequency band.

- If the room acoustics are perfect, the RTA should read equal levels at all frequencies. If there are peaks or dips in the acoustic frequency response, they'll be displayed as peaks and dips in the RTA display.
- Adjust the 31 equalizer bands to create a flat room response at the mix position.

............................Video Example 3-1

RTA Studio

TRACKING AND THE MIXDOWN

Tracking is important to the mixdown process. The more accurate and pristine your sounds are during tracking, the easier the mix will go. If you spend the time tracking clean, solid, exciting sounds, which are precise and well-crafted onto the multitrack, you'll be a happier person during mixdown.

Producers, engineers, and artists often throw around the phrase, "It's all right. We'll fix it in the mix." Although it is true that there are many problems that can be most efficiently solved during mixdown, avoid lowering your musical and sonic standards during tracking simply because you're tired or because folks are anxious to get on the Interstate before the afternoon rush. Spend the extra time required to track excellent musical takes. If you leave too many problems for the mixdown process, you could end up spending hours fixing something that could have been tightened up in a few minutes during tracking. If you're spending hours on anything during mixdown, it should be on enhancing and creatively shaping the production.

COMPARISON TO OTHER PROJECTS

A very effective mixing technique involves comparing your mix to a mix that you love the sound of or one that's held in high regard by the audio community at large. Listening to your favorite recording on the studio monitors is also a great way to quickly adapt to a new system. If you're mixing in a new environment, it is critical that you cross-reference the sound of your music to the sound of known hits.

Plug a CD player into one of your mixer's aux or tape inputs or into two channels of your main mix bus—have it there and ready to switch on for comparison. As you build your mix, turn the CD on occasionally. Evaluate highs, mids, and lows of your mix and the prerecorded CD. In addition, compare the use of effects and the basic orchestration. It helps if the reference mix is similar in style to the song you're mixing.

You'll often be surprised by the results when you try this. You might be amazed by how bad your mix sounds in comparison—but you might also be amazed by how good your mix sounds. Comparisons are inherent in the music business, so it's best to make them while there's still an opportunity to make changes.

Mixing & Mastering .... by BILL GIBSON

CHAPTER TEST

1. In the recording world, critical acclaim and commercial acceptance depends completely on how well the engineer likes the final sound in his or her listening space.
   a. True
   b. False

2. If your monitors provide an exaggerated amount of high frequency content, your mixes, when heard on a variety of systems, are likely to sound:
   a. dull and lifeless
   b. brittle in the high end
   c. weak in the low frequencies
   d. boomy in the low end

3. In most mixing environments, the far-field monitors provide the most trustworthy audio sound.
   a. True
   b. False

4. _____ is often confused with high-frequency content.
   a. Edge
   b. Transient information
   c. Distortion
   d. Dissonance

5. _____ is a major cause of ear fatigue.
   a. Earwax
   b. Dissonance
   c. Distortion
   d. Sensitivity

6. As a general rule, _____ provide the most reliable sound at a relatively affordable price.
   a. 1000-watt power amplifiers
   b. non-powered monitors
   c. self-powered monitors
   d. digital monitors

7. Near-field monitors are typically designed to be positioned about _____ the listener's ear and pointed at the ears. The monitors should also be about _____ apart and about _____ from the listener's ears.
   a. 10 degrees above, one meter, one meter
   b. 10 degrees below, one meter, one meter
   c. 20 degrees, 10 feet, 5 feet
   d. 30 degrees, 10 feet, 5 feet

8. Mixing at a low volume decreases the damaging effects of distortion and could increase the length of your career.
   a. True
   b. False

9. Far-field monitors are typically hung on, or built into, the wall behind the mixer. They're usually _____ from the mix position.
   a. 5 feet
   b. 1 meter
   c. between 10 and 20 meters
   d. between 10 and 20 feet

10. If your control room has not been designed and acoustically treated to optimize the mixing environment, it's usually best to:
    a. take the room out of play by using near-field monitors at a minimal volume
    b. monitor using headphones
    c. monitor at excessively loud levels so that you can override the detrimental acoustic interactions
    d. use a large power amplifier to minimize distortion

Chapter 3 .... MONITORING

11. RTA stands for:
    a. Rural Transit Authority
    b. Real-Time Analyzer
    c. Reflection Tester and Analyzer
    d. Radio Transmission Action

12. If you spend the time tracking exciting sounds onto the multitrack, which are well-crafted, you'll be a happier person during mixdown.
    a. True
    b. False

13. A very effective mixing technique involves:
    a. comparing your mix to a mix that you love the sound
    b. comparing your mix to one that's held in high regard by the audio community
    c. comparing your mixes to known hits
    d. All of the above

14. When evaluating a mixing studio, _____ is (are) just as important as the monitor speakers.
    a. the power amplifiers
    b. interior design elements
    c. the acoustical environment
    d. the type of cables used

15. Absorptive surfaces, such as foam, curtains, sofas, and egg cartons, control _____.
    a. low frequencies
    b. midrange frequencies
    c. high frequencies
    d. soft sounds

16. Problematic _____ are best controlled through the use of structural changes.
    a. high frequencies
    b. midrange frequencies
    c. low-mid frequencies
    d. low frequencies
    e. Both c and d

17. Very large venues tend to maintain their basic tonal response when filled with people and equipment simply because of the ratio of open airspace to variable acoustic components.
    a. True
    b. False

18. Specific acoustical interactions between sound and studio surfaces depend on:
    a. placements of walls
    b. structural designs
    c. material density
    d. structural rigidity
    e. All of the above

19. When you're not in a well-designed acoustical environment, use _____ to assess the recorded track, and use _____ to control ambient influences.
    a. an RTA, Tube Traps
    b. the waveform editor, the inverse ambience device
    c. your ears, portable acoustic treatments
    d. a spectrograph, automation

20. The center of the frequency bands on a(n) _____ typically correspond to _____.
    a. parametric equalizer, the width of the band
    b. RTA, the sliders on a 31-band graphic equalizer
    c. graphic equalizer, a 1/4 octave wide band of audio
    d. All of the above

Test answers are on page 298

Mixing Theories

CHAPTER 4

CHAPTER AT A GLANCE

Mix Approach	73
The Arrangement	74
Signs of an Amateur Musical Recording	76
Lack of Consistent Focal Point	77
No Contrast	77
Excessively Wide Dynamic Range	77
Low Levels	77
Noisy, Dull, and Lifeless Mixes	79
Level-Dominating Outbursts	79
Distant, Sterile Mixes That Lack Intimacy	80
Dull and Uninteresting Sounds	80
Unsatisfactory Instrumental Solo Levels	80
Characteristics of a Good Mix	81
Strong, Solid, Yet Controlled Lows	81
Mids Distributed Evenly Among Various Instruments	81
Strong, Smooth Highs That Are Easy To Listen To	81
Balance	82
Depth	82
Width	82
Momentum	82
Consistent Playback Quality	83
Sounds Good in Stereo, Surround, and Mono	83
Consistent Focal Point throughout the Song	83
Controlled and Appropriate Use of Effects	83
Motion	83
Inclusion of Acoustic Information	84
Simplicity	84
Mixing Styles	84
East Coast (New York)	86
West Coast (Los Angeles)	86
Southern (Nashville)	86
European (London)	87
Mix-Building Concepts	87
Ineffective Approaches to Mixing	87
Using Dynamics Processors to Create a Blend	88
Arranging during Mixdown	90
Multiple Mixes	90
Mix Versions	91
Stems	94
Different Mixes	95

It's best to approach each mix as a separate musical work. For the most natural and believable mix, imagine the music as if a live group was playing it. For panning, imagine where each instrument would be onstage. It's most typical in a live band to have the drums and bass in the center with the keys to one side, rhythm guitar to the other side, and the lead vocals in the middle. Any instrumental solos are typically placed in the center of the mix, as if the soloist had stepped forward for the solo section. There are, of course, infinite variations of precise placement in a live performance situation and multiple instrument combinations, but imagining your recorded music as a live group will result in consistent success and believability.

MIX APPROACH

The rookie recordist usually doesn't know where to start in the mixdown process. A mixdown requires great attention to how tracks blend together and to the specifics of maintaining a focal point while creating an undeniable musical flow. There's much more to creating a powerful mix than simply turning up all the faders and adjusting to taste. On the other hand, it's important to maintain a good balance between technical tweaking and simply mixing from the heart. There are occasions where a very cerebral and technical approach results in the complete loss of musical life and impact. However, if you understand and love music, there's a strong chance that you'll be able to focus on technical details while maintaining a strong musical feel.

Although I tend to take each mix as a separate entity and approach the mix from the angle that most suits the musical need, I've found the following approach works well to produce excellent mixes that maintain a constant focal point while still sounding musical.

- Focus on the drums and bass first. If these ingredients are punchy, balanced, and supportive, most of the work is done. This combination defines the structure and boundaries of the mix.
- Next, add the lead vocal. Start working on fitting the lead vocal together with the bass and drums. Once this combination is solid, you might be surprised at how full and complete the sound is. Many times we keep adding tracks to get a full sound when we probably should concentrate on choosing which tracks to eliminate.
- Then, start adding ingredients in order of importance. Once the bass, drums, and lead vocal are working together, you'll find it easy to tell what the level of the primary guitar and keyboard should be. Ease these ingredients into the mix. This is where you begin to consciously control the focal point. There should be a basic setting for guitar and keys that supports the singer without competing for the focal point. When the vocals are silent, it's often appropriate to boost the guitar or keyboard part to fill in the mix.
- Add all the miscellaneous percussion and sound effects after everything else is up. Use only what you need. Try not to run over the lead vocals with an instrument or solo. If the lead vocal is on, you probably don't need another lead instrument fighting for the limelight. Focus as you mix. Determine what the most important thing is at each point in the song and highlight it.

THE ARRANGEMENT

If the arrangement has been structured with the final product in mind, and if you've been disciplined enough to record only the parts that really need to be in the song, mixing is a much easier and more streamlined process. That's why arranging and production experience is so valuable to the success of a project.

Chapter 4 .... MIXING THEORIES

There are many situations when it's valid to record a few tracks that you might or might not use in the mix. Often those tracks will be turned up for just a portion of the song, at just the right time. In that context, it can be very valuable to record extra parts.

There's also definite value in planning your song out in detail before you start recording, and then sticking to that plan throughout the recording process—of course, you must also allow for creative freedom in the heat of the recording moment.

Keep in mind that there should always be a focal point that stands out to the listener at each point of the mix. As the mixing engineer, you must always give the

Planning Ahead

A little bit of forethought yields great payoff in the recording and music production process. When working with multiple creative sources, agreement on exactly how the production is expected to unfold promises to ward off many miscommunications and to set a tone of collaboration—plus, combined creativity often yields the most exciting and powerful music.

Be efficient and aggressive in this process. Work fast, especially at first, and start by getting all of your ideas on the table. This works very well in the songwriting and initial production phases, but it also works well in the mixing phase. There are several ways to approach any mixdown session. Compile a list of everyone's expectations and ideas for the final sound of the final mix. When there are conflicting opinions it is the job of the producer to choose which approach best serves the musical needs of the project.

The simple, handwritten outline at the right provides the essence of the intent for the final mix. Organization doesn't necessarily need to be beautiful and computerized—it just needs to be clear and concise.

listener a point of interest. This approach produces mixes that are fun and easy to listen to because they maintain listeners' interest while captivating and pulling the listeners through the song. Keeping a focal point normally involves many level, panning, and effect changes throughout the song. If you don't provide a mix that holds the listener's interest, your music has less of a chance for success.

Timing is critical when adjusting levels. Developing the touch necessary to change levels and to turn tracks on and off at just the right time takes practice. Selecting when and where to make a crucial change often requires the ability to push a button, turn a knob, or move a fader at a precise moment or within a very specific time period.

If you'd like to get people to listen to an entire song, give them a mix that builds from the beginning to the end and always has one focal point. Include some exciting and possibly surprising sounds, and structure your arrangement with the goal of keeping your listener's focus on the tune.

Remember this: If you're turning channels on and off and you've simplified to the point that there's only one or two instruments in the mix, it should sound like those were the only instruments you recorded. They should sound full and interesting, and the rest of the tracks should be off so they aren't adding electronic noises or inadvertent sounds that happened to leak into the mics during tracking. It's best if at any given time all tracks are muted expect the ones being heard in the mix. This is the safest approach to controlling errant and unwanted sounds in the final master recording. Sometimes, we're so inside the mix that we miss obvious flaws. If a track is empty, it should be muted. In the analog domain, each track adds a small amount of noise to the mix; therefore, it's increasingly important to mute inactive tracks. In the digital domain, noise isn't an issue as far as a blank track goes, but frequently a track that looks blank has something on it. If the

SIGNS OF AN AMATEUR MUSICAL RECORDING

Throughout this series I have tried to make positive comments about what we should do to make better recordings and I've avoided lists of what we should not do. However, there are certain procedures that result in amateurish mixes—we should avoid these.

Lack of Consistent Focal Point

A sure sign that the mix engineer doesn't really understand the musical impact of a mix is the lack of a consistent focal point. It's common to hear an unprofessional-sounding mix in which the mix is all right as long as the vocals are active. However, the spaces between the lyrics lose interest—the momentum drops quickly and the listener is left without a point of interest. Mixes like this are difficult to endure. A four- or eight-bar break between the chorus and the verse can be unbearably long without a specific ingredient moving to the forefront to hold the listener's interest.

No Contrast

A sure sign that a production is amateurish in every way is when all instruments play all the way through the song with no contrast or texture change. When there is too much going on throughout the production, the listener is not emotionally challenged to stick with the recording until the last note. It becomes obvious early in the song that the experience is over.

Excessively Wide Dynamic Range

Dynamic range is a good feature of a musical mix when used in proper context and when controlled to develop the emotional flow of a musical work. The reality of the commercial mix is that dynamic range is typically indicated by textural change rather than by actual level changes. The level of a good commercial mix usually remains fairly constant, but as the mix thins out, it creates the feeling of dynamic change and textural contrast. Even if the actual signal level decreases, the apparent loudness typically remains constant. It is a fact that one or two tracks at full signal level sound louder than several tracks combined to full signal level.

Low Levels

Low mix levels are unacceptable. The mastering process compensates for conservative mix levels, but for your mixes to realize the greatest sonic purity you must, in the digital realm, take full advantage of the available bit depth and, in the analog realm, record as far above the noise floor as possible. Craft your mixes so they use within two or three decibels of full signal level several times during the production—this will ensure that the mix will fare well in the mastering process and that you've taken advantage of all available audio fidelity.

The result of low digital levels is decreased accuracy at low levels. As the signal decreases there are fewer bits to define amplitude quantization; therefore, it is desirable to record at full digital levels. The advantage of increased digital levels is realized in increased clarity not so much in the louder passages, but in the softer passages. It is always advantageous to use the highest practical bit depth when recording your files. The increased quantization resolution of a 24-bit sample over a 16-bit sample is marked. Master mixes should be recorded, bounced, or rendered as 24-bit audio files even if the release will be 16-bit CD-quality audio.

The result of low analog levels is a decrease in the signal-to-noise ratio. Every decibel decrease in the maximum mix level equates to a decibel increase in relative level of the noise floor.

The Result of Low-Level Analog Mixes

When analog signals are unnaturally low they become clouded by the noise floor. For this reason it is important to keep mix record levels as high as possible. For most commercial and pop mixes, the mix level should remain constant and hot. For classical and other acoustic recordings, the wide dynamic range of the inherent stylistic nuance often surpasses the effective dynamic range of most analog tape machines. Noise-reduction systems, such as Dolby SR, can increase the dynamic range of a taped-based analog system to help facilitate recording a wide dynamic-range audio source.

Notice the graphic below and its representation of the constant noise floor in relation to the recorded waveform.

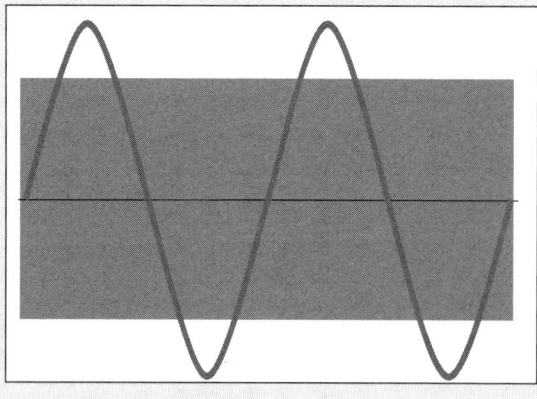

The noise floor, represented by the green shaded area, adversely affects the clarity and impact of the music, even though the waveform is typically accurate throughout most of the audible spectrum.

Chapter 4 ....MIXING THEORIES

Noisy, Dull, and Lifeless Mixes

A lack of understanding of the fundamentals of mixing often results in the production of mixes that lack excitement. The mix engineer must understand the concepts of blending levels, combining EQ, building the arrangement, and controlling dynamics in order to create a solid mix that is exciting and enticing.

Level-Dominating Outbursts

An experienced mix engineer looks for and minimizes mix level outbursts. Once the mix is built and the musical impact is satisfactory, the mix engineer should play the entire mix with the single intent of locating level peaks. Because low frequencies contain substantial amplitude, instruments such as the bass guitar, low toms, or even a very full electric guitar might create level peaks that control the maximum mix level but that have little impact on the apparent volume of the mix. Thorough scrutiny of the mix level and subsequent elimination of several

The Result of Low-Level Digital Mixes

The digital recording system contains a finite number of timeline steps, represented by samples, as well as a finite number of amplitude steps represented by wordlength (bits). It is best to maintain ample mix levels to optimize the vertical resolution of the sampled waveform. When mix levels decrease to unrealistically low levels, the digital sampling resolution could become insufficient to accurately indicate the original waveform.

Even though the sample rate remains constant, low-level signals can't be accurately depicted because of insufficient amplitude resolution. The illustrations below represent the analog sine wave along with an accurate and inaccurate digital representation of the same sine wave.

mix peaks results in the opportunity to increase the entire mix level in order to re-attain full signal strength.

When a peak is located that is the result of low-frequency accumulation, the proper fix is usually a decrease in the low-frequency level at the moment of the peak. The repair of low-frequency outbursts can easily result in a 3- to 6-dB increase in the entire mix level.

Distant, Sterile Mixes That Lack Intimacy

These mixes are usually the result of too much reverb or overuse of other effects. As a rule of thumb, there should always be at least one instrument in each mix that is dry—this serves as a point of reference for the listener. With at least one dry sound, the mix takes on much more of an intimate character than if everything has reverb. Remember, reverb is a tool that adds distance and space to a sound, so if every ingredient in a mix has reverb, the entire mix will sound distant.

Dull and Uninteresting Sounds

Learn what's considered good for your style of music and then start practicing. Develop excellent sounds that are appropriate for whatever style of music you're working with.

Unsatisfactory Instrumental Solo Levels

It's not always easy to judge the proper level for instrumental solos, especially when considering multiple types of playback systems. A guitar solo that utilizes an edgy, distorted sound might sound perfectly balanced on a large monitor system but far too loud on a small system. The sensitivity of small speakers to the dominant frequencies of a distorted guitar is brutally apparent when you listen to your mixes on your laptop computer.

This is where the value of multiple sets of monitors is obvious. Always check the sound of your instrumental solos on large, medium, and small speakers. The solution to a solo that is unacceptably dominant on one particular type of monitor is usually in the proper adjustment of equalization, rather than in simple level changes. If the solo sounds too loud on small speakers, try decreasing the frequencies between 1 and 3 kHz.

CHARACTERISTICS OF A GOOD MIX

Strong, Solid, Yet Controlled Lows

It's extremely important to build a mix that distributes low frequencies evenly among the low-frequency tracks. If the kick is boosted at 100 Hz, the bass should not be boosted at 100 Hz—in fact, most likely the bass should be cut at 100 Hz. Always consider the ramifications of boosting or cutting the same frequency on two or more instruments. If you're limited on your mixer to simple two-band, fixed-frequency cut/boost EQ, you must use good mic choice and technique along with educated EQ choices during recording of tracks.

Mids Distributed Evenly Among Various Instruments

The midrange frequencies contain most of the character of each sound. However, too much midrange results in a "honky" sound, and too little midrange results in a hollow, empty sound. It's important to control this frequency range. Midrange tones tend to help a mix sound blended and smooth, but overly accentuated mids can cause a mix to sound dull and lifeless in the high-frequency range or weak and powerless in the low-frequency range.

Strong, Smooth Highs That Are Easy To Listen To

A mix that has one particular high frequency boosted on several instruments can take on an abrasive and irritating character. Highs must be distributed evenly.

- High frequencies between 2.5 and 5 kHz typically create a piercing, harsh, and edgy sound when exaggerated.
- High frequencies between 6 and 9 kHz typically add clarity without a harsh timbre.
- High frequencies above 10 kHz add an airy quality to the sound with less of an apparent high-frequency boost.

Avoid boosting the same high frequency range on several tracks because this could result in a harsh-sounding mix. It is best to use proper mic selection technique, avoiding drastic equalization settings; however, once the tracks are recorded and it's time to mix, you simply need to do whatever it takes to produce an excellent mix, including correctly applying extreme equalization and other processing. Therefore, if you need to boost the high frequencies on several tracks, combine cuts and boosts across the high-frequency spectrum to create an even dispersion of tones.

Balance

A mix that sounds like it's stronger on one side than the other can be distracting. A good way to check the balance of a mix is on headphones. I'll usually listen to a mix on the phones just before I print the master. Headphones are very telling when it comes to stray instruments that might distract if not placed properly.

Depth

A mix can sound okay if it's two-dimensional (just left-right), but when a mix sounds three-dimensional—or if the sounds seem distributed from near to far as well as left to right—it becomes much more real-sounding.

Reverberation and delays add depth. It's usually best to have one instrument define the near character and one instrument define the far character. A simple dry percussion instrument is usually a good choice for the closest instrument. A synth string pad or guitar part might be a good choice for the most distant-sounding instrument. These choices are all dependent on the desired musical impact.

Width

A stereo mix is more interesting if there are one or two instruments defining the far left and far right boundaries, although you must take care to ensure that the mix sounds good in both mono and multi-channel formats. Mixes with boundaries closer in toward the center position—3:00 and 9:00 or 10:00 and 2:00—transfer very well to mono, but they aren't as fun to listen to in stereo.

Momentum

If a song maintains the same intensity and texture from start to finish, it probably won't hold the listener's interest. As a mixing engineer, you should always strive to give the song the appropriate flow. A mix with strong momentum might start with only one instrument and the lead vocal, building to a full orchestration with exaggerated effects; or it might include subtle changes throughout the song that are barely noticeable but add enough variation to maintain the listener's interest.

Consistent Playback Quality

A mix is only good if it sounds good on any system it's played on. Too often a mix sounds great in the studio or on your own recording setup, but when you play the mix in your car, in your living room, on the club sound system, on the radio, or on your friend's mondo home entertainment complex, it sounds embarrassingly bad. Use near-field reference monitors to monitor most of your mix and, as a cross-check, include some larger far-field monitors and some very small radio-like monitors in your setup. Being able to check your mix on two or three sets of speakers can make the difference between good, usable mixes and bad, waste-of-time mixes.

Sounds Good in Stereo, Surround, and Mono

Continually cross-reference the sound of your stereo mixes in mono. Also, check your surround mixes in stereo and mono. Multitrack mixdowns are fun because they sound great. Don't ignore the fact that your multitrack mixes are likely to be heard in mono or stereo. Even though they might sound great in one format, they could sound terrible in another.

Consistent Focal Point throughout the Song

It's very important that the listener not be left wondering. As the mix engineer, it's your job to control the focus—to build a mix that is undeniably easy to follow. Lead vocals provide the obvious focal point in most genres, but in the spaces between lyrics or musical sections, some mix ingredients need to take over, providing a bridge for the listener to the next musical section.

Controlled and Appropriate Use of Effects

The use of effects must create a discernable depth in each mix. Most mixes should sound very large and impressive, yet somehow they must also feel very intimate and personal. Each mix must be shaped and molded to fit within the soundscape that projects the most realistic musical emotion for that specific song.

Motion

There should be a feeling of motion and flow within the mixing panorama. Tracks don't necessarily need to sweep across the panorama, but there should be strategic pan positioning so that, as mix ingredients come and go, the listener feels the natural ebb and flow across the soundscape.

Inclusion of Acoustic Information

Acoustic ambience adds a unique sonic character to most mixes. The inclusion of appropriate amounts of natural ambience around a few recorded tracks helps the mix achieve realism that is otherwise difficult to create.

Acoustic ambience can be captured during tracking; however, it can also be added during mixdown. Simply play back the track or tracks through high-quality monitors in the desired acoustic environment, set up a stereo pair of condenser mics away from the monitors, and blend the room sound into the mix.

Simplicity

This is an incredibly important mix characteristic. The more I've mixed, the more I've learned that, when it comes to mixing, it's usually better to take away than it is to add. Keep it simple and you won't go wrong. It's easier to build power and impact with fewer ingredients than with many. There are certainly times when the music demands a more complex and thick texture, but the power of simplicity is real. Strip away ingredients so you can hear the important aspects of your music. This approach demands a high standard of excellence because as the forest thins, there are fewer places to hide. But it is very worth the time and effort to get the track performed and recorded well and to create a strong and powerful mix that shows it off.

MIXING STYLES

Each major music production region develops its own personality. This personality manifests itself in the local community and the sonic character of the music produced therein. This is beneficial for the successful producer and musician because they can choose to take their music to the region that matches the personality of the artist or the character of the music.

For most recordists, these styles serve primarily as points of comparison and as learning tools. Your favorite type of music probably defines your personality. In a similar way, the type of music that is popular in a certain region defines the

Use Visual Imagery to Guide Your Mixes

An excellent mix is a lot like an excellent photograph or painting. There is a balance and form that is appealing—it is often symmetrical, although sometimes the appeal of a visual or auditory image resides in its attractive asymmetry. Certain parts of a photograph are in crystal-clear focus, yet other supportive ingredients are slightly out of focus. An excellent mix relies on the same principles, positioning some ingredients up close and personal in the mix and intentionally hiding and obscuring other ingredients to create an appealing backdrop for the focal point. You should see the mix in your mind's eye as much as you hear it in your soul.

The image below is simple. It offers a focal point with supportive imagery. Like photography and other art forms, musical appeal is subjective. Some might look at this photograph and call it unbalanced, yet others might be enthralled by its asymmetry. In your musical productions, be attentive to detail and provide your listeners with intentional surprises and contrasts.

industry personality within that region. This is neither a good nor a bad factor; it just is what it is.

It is helpful for us to realize and learn from global regional production tendencies. The onset and growth of rap and urban music has influenced music production around the world and has aided in the globalization of aggressive, highly compressed, in-your-face mixes. Although the lines are blurring between regional tendencies, they are still recognizable in the big picture.

East Coast (New York)

Traditionally, the East Coast sound was much more matter-of-fact and to-the-point than other styles. Arrangements tended to include fewer instrumental and vocal parts, but each ingredient was more finely crafted into a musical entity than in some other styles. For example, East Coast producers preferred to create one great guitar part that functioned exceptionally well throughout the mix, rather than layer several guitar parts.

The East Coast sound still retains much of its attitude from the past, but it has also become very punchy and in-your-face. There is extreme use of compression and limiting as the mix and mastering engineers strive to be the loudest and baddest birds in the nest.

West Coast (Los Angeles)

Traditionally, the West Coast mixing style has drawn on the slick and smooth LA style, layering parts—sometimes beyond reason—and creating lavish beds of sound that are silky smooth and clean. The West Coast production tendency has been to add more parts to create a huge mix, rather than to simply craft the existing ingredients into better music.

The West Coast sound still remains a little more layered and polished than the East Coast sound, but the modern era has seen increased melding of all regional characteristics.

Southern (Nashville)

Nashville has become a melting pot of recording producers and musicians. Previously known primarily for country and Christian music, it has broadened its scope in recent years. The Nashville sound has long been very clean, simple, and straightforward (much like the general population). Although Nashville has been a music hub for many years, it still retains a down-home feel. The Nashville sound is also traditionally more transparent than other regional styles, with a very polished and open feel.

As country-western music has evolved, spawning new country music, Nashville has retained much of its original character with some new faces and a more aggressive musical style. Most of the new country music sounds and feels very reminiscent of rock-and-roll from the '70s and '80s. The production style is relatively wide open—productions are equally likely to have a heavy R&B, rock-and-roll, or southern gospel feel, and the production styles range from hillbilly to pop rock. So far, there is relatively little rap influence in Nashville.

European (London)

The European sound is as regional as the American sound. London productions are historically very layered and prone to including multiple ingredients that possess their own space. You might hear a relatively intimate mix with a flash of an open ambient sound added once or twice just for impact.

Germany, Italy, and many other European regions are very heavily techno-dance or trance oriented. These styles are very groove oriented. Producers and musicians are willing to let the groove ride for a while with sonic textures sprinkled in like spice, just to keep the listener involved.

MIX-BUILDING CONCEPTS

It pays to develop a consistent plan of attack for creating a solid mix. If you randomly approach this important part of the recording process, you'll probably miss an opportunity to get the most out of your productions.

With today's modern mixing technologies, it is very likely that you'll have plenty of time to develop and save the basic mix layout before the actual mixdown process begins. If you're using a digital mixer with snapshot capabilities, store each basic mix as you develop your music. Listen to the rough mixes in your car or on your home entertainment system. These pre-mixes are very instructive and they help shape the overall sound of any project. By the start of the mixing process, you'll have informed and valid opinions about the tonal and musical character of the perfect mix for your production.

Ineffective Approaches to Mixing

The following mix approaches are common to the beginning mix engineer. They are generally ineffective and don't usually lead to the best possible mix for any project. As a disclaimer, mixing is a very subjective process. Each engineer develops his or her own style—many are unconventional, and yet they still result in usable mixes.

Most experienced engineers avoid the following approaches to mixdown, and you probably should, too.
- Quickly get all of the tracks to sound good together and then add the lead vocal.
- Turn everything up and adjust until it sounds good.
- Get the rhythm section sounding good first, then the filler keys and guitars, then the backing vocals, then the lead vocals.

There are, of course, individual preferences for how each mix is built, and there are times when a quick and easy mix is appropriate, especially when you're just learning the song before the real mixdown process begins. If you do set up a quick mix and it sounds good, be sure to print a copy to whatever mixdown format you're using. Sometimes these intuitive mixes end up being the most musical and exciting.

Using Dynamics Processors to Create a Blend

Dynamics processors are important in the recording process. They're used to help control levels during tracking, monitoring, mixing, and mastering. They also help blend mix ingredients together in a way that simple level control can't.

On one hand, dynamics processors are very useful in the recording process—they can aid in the effort to increase vocal intelligibility, they can control the overall mix level so that the entire mix increases in intimacy, and they can blend tracks together so that they possess a cohesiveness that would otherwise be difficult or impossible to achieve. On the other hand, dynamics processors hold the potential to suck the life out of any mix when overused. If you want your mix to sound big and powerful and impressive, disciplined and intelligent compression can help. But if your mix is sounding small and weak and anemic, overuse of compression is probably to blame.

Any time you implement dynamic control using a compressor or limiter, be sure that the device is not affecting the signal most of the time. If the compressor circuitry is always active, the audio passing through it will be degraded all of the time. A simple single-band compression circuit compresses the dynamic range into a small dynamic space; however, when it acts on the signal it changes the tonal and timbrel balance and texture, rarely for the better. When the signal is only affected at the peak dynamic levels, the majority of the track is as powerful and dynamic as you created it to be in the first place, but the peak levels are controlled and compressed.

Engineers and producers don't all agree on the integration of dynamics processors into the mixdown process. Some recordists overuse these devices, while others never use them. The style of music, genre, and producer's taste determine the relevance of dynamics processors to any specific mixdown situation.

Blending Rhythm Instruments

A stereo compressor is often used on the drum set overhead or room mics. These tracks are often severely compressed, resulting in a smooth-sounding drum track that remains forward in the mix.

Patch the tom tracks through a stereo compressor to highlight a warm, blended tom sound with ample tone and length. Depending on the compressor settings, both the drum tone and attack are accentuated.

Bass guitar is frequently compressed heavily. Because low-frequency level inconsistencies result in sporadic mix levels, the bass must be blended and controlled. Synthesizer bass is much easier to mix than electric bass guitar because its output is typically much more consistent.

Blending Vocals

Lead vocal tracks are typically compressed during recording and often they're often recompressed during mixdown. Many mix engineers prefer to simply ride the lead vocal level, rather than recompress the entire track. You get to choose how you work. In some ways, recompressing during mixdown makes the lead vocal track easier to fit into the entire soundscape. In other ways, recompressing the track could result in a reduction of life and transparency.

In many pop songs, compression on the vocal track is used as an effect that smooths out all the rough edges. The constant overcompression serves to accentuate the intimacy of the mix sound, and the continual action of the VCA or DCA becomes a mix ingredient.

Additionally, the more compression you use on the other mix ingredients, the more appropriate compression becomes on the vocal tracks.

Dynamic and Special Effects

In a very open production with important subtleties in the vocal track, compression often acts to supernaturally accentuate the intimacy-defining breaths, moans, and sighs. Frequently, the setting of the release control is as important as the setting of the attack control. Often, the timing of the track turning back up after being compressed should match the tempo of the production in some relevant way.

ARRANGING DURING MIXDOWN

Often during mixdown, radical adjustments are made to the musical arrangement. Once you've critically evaluated the production, you could end up turning off everything but the acoustic guitar and the lead vocal during the intro or the first quarter of the song. In addition, you might leave some tracks completely out of the song or just include them on the choruses—the options are vast.

Spend some time analyzing your rough mixes. It's very important to listen to your song with analytical ears before you begin the final mix. This could take a few hours, but it is definitely time well spent. Try to consider all the options; make a list of different ideas and attempt to separate your heart from the song. If you listen as though you were hearing the song for the first time, you might come up with ideas that add a fresh, new interest to your music. One thing that takes quite a while during mixdown is experimenting with different approaches to the music.

Multiple Mixes

Don't be afraid to try something really "out there" with your song. Go ahead and work through your ideas, printing each idea to tape or disc. I like to print as many versions of each song as I can come up with. Sometimes you'll listen to all of your final mix versions and fall in love with the one that seemed like your least favorite in the studio. You might even end up editing parts of different versions together.

I start laying mixes to the mixdown machine as soon as each version is even close to complete. Often your first impressions of balance, pan, and level are the most natural and will best suit the song. Printing that primal, gut-level mix frequently pays off.

Once you've printed the first couple "safe" mixes, try different approaches that come to mind. It's much quicker and easier to print mixes when everything's set up than to reset later. If you have a question about whether or not the bass is too loud or soft when the mix is played on your home hi-fi stereo, print the song once with the bass louder and once with the bass softer. You could end up with several mixes of each song—it's common to end up with 10 or 20 or more. Chances are good that you'll be happy with one of the versions, and you'll possibly save yourself from personal embarrassment and wasted time.

MIX VERSIONS

As you develop your mixing skills, print several mixes just to make sure you've gotten the most out of your mixing sessions. As you become more comfortable with the mixdown procedure and confident that the mixes you hear in your studio translate well to the rest of the listening world, you'll probably need to print fewer mix versions.

In the era of analog multitrack recorders and tape-based mix recorders, mixes were performed and committed to the mixdown machine—that was "printing" the mix. Although that process still exists when mixing to real-time CD-R or analog multitrack, the modern mix is typically bounced within the digital realm. So, a mix is merely a digital bounce of the mix that lives inside the DAW—it never needs to leave the computer. If this is your workflow, it's still important to create different mix versions for review. These mixes might not need to be rendered or bounced until they're called for, but you should have them ready and be prepared for the request to hear them.

Get into the habit of saving multiple versions of your mixes. When you open the session file, do a Save As... and add the date to the end of the mix title. If someone asks for an instrumental version, first do another Save As...with the suffix "-trax" or "-instrumental" or whatever helps you keep track of the different versions. Saving mix versions takes up very little data space and it is important to keep a mix path so you can find your way back to the beginning of the mix stream if necessary. Sometimes the first mixes are the best and we tend to lose them in the digital realm if we don't keep saving new versions of the session file. It is not necessary to save the digital audio with every version because each new session file references the same folder full of .WAV or .AIFF audio data.

No matter how you build and save your mixes, and even if you're a mix master, four mixes are the basis of every mix package.

- The master mix
- The master mix—Vocals up 1 dB
- The master mix—Vocals down 1 dB
- The TV mix—No lead vocal

The following sections describe some of the basic mixes that I consistently print. Some of these might not be rendered but they are part of the session file and are readily available.

The Gut-Level Mix

This is my first reaction to the music and how it should go together. Sometimes these instinctive mixes are the most punchy and real-sounding. Always print your first guess. You might use it less than 10 percent of the time, but on those occasions where it's the best mix, you'll be the hero for having had the foresight to print it.

The Guitar-Heavy Mix

This mix is heavy on the guitars, often with no keys except when they're absolutely necessary.

The Keyboard-Heavy Mix

This mix is heavy on the keys, often with no guitars except where they're absolutely necessary.

The Streamlined Mix

Take away everything except the lead vocals, and then add only the instruments absolutely necessary to provide harmonic structure.

The Build Mix

This mix starts as simply as possible, with parts added as the music requires until the end, at which point all the tracks and instruments might be included.

Vocals Up or Down

I like to print each version with the vocals a little louder and softer than normal. Even engineers who are very confident in their mixing abilities print alternative mixes with the lead vocals turned up 1 dB and down 1 dB.

Bass Up or Down

Bass can be one of the toughest instruments to judge at first. Monitor speakers are very important. They influence every decision you make during mixdown, whether it involves high, mid, or low frequencies. Only time, practice with your own equipment, and cross-referencing on other systems will give you confidence that what you hear in your studio is compatible with what you'll hear in the real world. If you have any question at all about the bass, print versions with the bass louder and softer than your primary mix.

Solos Up or Down

If there's any question, print mix versions with the solos turned up and down 1 or 2 dB. Sometimes you'll end up with the perfect solo level except for that one high note that kills. If you have a version with the solo turned down, you can always edit that part of the solo in from the "soft solo" version. Like I said before, part of the beauty of having all these mixes is the flexibility to mix and match parts later.

No Backing Vocals

Sometimes the simple version without backing vocals has more punch and believability. This version is also handy for editing purposes. Maybe you'll end up wanting the backing vocal out during the first half of the song. If you don't print a version without backing vocals and you end up needing it at a later date, you'll need to set up everything again, try to get together everything you like about the current mix, and then print the version without the backing vocals. You'd be better off investing the time to print this option in the first mixing session.

Instrumental with Backing Vocals (The TV Mix)

With the popularity of instrumental "trax" and karaoke, there might be a need for the instrumental version of your song. This is often referred to as the TV mix, for the obvious television performance reasons. I've found a definite need to print these, especially in the pop, country, and Christian markets. It's painless to turn the lead vocal off and spend three or four minutes printing this version, but it is usually painful and expensive to go back later to duplicate your complete master mix without vocals. Saving time is always good! Besides, when these versions are needed and you've shown the foresight to have them instantly available, you look good and you solidify the ever-important client/artist relationship.

Instrumental without Backing Vocals

The instrumental version of the mix without backing vocals is convenient for editing flexibility, but it can also be used for a backing track in live performances.

Stems

Stems have become more and more common in the music production world, but they have always been a requirement in the film industry. A stem is simply a submix of a component of the final mix. Where stems are traditionally differentiated from random submixes of some ingredients of the production is that stems are a mixed and effected components of the final master mix, just exactly as they are in that mix. So, if the mix is done and printed, you might be requested to provide a submix of the instruments—exactly the way they were mixed for the final product—and a separate submix of the lead vocal with effects and yet another mix of the backing vocals with their effects. Each of these separate mixes would be a stem derived from the master mix and are typically presented in stereo or surround depending on the master mix format.

The audio post production industry traditionally provides stems for films, including an M&E mix, which stands for "music and effects," and a dialogue stem along with its respective effects and Foley. Sometimes, a film post engineer is asked for music, effects, and dialogue all on separate stems. This makes it much easier to fine-tune the final mix prior to release.

Stems have become a more important consideration in the music production world, largely because of the video game phenomenon *Rock Band*. To author a song for *Rock Band* the following nine 16-bit, 44.1 kHz stems are required, all at levels not to exceed -0.5 dB:

1. Kick drum in mono
2. Snare drum along with its effects
3. Stereo toms
4. Kit mix, including a stereo mix of cymbals, rooms, toms, and so on

5. Bass: playable bass guitar part in stereo
6. Guitar: playable guitar part in stereo
7. Vocals: playable vocals part in stereo with effects
8. Track: any music not already part of a stem, including backing vocals, in stereo
9. Reference dry lead vocal in mono. This is for reference only and will not be used on playback.

Different Mixes

Listen to the different mixes and stems in Audio Examples 4-1 through 4-4. Take note of the things you like and dislike about each. Each mix has a different feel; notice that each stem is complete from the master full mix.

·············· Audio Example 4-1
Complete Mix

·············· Audio Example 4-2
Minimalist Mix

·············· Audio Example 4-3
Band Stem

·············· Audio Example 4-4
Vocal Stem

CHAPTER TEST

1. For the most natural and believable mix:
    a. imagine the music as if a live group was playing it
    b. pan the ingredients evenly across the panorama
    c. use hardly any reverberation
    d. avoid all compression

2. A mixdown requires great attention to:
    a. how tracks blend together
    b. the specifics of maintaining a focal point
    c. the specifics of creating an undeniable musical flow
    d. All of the above
    e. Both a and c

3. In most cases, the best way to set up the mix is to turn all the faders up to about the same level and adjust until you find the sound you want.
    a. True
    b. False

4. Many times we keep adding tracks to get a full sound when we probably should:
    a. increase the amount of reverberation
    b. think of layering sounds instead
    c. concentrate on choosing which tracks are unnecessary
    d. All of the above

5. Mixing is much easier if:
    a. the arrangement has been structured with the final product in mind
    b. you've been disciplined enough to record only the parts that really need to be in the song
    c. the entire band is there to share their opinions
    d. All of the above
    e. Both a and b

6. When there are conflicting opinions, it is the job of _____ to choose which approach best serves the musical needs of the project.
    a. the producer
    b. the mix engineer
    c. the band leader
    d. the manager

7. As the mixing engineer, you must always give the listener:
    a. layers of primary and subliminal sounds
    b. at least three ideas happening simultaneously so there is always something interesting to discover in the mix
    c. a focal point
    d. lots of activity

8. If you'd like to get people to listen to an entire song:
    a. give them a mix that builds from the beginning to the end
    b. build a mix that always has one focal point
    c. include some exciting and possibly surprising sounds
    d. All of the above
    e. Both a and c

9. If there are only one or two instruments in the mix:
    a. be sure to use plenty of reverberation so they'll sound impressive
    b. pan them hard left and right for the best sound
    c. you might want to consider adding more parts for a bigger sound
    d. it should sound like those were the only instruments you recorded
    e. All of the above

10. So there will always be a constant and natural sound quality, be sure to leave all of the tracks turned on and up during the mix.
    a. True
    b. False

Chapter 4 ....MIXING THEORIES

11. In a commercial mix, dynamic range:
    a. is controlled through mix-level changes
    b. is typically indicated by textural change
    c. is a non-issue
    d. is established by the expander

12. To ensure that your mix will fare well in the mastering process and that you've taken advantage of all available audio fidelity:
    a. craft your mixes so they use within one or two decibels of full signal level several times during the production
    b. be sure there are a few places where there is no level as a contrast
    c. mix to analog tape
    d. mix to 192-kHz sample rate

13. The most dramatic result of low digital mix levels is:
    a. substantially decreased accuracy at the highest levels
    b. high-frequency emphasis
    c. a decrease in the signal-to-noise ratio
    d. decreased accuracy at low levels

14. The result of low analog mix levels is:
    a. substantially decreased accuracy at the highest levels
    b. high-frequency emphasis
    c. a decrease in the signal-to-noise ratio
    d. decreased accuracy at low levels

15. The mix engineer must understand the concepts of _____ in order to create a solid mix that is exciting and enticing.
    a. blending levels
    b. combining EQ
    c. controlling dynamics
    d. All of the above

16. Once the mix is built and the musical impact is satisfactory, the mix engineer should play the entire mix with the single intent of:
    a. finding the minimum levels
    b. locating peaks in level
    c. adding reverberation to the overall mix
    d. All of the above

17. A mix that has one particular high frequency boosted on several instruments:
    a. can take on an abrasive and irritating character
    b. is bound to sound crisp
    c. runs the risk of cancellation at that frequency
    d. will be okay if there is an offsetting boost at the correct low frequency

18. If a song _____, it probably won't hold the listener's interest.
    a. doesn't contain a modulation
    b. doesn't have enough reverberation and delay effects
    c. maintains the same intensity and texture from start to finish
    d. doesn't have enough textural layers

19. _____ adds a unique sonic character to most mixes.
    a. High-quality cable
    b. Balanced circuitry
    c. Acoustic ambience
    d. Condenser mics

20. Dynamics processors:
    a. are important during the recording process, especially when tracking to analog tape
    b. are used to help control levels during tracking, monitoring, mixing, and mastering
    c. help blend mix ingredients together in a way that simple level control can't
    d. can suck the life out of a mix
    e. All of the above

Test answers are on page 298

Imaging

CHAPTER 5

CHAPTER AT A GLANCE

The Spherical Approach to Panning
  and Positioning............................. 100
Speaker Position and Choice 103
Mic Techniques.............................. 103
Panning..110
Reverberation.................................114
Space in a Space............................117
Combining Wet and Dry 119
Delay... 120
Panning... 123
Chorus, Flanger, and Phase
  Shifter Effects............................. 125
Monitors and Your Stereo Image 126

When you're mixing down, you must be in control of the precise positioning of each mix ingredient. You'll achieve the most impressive mixes when you intentionally place instruments so they are either very visible or blended into the mix. The following examples and explanations will help you control the stereo image in your productions.

I consider stereo imaging primarily in this chapter because the techniques used transfer well to any playback format. When you thoroughly understand the concepts in this chapter, you'll be able to envision nearly any image position and achieve that placement in your music.

Given a stereo system, it is possible to place any mix ingredient at a specific point into a global panorama using reverberation and delays. However, given a surround system, positioning becomes much simpler. Positioning ingredients behind the listener is easy, whereas implications of sounds behind the listener are difficult to achieve using a stereo system, and they don't transfer well between differing systems.

Whether you're using a stereo or surround monitor system, always imagine your mixes in a global panorama and strive to specifically place mix ingredients so they combine to form a wonderful and emotion-filled mixdown.

THE SPHERICAL APPROACH TO PANNING AND POSITIONING

Before the 1950s, all commercially recorded and transmitted audio was monophonic. You got one channel, and that was it. The home entertainment industry has helped the left-center-right and surround approach gain public recognition and acceptance, and the theater industry brought multiple-channel audio to the masses years ago. Our current practical standard is still stereo, but that is being threatened by surround sound. The newer playback formats of 5.1 and 7.1 systems are standard for home entertainment and are very common in the automobile sound system industry.

When one uses the term stereo, most people envision a sound system that plays back through two loudspeakers. Stereophonic sound, though, actually refers to a system that provides the listener with an illusion of directional realism, no matter how many channels or speakers are used. Our two-ear hearing system is stereophonic even though we can perceive sound localization accurately around a virtually limitless three-dimensional panorama. It's the engineer's goal to produce a sound that contains complete directional realism, and that's usually accomplished using just two speakers.

What does directional realism really mean? For a recording to sound natural and interesting, it must be more than two-dimensional. When sounds are panned left and right in a mix you can separate the instruments across the left-to-right spectrum, and when levels are adjusted, you can vary the relative intensity of each ingredient in a recording. But there's much more to shaping the sound of your music than simple volume and left-to-right adjustments.

Natural acoustic sound is more than two-dimensional. A sound might appear to come from the left or right, or one sound might seem louder than another, but also, some sounds appear to be closer and others appear to be distant. The human hearing system has an amazing ability to determine direction and distance. Even though we only have two ears, we can tell whether a sound is in front of us, behind us, close to us, far away, to the left, to the right, above, below, up high, or down low. We can hear very loud sounds, and if our ears were much more sensitive, we could hear the sound of molecules colliding in the air.

It's our job to try to approximate the intricacies of the ears' perceptions by sending sound out of left and right speakers. It's possible to give a very dimen-

Chapter 5 .... IMAGING

Imagine a Visual Image for Each Mix

Picture the final mix in your head. All of the ingredients should be intentionally positioned for just the right impact on the listener. A clear mental picture aids in the process of developing a mix that displays controlled symmetry, balance, and a sense of structure. Imagine a three-dimensional image along with ambient content.

In this illustration, the vocal glows (reverberates) throughout a specific space that's shared with the guitars. The band tracks are clear and dry—imagine what a mess an image such as this could be if all the instruments spread into each other's mix territory. That's the way reverberation tends to create a muddy, cloudy mix. This images displays a visual balance and clarity.

In addition, notice the synth keyboard behind everything in a soft and supportive role, much like the role of the warm stereo synthesizer pad in many mixes.

sional rendition of your music, even when it's played through a stereo system. That's what this chapter is all about.

The possibilities of instrument placement in a mix are far more complex than a simple left-to-right array of multiple tracks, but through the use of good miking and mixing techniques, sounds can be placed in the mix so that they seem to come from left, right, near, far, above, below, or even behind.

Depth—the feeling that a sound is close to or distant from the listener—is created through the use of reverberation and delay. This reverberation and delay might occur naturally or be electronically created. I've already covered some of the techniques to make a sound fuller throughout the stereo spectrum using delays, chorus, and reverberation, as well as room ambience and mic technique.

Stereo imaging is the realization of specific points of origin across the listening panorama of each ingredient in a recorded work. Where we hear the sound

The Stereo Image and the Global Perspective

Keep in mind that each mix ingredient occupies a three-dimensional space. The two-dimensional left/right plane is not enough to create a realistic and inspiring musical mix.

Acoustically, room reflections combine with direct sound waves from the sound source to provide mental cues about the environment in which the audio is heard. Technically, in a musical mixdown, reverberation and delay provide an electronic simulation of acoustic surroundings.

Notice the difference in the imagery between this illustration and the previous illustration.

coming from and what its acoustical space sounds like are key ingredients in the creation of a pleasing stereo image. If the acoustic guitar sounds like it's coming from four feet to the right of center at a distance of 20 feet from the listener, at 45 degrees above the horizon in a large concert hall, that's its stereo image. Keep in mind that low frequencies below about 150 Hz are omnidirectional, so an effort to give a primarily smooth low-frequency instrument a specific stereo image is usually futile.

SPEAKER POSITION AND CHOICE

When you are trying to control the stereo imaging and panning in a song, the choice of monitor speakers, their placement, and the quality of amplifier and listening environment become crucial. When recording tracks, it's important to have an accurate monitoring system, but as you reach the point of choosing levels and positions for the ingredients in a completed mix, you must be able to trust that what your monitors tell you is true and accurate.

As I mentioned before, good near-field monitors are more dependable than far-field monitors in most monitoring situations—and that includes final mixdown, where crucial placement choices are made. As a word of advice, get the best near-field monitors you can find and afford. Choose a product that's made by a well-established and respected manufacturer and has an excellent reputation for being reliable and accurate. Each monitor sounds different when it comes to stereo imaging and specific panning placements. Your ability to predict how effective or impressive your mix will be when it's played on many types of systems is very dependent on the monitors you use while mixing.

MIC TECHNIQUES

Much of the stereo imagery that's included in your recording starts with fundamental mic technique during the initial tracking. To achieve depth, acoustical interest, and space in the initial recordings, good mic technique is a must.

On the surface it might seem odd to include stereo miking techniques in a mixing book. However, it is common mixdown procedure to send a channel or group of channels to a speaker system, set up the speakers in a room and mike those speakers, and then include the miked sound in the mix. This procedure, typically called "reamping," uses existing acoustic environments as natural reverberation chambers. This technique is very effective in helping drum machine samples and loops sound natural and blended. It also works very well on synth and guitar sounds, live drums, or virtually anything that can be enhanced by a room.

................................Video Example 5-1
Reamping Electric Guitar

................................Video Example 5-2
Reamping Acoustic Drums

It would seem that, in order to hear the specific stereo location of several instruments recorded at once, you'd need many mics to control their panning placement and to adjust the amount of reverberation separately on each track. It's possible to achieve good results this way, but there is a method that's much more reliable and predictable for recording a very accurate stereo image, especially in a room that sounds good.

Using two mics in one of several different stereo miking configurations, you can produce wonderfully interesting stereo sounds. It's amazing how clear the differences between left and right and near and far are with most of the standard stereo miking configurations.

Always check the combination of the two mics in mono to guard against phase cancellation. Coincident miking techniques, such as X-Y or MS (mid-side), have the most reliable stereo images when it comes to summing left and right to mono, but there are plenty of situations in which these techniques aren't appropriate or practical.

Let's examine a few of the standard stereo miking configurations. Each one of these techniques is field tested and has proven functional and effective. Listen very carefully and analytically to these examples. Listen for left/right positioning and for the perception of distance. Are the instruments close or far away? Can you hear a change in the tonal character as the different sounds change position? Do you perceive certain instruments as being above or below other instruments? Can you hear the room sound? In other words, pick these recordings apart bit by bit.

Chapter 5 .... IMAGING

X-Y Configuration

On each of the following diagrams, 0 degrees represents the position of the sound source.

This is the most common stereo miking configuration. The fact that the microphone capsules are as close to the same horizontal and vertical axes as possible gives this configuration good stereo separation and imaging while also providing reliable summing to mono.

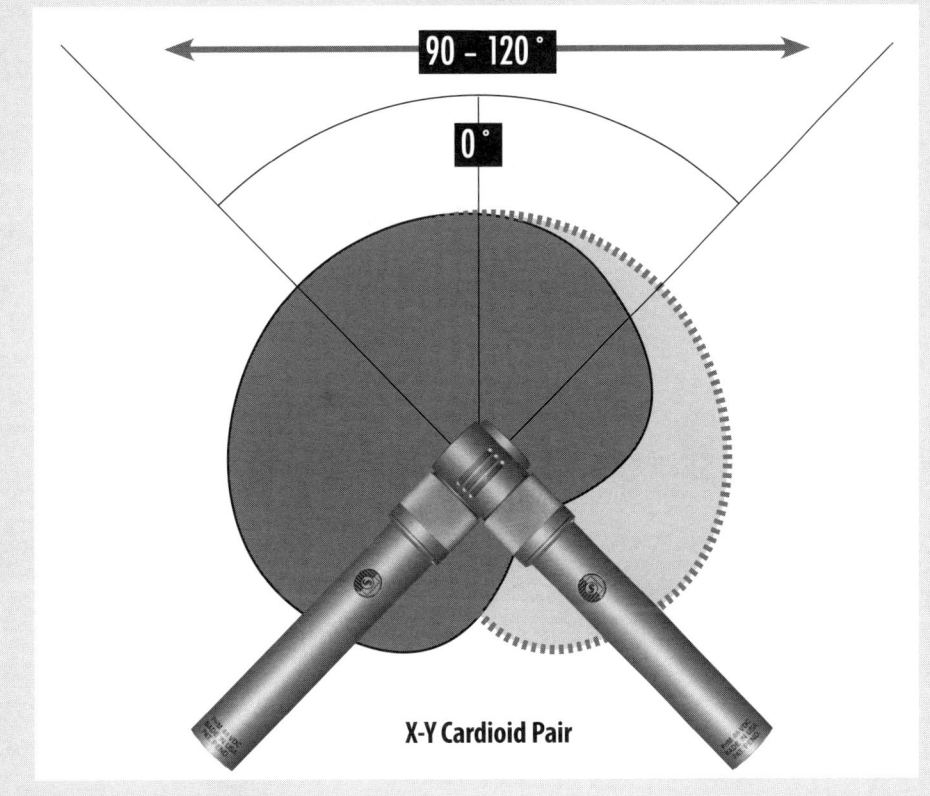

X-Y Cardioid Pair

You've heard the X-Y in a number of situations so far. In Audio Example 5-1, listen very closely to the sound of each ingredient in the stereo recording. Listen to the changes in the sounds as they move around the room.

.... Audio Example 5-1
X-Y Configuration

Two omnidirectional mics spaced between three and ten feet apart can produce a very good stereo image with good natural acoustic involvement. When you are recording a small group, such as a vocal quartet, keep the mics about three feet apart; for larger groups increase the distance between the microphones. Use this

Spaced Omni Pair

This configuration uses two omnidirectional mics. The ambience of the recording environment will color the sound of the recording. This setup is capable of capturing beautiful performances with great life—especially if the recording environment has an inherently good sound.

"D" on the diagram represents the distance from the center of the sound source to its outer edge. Notice that the distance from the center of the sound source to each microphone is one-third to one-half of D.

technique only if the room has a good sound. In Audio Example 5-2, listen closely for the panning placement and perceived distance for each instrument. There's a definite difference in the apparent closeness of these percussion instruments.

.... **Audio Example 5-2**
Spaced Omni Pair

A variation of the spaced omni pair of mics involves positioning a baffle between the two mics, which increases the stereo separation and widens the image. Notice, in Audio Example 5-3, how clearly defined the changes are as the percussion instruments move closer to and farther away from the mics.

Spaced Omni Pair with Baffle

This technique retains much of the openness of the regular spaced omni pair; however, the addition of a baffle between the microphones increases stereo separation. When miking a blended acoustical group or a stereo send from the multitrack of specific mix ingredients, this configuration provides a striking stereo image.

·· Audio Example 5-3
Spaced Omni Pair with a Baffle

The crossed bidirectional configuration uses two bidirectional mics positioned along the same vertical axis and aimed 90 degrees apart along the horizontal axis. This is similar to the X-Y configuration in that it transfers well to mono, but the room plays a bigger part in the tonal character of the recording.

·· Audio Example 5-4
The Crossed Bidirectional Configuration

The MS technique is the most involved of the techniques I'll cover, but it's the best in terms of combining stereo to mono, and it also gives a very true and

Crossed Bidirectional Blumlein Configuration

The crossed bidirectional configuration (also called the "Blumlein" configuration) has the advantage of being a coincident technique in that the overall sound isn't significantly degraded when the stereo pair is combined to mono. The sound produced by this technique is similar in separation to the X-Y configuration but with a little more acoustical life.

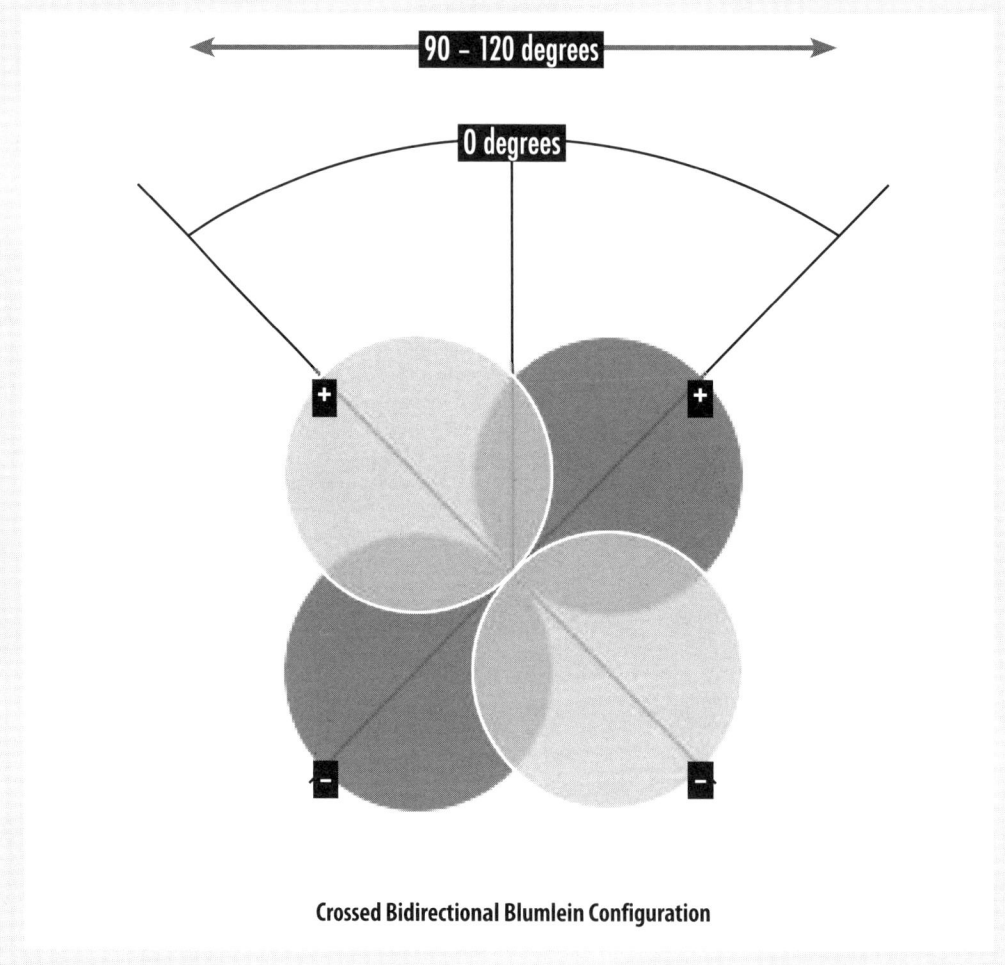

Crossed Bidirectional Blumlein Configuration

reliable stereo image. Most stereo mics contain two condenser capsules that are positioned in an MS configuration.

................................Audio Example 5-5

Mid-Side Configuration

MS (Mid-Side) Configuration

Position the mid mic and the side mic in the closest proximity to each other possible. Both mikes should be along the identical vertical axis and as close as physically possible to the same horizontal axis—without touching. The MS (Mid-Side) technique is the most flexible of the stereo miking configurations. Its drawback is that it isn't simple to hook up. You must use a combining matrix that'll facilitate sending the sum of the mid and side mics to one channel and the difference of the mid and side mics to the opposite channel. In other words, you must be able to:

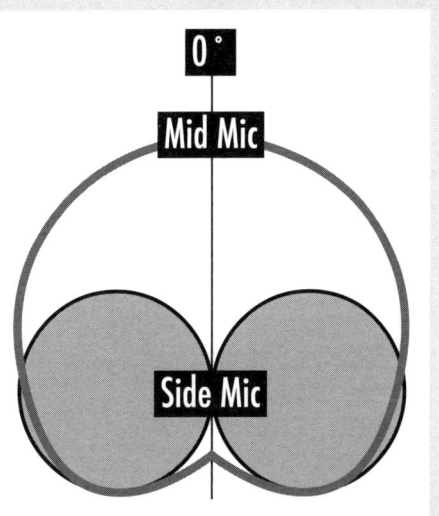

1. Split or Y the output of the mid mic and send it to both channels (or simply pan it to the center position.)
2. Split or Y the output of the side (bidirectional) mic and send it to both channels.
3. Invert the phase of one leg of the side mic split. A leg is simply one side of the Y from the side mic.
4. Leave the other leg of the side mic split in its normal phase.
5. Adjust the balance between the mid mic and the side mics to shape the stereo image to your taste and needs.

High-quality, double-capsule stereo mics typically use this configuration. They demonstrate the advantages of coincident technique—minimal phase confusion between the two microphones. Also, and possibly more important, since the side mic signal is split to left and right—and left and right are made to be 180° out of phase with each other—when the stereo signal is sent through a mono playback system, the side mic information totally cancels. This leaves the mid mic signal as simple and pure as if it were the only mic used on the original recording.

PANNING

Let's start with a very simple arrangement of a rhythm section with a single melody line. When all instruments are panned to the center it's possible for each part to be heard, but the overall sound isn't very natural or spatially interesting. Audio Example 5-6 demonstrates the mono reference point.

.... Audio Example 5-6
Mono Mix

Using simple panning, you can obviously build a more interesting audio picture. Here's the same piece of music but, as the music plays, I'll pan the guitar and keyboards apart in the left-to-right spectrum. This is the beginning of—but definitely not the culmination of—a stereo image. Notice how much easier it is to hear everything when these two instruments claim a different space in the soundscape.

.... Audio Example 5-7
Guitar Right, Keyboard Left

I'll continue to use visual references with the Audio Examples; they're some of the most important considerations when mixing your music. In the previous Audio Example, as soon as the guitar and keys moved out of the way, you could hear the bass, drums, and melody better. Also, you could pinpoint the origin and

Mono Sound

This is the graphic equivalent of mono sound. Like a good mono mix, it is possible to see everything, though it is not very easy or fun to look at.

Guitar Right, Keyboard Left

We consider these audio placements in graphic reference because it provides a means of comparison. When I envision a mix I do exactly that—I visualize the audio components in a three-dimensional thought plane. Now that the keys and guitar are moved from the middle, you not only hear the keys and guitar better, but also the bass, drums, and melody.

tonal character of the guitar and keys in greater detail. Panning is important, but the stereo image you provide for the listener is even more important.

In a previous Audio Example, I split the bass across the stereo spectrum. By sending the dry bass track to one side of the mix and panning a short delay of the bass to the other side of the mix, I created a bass sound that seemed to come equally from left and right, but didn't seem to come from the center of the mix. In

Splitting the Bass

Now we're getting somewhere. The big pieces of the puzzle are all visible. Be sure to check this kind of setup in mono—it can truly sound wonderful in stereo and totally awful in mono.

Audio Example 5-8, I've set up a stereo bass sound with the original panned to one side and a short delay of the bass panned to the other. Using this arrangement, I'll split the bass hard right and hard left. I'll also bring the guitar and keys in to about 3:00 and 9:00 so they don't conflict with the bass.

· Audio Example 5-8
Splitting the Bass

Notice in the illustration below that each ingredient is claiming a space in the stereo soundscape. So far, we're only dealing with left-to-right placement of instruments that might or might not have a natural imagery on their own. We're also only dealing with the two-dimensional left-right/up-down plane. Left-to-right positioning is adjusted with the pan control. Up-and-down positioning can be a function of EQ, with the bass frequencies low in the image and the treble frequencies high in the image. Up-and-down positioning can also be indicated by combining a signal with a short delay of that signal in the same pan position. Notice in the last few illustrations that the bass is placed on the bottom, representing the low frequencies, and the rest of the instruments occupy different top-to-bottom positions. When you're creating your own stereo imagery, always keep

Adding the Triangle: Asymmetry

When you look at this picture, the visual imbalance is instantly recognizable. The audio version of this picture might not seem unbalanced instantly, but eventually a glitch like this will stick out.

Chapter 5...IMAGING

these pictures in mind. Strive for a visual balance, and you will usually achieve in an aural balance. Listen to Audio Example 5-9. What's wrong with this picture?

·· **Audio Example 5-9**
Distracting Pan Position

You probably caught the triangle on the left that made the mix seem lopsided. This only happened because there wasn't another similarly textured instrument on the right side of the mix to balance things out. This problem seems obvious once you focus on it, but if you aren't thinking visually while you mix, this could end up in the final product. Again, think of your mix in visual terms.

If there was just one triangle and no other similar percussion instrument to offset it, the triangle would need to be placed in the center of the mix to provide a balanced sound.

Listen to Audio Example 5-10. I'll pan the triangle to the center and adjust the level. Notice how much easier this mix is to listen to.

·· **Audio Example 5-10**
Panning the Triangle

In Audio Example 5-11, I'll add a cowbell on the other side of the mix from the triangle to offset the imbalance. Even though I've added an instrument, this mix has a balanced, even sound and is easier to listen to. The distraction caused by the imbalance no longer exists.

·· **Audio Example 5-11**
Adding the Cowbell

Stereo imagery is much more involved than this simple panning exercise. Panning is important, but reality demands much more than simple left/right comparison. If you are to create a realistic musical image, you must include left, right, up, down, in front, behind, inside, outside, and anywhere in between.

Try this exercise. Sit in any normal environment and just listen. Notice the different sounds. Even in a fairly quiet and serene setting, you'll be able to pick out several different sounds. Next, notice where each sound comes from.

The extreme localization accuracy of the human hearing system is amazing. We can very closely pinpoint the origin of each sound we hear. In real life, we're engulfed in a three-dimensional globe of audio stimulation, and in recording that's what you should always try to provide for the listener. Some of the tools required to fully accomplish this feat are either very expensive or haven't been designed yet, but there are several techniques you can use to more closely approach the ideal of three-dimensional audio. Some of the four- and six-channel systems that are common in the film business are very good at providing a surrounding image, but for everyday life most recordists have to primarily consider the normal two-speaker stereo system. This chapter focuses on practical and accessible techniques.

You can accomplish a lot on a two-speaker system. As I've mentioned before, you can create the dimension of depth by adding delays and reverberation. This is a very complex subject and requires you to consider many environmental and psychoacoustic variables. At this point, I'll keep things fairly simple and straightforward.

REVERBERATION

Listen to the reverberation on the snare drum in Audio Example 5-12; I've selected a long decay time. Listen intently to the effect it creates. Listen to the changes that occur as the reverb fades away. Try to imagine a real room that would sound like this. How big would it be? What kind of surfaces would be around?

............................Audio Example 5-12
Snare Reverberation

Audio Example 5-12 was an example of stereo reverberation. Stereo reverb is designed to have slightly different combinations of reflections and tonal character from left to right. A stereo reverb is very helpful in opening up the stereo spectrum and leaving more space for the music. Audio Example 5-13 demonstrates the same reverb sound as the previous example, but this time it's in mono. At the end of the Example, I'll open back up to stereo. Mono reverberation can be very useful when placing an instrument or voice within one area of a large stereo image, but generally stereo reverberation is preferable.

............................Audio Example 5-13
Mono Reverberation

When considering placement of an instrument, you must also determine where the listener should be in relation to the instrument. Placement of an instrument in a large concert hall is one consideration. Do you want the listener to feel that he or she is close to the instrument and inside the concert hall, or do you want the listener to feel as if he or she is standing at the opposite end of the hall from the instrument? Do you want the instrument to be far away and in the corner of the concert hall? Do you want the listener to feel that he or she and the instrument are close together, but closer to one side or the other? The list of considerations

Moving Close to the Snare Drum in the Hall

With the mic close to the drum and at one end of the hall, the recorded sound contains mostly direct sound and close reflections. The distant reflections still influence the sound of the drum but aren't always instantly recognizable. The reflections from the back wall of the hall, in this situation, are delayed substantially. In a hall that's 150 feet long, it takes about 265 milliseconds for sound to get from the instrument to the back wall, then back to the mic—since sound travels at the rate of roughly 1,130 feet/second.

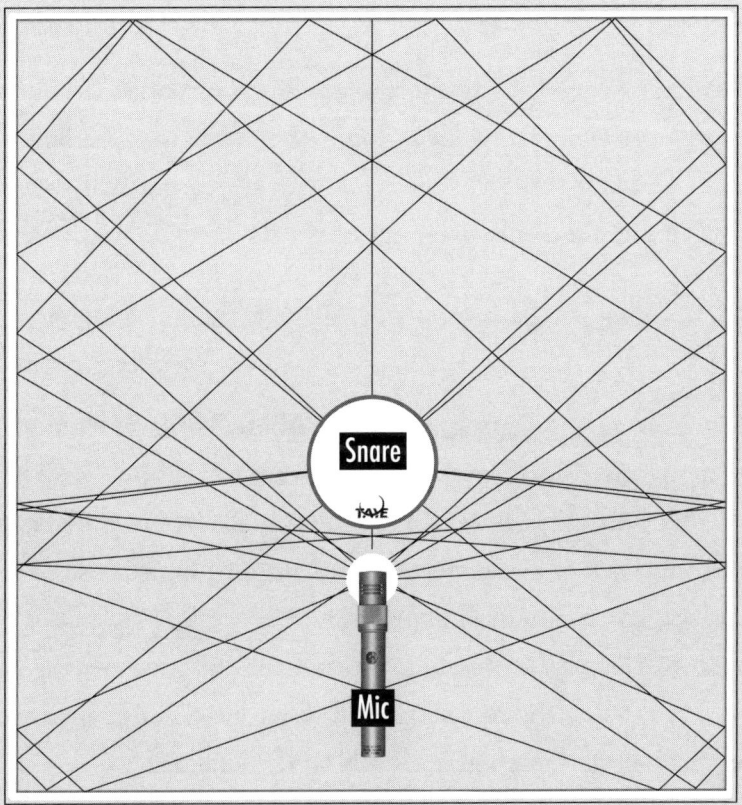

goes on and on. If you want to create a mix that has clear imagery, you'll need to consider these kinds of options for each instrument or voice in the soundscape.

Now, let's move the snare drum and ourselves around the room. If you want the instrument to appear to be close to the listener and in a very large hall, you must consider that the listener would naturally hear a strong, direct sound followed by a slightly delayed reverberation as it comes back to the listener from the hall. Changing the predelay on the reverb and the relative volumes of the reverberation and the direct instrument sound, let's vary the apparent closeness of the listener to the instrument—the longer the predelay, the larger the perceived size of the hall. Listen as I change the stereo image of the drum. I'll start with the drum far away in a large hall. Then I'll move the drum closer to you by increasing the level of the direct sound and lengthening the predelay. I'll pan the drum slightly, and while I pan the drum, I'll also vary the balance of the reverberation. As the drum moves left, I'll increase the level of the right-side reverb return. Try to picture the placement of this drum in your mind.

··························· **Audio Example 5-14**
Moving the Drum Around the Room

In Audio Example 5-15, I'll select a smaller reverberation sound and move the snare drum around in that image. Some of the changes are not as noticeable with this smaller room sound as they were with the larger hall sound, but these changes are still a dramatic enhancement of the dry original mono snare sound.

··························· **Audio Example 5-15**
Moving the Drum Around a Smaller Room

There are several good applications for these kinds of changes. Film and video sound demands control over sound imagery, and you must be capable of moving the audio image in tandem with the visuals. There are also appropriate settings for these types of movements in music, although most of the time the musical soundscape is stable and balanced.

With your own equipment, select a sound and practice moving it around the stereo image. Try moving the image around different-sized environments—from very large to fairly small. Listen very closely to the changes.

With the control available to the modern-day engineer, there are plenty of opportunities to create sounds that would never occur naturally, and these sounds can be very powerful and appropriate. The ability to recognize and create a natural stereo image facilitates much more control in creating usable unnatural stereo images.

Space in a Space

It's common when shaping sounds to combine reverbs and delays to add interest and realism. Combining a small-room reverb with a concert-hall reverb is fairly common. Combining a tight-room reverb with a large stereo-hall reverberation adds depth to the stereo image.

Stereo Distant Mic Setup

This stereo distant mike setup represents a scenario where the reflections might be as strong as the direct sound. The reflections shown are only a small representation of the reflections that occur in reality. Low frequencies carry more energy than high frequencies and therefore can set up repeating patterns of reflections called standing waves. As these patterns combine they either sum or cancel at specific frequencies, causing acoustic coloration of the sound.

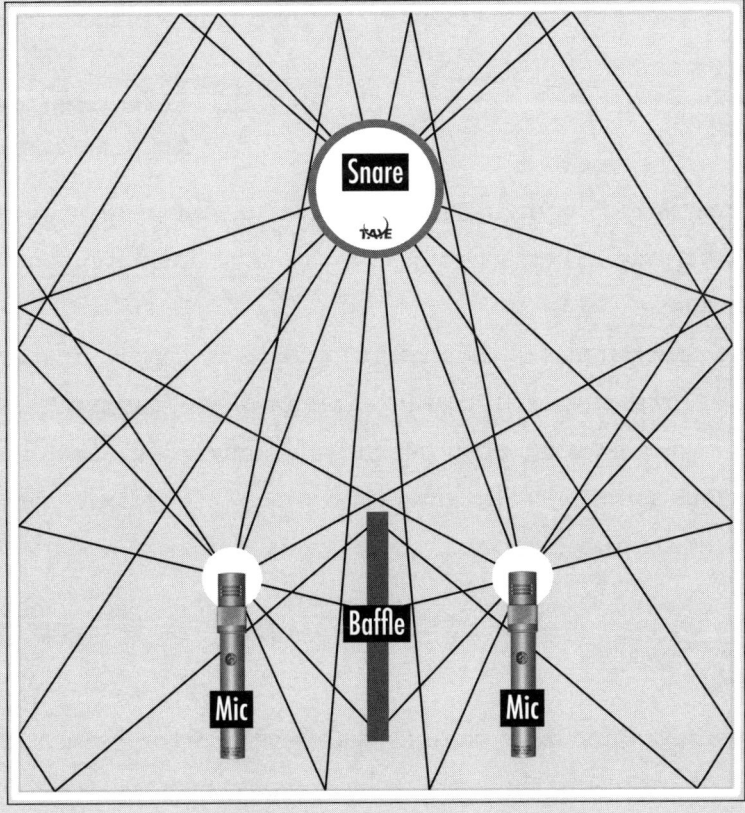

The combination of effects is used to help build a pronounced stereo image. When I add a very tight room sound to the marimba in Audio Example 5-16, I increase the acoustic interest of the sound.

·····························Audio Example 5-16
Marimba with Tight Room Reverb

Adding a large-hall sound with a fairly long predelay (around 200 ms), the sound takes on a completely different feel.

·····························Audio Example 5-17
Marimba with Large Hall Reverb

Add the tight room sound to the marimba and then pan the marimba and the room sound toward the right, then pan the large hall sound to the left. This creates a stereo image that puts the listener in a small room with the marimba, but there's a door open on the left side of the room that leads into a concert hall. This technique of panning the instrument apart from the large room or hall sound, dry or with small-room reverberation, is very effective and provides an interesting stereo image in a song or a mix. Listen to the imagery in Audio Example 5-18.

·····························Audio Example 5-18
Marimba Next to the Concert Hall Door

These images add depth and sound quality to your recordings that can't be achieved in other ways. There's a lot of room for experimentation and innovation with these options.

Listen to the examples of different placements and stereo imaging in Audio Example 5-19. Try to envision the audio space for each of the examples. They will help fine-tune your listening, plus they provide some useful stimuli for creating your own unique sounds. Write down your impression of each example's stereo image, then recreate that image with your own equipment.

·····························Audio Example 5-19
Stereo Images

When you combine basic panning with reverb in the context of a song or instrumental arrangement, the options for mix placement increase dramatically. If the guitar is panned right, should it be up front and dry in the mix, or should it sound like it's coming from behind the rest of the instruments? Should an instrument's reverb be wide and stereo, or should it be mono and localized to the point of origin for the instrument? Should the entire mix sound like it's being heard in an auditorium? The list of considerations goes on and on.

Listen to the difference in Audio Example 5-20 as I change the position and reverb on the guitar track. I'm changing the pan position of the guitar and/or the reverb, decay time, and predelay. Notice how the stereo image of the guitar changes from close to distant and how the size of the image changes from very small to very large.

Audio Example 5-20
The Roaming Guitar

Combining Wet and Dry

If you're designing textures with multiple instruments performing the same musical part, it isn't usually necessary to add reverb to all pieces of the texture. In fact, the overall image can change substantially depending on what part of the texture you send to the reverb. If you have similar timbres in the different sounds you're layering, try adding reverb only to certain sounds.

As a practical example, it's common on the chorus of many songs to hear the lead vocal singing along with the background vocals. When this scenario occurs with vocals or other textures, you need to determine which part of the texture you want to be in front of the other parts. With the vocal chorus section, try adding reverb to the background vocals but leaving the lead vocal totally dry. The fact that the background vocals have a similar timbre to the lead vocal will give the impression that there is really reverberation on all of the vocals, including the lead part, because the other parts will activate the reflections. But the overall image will be that the lead vocal seems more present—further forward or closer to the listener—in the mix. This technique is commonly used in the recording industry.

Sometimes you end up combining two or more sounds for a texture, and the sounds are totally different in their frequency content. Reverberation can be applied to either or both sounds; the result of each combination produces a completely different musical feel. Audio Example 5-21 demonstrates a combination of a low-end pad sound with a high-end string sound.

·························· **Audio Example 5-21**

Low Pad, High Strings

In Audio Example 5-22, hall reverb is added to the low pad sound, but the high-end strings remain dry. Notice the clarity of the high end and the fullness of the low end.

·························· **Audio Example 5-22**

Reverb on the Low Pad

In Audio Example 5-23, with the same sounds used in Audio Example 5-22, plate reverb is added to the high-end strings, but the low-end pad remains dry. Notice the sizzle of the high end and the closeness of the low end.

·························· **Audio Example 5-23**

Reverb on the High Strings

Delay

In the chapters on guitar, keyboard, and vocal sounds, and in Books 1 and 2 of this method, we use digital delay to widen the image of a single instrument. With the original instrument sound panned to one side of the stereo spectrum and a short delay—below about 35 ms—panned to the opposite side of the spectrum, the originally mono image spread across the panorama, leaving more room to hear the rest of the instruments. This technique widens the stereo image, but almost more importantly, it makes room in the mix to hear other instruments and their images in the stereo soundfield. As a quick review, listen to the guitar in Audio Example 5-24. It starts mono in the center, and then I pan it left and turn up a 17-ms delay on the right.

·························· **Audio Example 5-24**

Creating a Stereo Guitar Sound

Each time you use short delays to widen the stereo image, be sure to keep these three points in mind:
- Always check the mix in mono to be sure the original and the delay don't combine in a way that cancels the predominant frequencies of the track.
- If you've hard-panned the delay and the original apart in the mix, be sure that when the mix is summed to mono the instrument is still audible in the mix.

Stereo to Mono Hard Split (Stereo Image)

In this stereo image, the guitars are clear and visible because they're hard-panned out of the way of the rest of the instruments. This is typically very effective in a stereo mix, but when the mix is summed to mono the instruments or voices that are hard-panned disappear to a greater degree than instruments that are distributed closer to the center position.

As music radio and television eliminate mono broadcasts, concern about mono compatability will fade; however, so long as there is any chance that your hard work will be heard on a mono system or broadcast format, be sure to verify that your mixes sound good in stereo and mono.

The illustrations that follow demonstrate the visual equivalent of stereo/mono comparisons.

- When choosing delay times, keep in mind that short delays—below about 11 ms—usually cause the most problems when summing to mono.

Audio Example 5-25

Short Delays from Mono to Stereo

Stereo to Mono Hard Split (Mono Image)

Once the mix is summed to mono the guitars are hidden among the rest of the orchestration. The only way to minimize this situation is to avoid hard-panning in the stereo mix. The closer in to the center position you keep each ingredient of the mix, the better the mix will sound in mono. You must compromise and constantly cross-check your mix if you want a product that sounds good in both stereo and mono.

Sometimes, even if there's no phase problem when summing to mono, the split instrument seems to disappear when the mix goes to mono. The hard-panned split tracks are very visible in stereo because there's nothing in the listener's way. As soon as everything comes together in the center in mono, however, the split tracks are simply buried in the mix. The only way to avoid this situation is to avoid hard-panning tracks in the mix. The closer you keep all of the ingredients in your song to the center position, the better the mix will transfer to mono.

It's up to you to decide whether your music should have a huge stereo image or sound good in both mono and stereo. It is possible to get a mix that sounds huge in stereo and still great in mono, but it takes several comparisons, compromises, and fine adjustments throughout the mix process. Each instrument must be deliberately placed in the mix, the spread across the stereo spectrum should be very even from hard-left to hard-right, and all stereo images must be aurally calculated and compared to provide width and fullness in stereo while maintaining visibility and clarity in mono.

Delay times above 11 ms and below 35 ms tend to transfer well to mono, but they still must be cross-checked and fine-tuned in both mono and stereo. Audio Example 5-26 demonstrates a 25-ms delay that sounds pretty good in stereo. When I switch to mono, I'll fine-tune the delay time to get the best sound.

······················· Audio Example 5-26
Fine-Tuning the 25-ms Delay for Mono

Delay times between 35 ms and 50 ms often sound very large and impressive in stereo, but when they are summed to mono they tend to sound roomy with a very short slapback effect. Audio Example 5-27 demonstrates a 50-ms delay, cross-checked from stereo to mono.

······················· Audio Example 5-27
Fine-Tuning the 50-ms Delay for Mono

In understanding the stereo image, it's helpful to realize that when these short delays are panned apart, our ears will prefer the original over the delay. A phenomenon known as the Haas effect indicates that the delay is suppressed by as much as 8 to 12 dB. In other words, our hearing system is doing its best to ensure that localization is cued from the initial, direct sound wave. If you want to split an instrument in the mix and you want that instrument to sound like it's coming equally from both left and right, you have to turn the delayed signal up higher in actual level than the original. The amount depends on the amount of transient and the overall sound quality of the instrument.

Panning

If the wide stereo image has been created with a good 16-bit, 24-bit, or better digital delay, the sound quality of the delayed signal should be nearly identical to the original sound. To increase the stereo effect, try equalizing the left and right sides differently. Listen to the split of a simple keyboard sound in Audio Example 5-28. The original is panned right and the delay is panned left. On the left, 8 kHz is boosted and 4 kHz is cut; on the right, 8 kHz is cut while 4 kHz is boosted. This way, the difference between left and right is enhanced; the frequencies that I've selected should be well represented in nearly all possible monitor systems.

Audio Example 5-28
Equalizing the Stereo Split

Short delays are good for widening images, but they're also useful for creating more subtle changes. When short delays, below about 17 ms, are combined with the original dry signal in the same pan position, the image can seem to rise or lower on the vertical plane.

Depending on the tonal character of the instrument you're recording and the accuracy of your monitors, these short delays produce different effects. Listen to the acoustic guitar part in Audio Example 5-29. It starts clean and dry, and then a 17-ms delay is slowly added. The original guitar and the delay are both panned to the center position.

Audio Example 5-29
17-ms Delay

Audio Example 5-30 demonstrates the same example, this time with a 15-ms delay. Notice the audible vertical position of the guitar as the delay is added. Does it rise or lower?

Audio Example 5-30
15-ms Delay

Audio Example 5-31 demonstrates the same example, this time with an 11-ms delay.

Audio Example 5-31
11-ms Delay

Audio Example 5-32 demonstrates the same example, this time with a 7-ms delay.

Audio Example 5-32
7-ms Delay

Audio Example 5-33 demonstrates the same example, this time with a 3-ms delay.

.... Audio Example 5-33
3-ms Delay

The previous five Audio Examples are designed to provoke your thoughts on positioning and stereo imaging. When you listen with ears tuned to analyze these subtle sound differences, you're just beginning to hear the music.

Use these techniques to serve the purpose of the music. If some of these simple techniques can add to the musical power and impact and provide a clear visual image, they're serving their purpose well.

Combining each of the topics I've discussed in this chapter starts to become a bit of an organizational mental task. You've learned how to move instruments closer, farther away, into more than one acoustical space at a time, and up and down along the vertical axis.

In your head, develop a global picture of each mix. Keep track of the three-dimensional positioning of each ingredient. Create a balanced visual image; it will help you produce a mix that's easy to understand, powerful, and fun to listen to.

CHORUS, FLANGER, AND PHASE SHIFTER EFFECTS

The use of stereo chorus, flanger, and phase shifter effects can definitely widen an image. As I've discussed, these effects—although pleasing in stereo—can spell trouble in mono. They can be more trouble than a simple delay because their constantly changing and sweeping delay times cause sweeping changes in the frequencies that sum and cancel. These effects produce excellent results when adjusted to optimize their impact in both stereo and mono, but whether or not they are appropriate is mandated by the genre and era. Right now, it's not very common to hear a first-class mix that relies on these modulated effects. That is likely to change and it might change in the next month or year. It's up to you to assess the stylistic validity of any mixing technique but, for our purposes, you should be familiar with as many techniques and sounds as possible so you can respond quickly in the creative moment.

MONITORS AND YOUR STEREO IMAGE

Keep in mind that the stereo image will change depending on the monitor system. If many of your stereo placement cues are indicated by very high frequencies, everything will sound fine as long as your music is being heard on a system that reproduces the very high frequencies. As soon as your music is heard on a below-par system with limited highs, the image that you've worked so hard to create will probably be gone. This is a frustrating fact that we all must face.

If you check your mixes on large, medium, and small speakers, you should be able to build a mix that has good imaging and transfers well to most monitor systems. It's all a matter of compromising a little here and there for the good of each listening situation.

High-quality near-field reference monitors are typically your best tool for accurate mixing. The preferred monitor du jour changes occasionally, but it's never a secret. I have my current favorites that work well for me and help me build mixes that sound good on a lot of different types of systems—that's really the goal in monitor selection. Try out as many monitors as you can. This is another circumstance where an excellent relationship with a professional audio supplier is very valuable. Between your dealer's recommendations and the information you discover in industry trade magazines, you should be able to find several monitors that might work well for you. However, to find reliable monitors that actually work well in your mixing environment, you must mix something on them, leave the studio, and then listen to that mix everywhere possible. If the mix that sounds good to you on your studio monitors sounds good everywhere else, you're using the right monitors.

Chapter 5 ....IMAGING

CHAPTER TEST

1. Our two-ear hearing system is stereophonic even though we can perceive sound localization accurately around a virtually limitless three-dimensional panorama.
    a. True
    b. False

2. For a recording to sound natural and interesting, it must be:
    a. full-bandwidth
    b. recorded at maximum digital or analog level
    c. more than two-dimensional
    d. reverberated

3. _____ aid(s) in the process of developing a mix that displays controlled symmetry, balance, and a sense of structure.
    a. An RTA
    b. The intelligent use of dynamics processors
    c. A clear mental picture
    d. Peak meters

4. A mix can be made to sound fuller throughout the stereo spectrum using:
    a. delays
    b. chorus
    c. reverberation and room ambience
    d. mic technique
    e. All of the above

5. Low frequencies below about 150 Hz are _____.
    a. bidirectional
    b. not measured accurately by most RTAs
    c. omnidirectional
    d. directional
    e. None of the above

6. Your ability to predict how effective or impressive your mix will be when it's played on many types of systems:
    a. is very dependent on the monitors you use while mixing
    b. depends on the quality of your equalizers
    c. depends on the quality of the cable in your system
    d. All of the above
    e. None of the above

7. When all instruments are panned to the center:
    a. it's impossible to get a good sound
    b. conflicting phase relationships can degrade the sound quality
    c. it's possible for each part to be heard, but the overall sound isn't very natural or spatially interesting
    d. All of the above
    e. Both b and c

8. The technique of panning the instrument apart from the large room or hall sound, dry or with small-room reverberation, is very effective and provides an interesting stereo image in a song or a mix.
    a. True
    b. False

9. Using short delays, below about 35 ms, panned away from the original track:
    a. spreads the original mono image across the stereo panorama
    b. eliminates concerns about phase interactions in mono
    c. opens up more room in the mix to hear the rest of the mix ingredients
    d. All of the above
    e. Both a and c

10. Often, instruments that are _____ are hidden _____.
    a. radically reverberated, at low volume levels
    b. harsh-sounding, by low frequencies
    c. hard-panned in the stereo mix, when the mix is heard in mono
    d. dry, by wet instruments

11. A delay of _____, panned away from the dry signal, often sounds very large and impressive in stereo; however, when the dry and delayed signals are summed to mono they tend to sound roomy with a very short slapback effect.
    a. between 3 ms and 7 ms
    b. between 11 ms and 17 ms
    c. between 17 ms and 21 ms
    d. between 35 ms and 50 ms

12. When delayed signals are panned away from the original dry signal:
    a. a phenomenon known as the Haas effect indicates that our ears will prefer the original over the delay
    b. the delay is suppressed by as much as 8 to 12 dB
    c. the delayed signal must be louder than the dry signal for the listener to perceive a balanced image
    d. All of the above
    e. None of the above

13. When creating a stereo sound by panning a delay apart from the original, the stereo effect is decreased by equalizing the left and right sides differently.
    a. True
    b. False

14. When delays below about 17 ms are combined with the original dry signal in the same pan position, the image can seem to rise or lower on the vertical plane.
    a. True
    b. False

15. The closer you keep all of the ingredients in your song to the center position, the better the mix will transfer to mono.
    a. True
    b. False

16. It is important while creating a mix to:
    a. keep track of the three-dimensional positioning of each ingredient
    b. create a balanced mix image
    c. listen to your mix on different speaker systems as well as headphones
    d. All of the above
    e. Both a and c

17. Stereo chorus, flanger, and phase shifter effects:
    a. don't cause problems when summed to mono because of their LFO sweep
    b. cause sweeping changes in frequencies that sum and cancel
    c. can help widen an image
    d. All of the above
    e. Both b and c

18. The stereo image you hear during mixdown is not dependent on the monitor system.
    a. True
    b. False

19. High-quality far-field reference monitors are typically your best tool for accurate mixing.
    a. True
    b. False

20. The goal in monitor selection is:
    a. to find speakers that look really impressive in your control room
    b. to find monitors that help you build mixes that sound good on a lot of different types of systems
    c. to find speakers that either support or minimize the acoustics in the control room
    d. All of the above
    e. Both b and c

Mixing

CHAPTER AT A GLANCE

Equalization: The Cumulative Effect..	130
Combining EQ	130
Allocating EQ across the Audible Spectrum	132
Fitting the Puzzle Together	132
Practicing	132
Sweeping a Peak to Find a Problem	132
Basic Procedures for Building the Mix	133
Drums	134
Combining an Excellent Drum Kit and an Excellent Drummer	134
Kick Drum	135
Snare Drum	136
Live Toms	136
Drum Set Overheads (Live)	137
Drum Machines, Sound Modules, and Sample Libraries	137
Bass Guitar	140
Mixing Guitars	141
Acoustic Guitar	141
Dynamic Control	142
Electric Guitar	143
Keyboards	145
Lead Vocal	147
Intonation	149
Compression	152
Expander	152
Vocal EQ	153
Exciter	153
Simple Delay	153
Add Backing Vocals	154
Rhythmic Keyboards and Rhythm Guitars	156
Filling in the Holes with the Guitar or Keys	156
Lead Lines and Solo Parts	157

The techniques and guidelines in this chapter are designed to provide a point of reference for the development of your own specific style. There are several theories and procedures that are common through the mixing process, no matter what genre you happen to be producing; however, each type of music brings its own expectations.

Listeners, producers, and musicians aren't usually short on opinions when it comes to music they love. Become intimately familiar with the styles you're mixing. In addition, maintain an open mind during the process. Only when you are very familiar with the expectations of those who love the style of music you're producing can you legitimately and authentically push the creative boundaries—you should always strive to add your personal edge to the music you mix and produce.

Take note through this chapter of specific techniques that will help you develop better mixes. Many techniques involve adjusting frequency ranges, pan settings, and effects that primarily increase the power of the mix without dramatically affecting its sound. Other techniques radically affect the musical, emotional, and sonic impact of the mix.

Mixing music involves several factors other than the basic sound of the music. Although the artistic and musical aspects of mixing are very important, many of the techniques described herein are designed to maintain the musical sound while increasing the musical impact and power.

Mixing & Mastering .... by BILL GIBSON

EQUALIZATION: THE CUMULATIVE EFFECT

During mixdown you must make many decisions concerning the use of equalization, levels, panning, effects, and so on. When it comes to equalization, the big picture is what matters. The sonic character of an individual track is frequently secondary to considerations about how the tracks all work together to form a complete mix.

Combining EQ

As you build each sound, always keep in mind that boosts and cuts at specific frequencies accumulate. Boosting the same frequency on several tracks at once causes the entire mix level to increase artificially. Even though you might like the

Combining EQ Curves

When the same frequency is boosted on several full-range instruments, the mix quickly elevates to an unnecessarily hot level. In addition, the similarly equalized tracks conflict with each other, losing the individual character and personality.

Instruments such as the bass guitar and kick drum, when boosted in the same low-frequency range, quickly raise the overall mix level. Since both instruments contain ample content at 100 Hz, when they're both boosted by 6 dB at 100 Hz the entire mix level could be increased by 12 dB.

Kick Drum EQ Curve

Bass Guitar EQ Curve

Allocating EQ

Distribute equalization boosts and cuts across the audible spectrum. For example, if you need to boost the low frequencies on the kick drum, bass guitar, and synth pad, choose different frequencies to boost on each track. This procedure distributes the lows across a broader bandwidth, helping to minimize amplitude accumulation.

In this illustration the kick drum, bass guitar, and synth EQ curves reveal a 4-dB boost at separate and unique low-frequency bands.

Bass Boosted 4 dB at 50 Hz

Kick Boosted 4 dB at 100 Hz

Synth Pad Boosted 4 dB at 150 Hz

individual sound of each instrument, boosting one frequency band constantly causes that band to accumulate, adversely affecting the overall mix level.

For example, if you boost 100 Hz on the kick drum by 6 dB, then boost 100 Hz on the bass guitar by 3 dB, then boost 100 Hz on the synth pad by 4 dB, you could increase the mix level by up to 13 dB when all three instruments play aggressive full musical parts.

This concept also applies to cutting similar frequencies on multiple cuts. Multiple cuts at the same frequency create a mix that is unpredictable when cross-referenced on several systems. The hole in the broadband spectrum caused by multiple cuts at the same frequency could result in a mix that sounds fine on one system but completely unacceptable on others.

Allocating EQ across the Audible Spectrum

It's the mix engineer's job to build a mix that is strong, full, and balanced. Rather than boosting the same frequency on several tracks, allocate varying bands to each instrument. Instead of boosting 100 Hz on the kick, bass, and pad, try boosting different low-frequency bands on each to spread the low-frequency energy across a broader range. This way, there won't be such dramatic impact on the overall mix level.

Fitting the Puzzle Together

An experienced mix engineer allocates equalization boosts and cuts across broad frequency bands with the tracks fit neatly together like puzzle pieces. For example, if you need to fill out the kick drum and bass guitar tracks, try boosting the kick slightly at 60 Hz and then boosting the bass guitar at 120 Hz. With this done, create a dip in the EQ curve of each of the two tracks to create a space for the boost in the other. In other words, boost the kick track at 60 Hz and then cut the kick track at 120 Hz. Next, boost the bass track at 120 Hz and then cut it slightly at 60 Hz.

Using equalization in this way will produce a mix that sounds fuller on each track while the mix level is relatively unaffected. Without the accumulation of equalization boosts, the entire mix is more powerful and will end up sounding much louder when completed.

Practicing

Build some mixes and test these theories. You'll be surprised at how much more powerful a mix sounds when you use these intelligent equalizing principles.

Sweeping a Peak to Find a Problem

Sometimes you'll run across tracks that possess interesting tone problems. Annoying rings from a snare drum or tom can adversely affect the overall mix impact. An irritating high-frequency edge on certain guitar sounds can ruin the best of mixes.

If you find a problem that needs to be eliminated, try sweeping a very narrow peak across the suspected problem area.

Create Complimenting EQ Curves

The previous two illustrations demonstrated two valuable concepts: EQ accumulation and EQ allocation. In this illustration we create equalization curves for instruments with similar frequency content that fit together like puzzle pieces—if 120 Hz is boosted on the kick drum, cut 120 Hz on the bass guitar. Likewise, if you boost 60 Hz on the bass guitar, cut 60 Hz on the kick drum.

If you simply use this technique on these two instruments alone, the resultant power and punch in your mixes will increase dramatically. Whereas boosting both the kick and bass guitar at 120 Hz by 6 dB could result in a 12-dB increase in mix level, using the technique described in this illustration could create a more impressive sound while affecting the mix level very little.

The slider positions on the graphic equalizers below provide an excellent illustration of this concept of creating complementing EQ curves.

- Use a parametric EQ with the narrowest bandwidth selected.
- Create a severe boost.
- Sweep the boost until the problem frequency is most noticeable.
- Cut the selected frequency to eliminate or minimize the problem.

Video Example 6-1
Equalization Techniques

BASIC PROCEDURES FOR BUILDING THE MIX

Each instrument and voice demands individualized treatment during mixdown. You must assess every mix ingredient and determine how you feel it can best support the impact, power, and musicality of the production. The following considerations will help you build a high-quality mix; however, it is completely up to each individual to develop a sense of what high-quality music is. If you listen to a lot of great-sounding music and incorporate the principles described in this chapter, as well as the other books in *The Hal Leonard Recording Method*, there's a good chance that your mix decisions will lead to great-sounding mixes.

DRUMS

A real drum set played by a live person presents the mix engineer with a completely different set of concerns than a drum machine track. Whereas the drum machine offers great sounds that are easy to get, it lacks a blended sonic quality and usually is devoid of emotional life. Even though an excellent programmer can get the most out of a drum module, a musical edge is almost always missing when compared to a live drum track.

Live drums are sometimes difficult to make sound good, but they almost always offer excellent musical and dynamic expression.

Combining an Excellent Drum Kit and an Excellent Drummer

An excellent drummer will almost always provide a very usable drum part, even on a substandard kit. On the other hand, even with the best of drums, a mediocre drummer almost always provides a mediocre drum track. There are many tools available to help the sound of a bad drummer, but virtuosity can't yet be simulated by a plug-in. If you're hiring drummers, pay the price to hire the very best players. This is the best way to help the mixdown process go smoothly and efficiently.

Marginal drummers usually bring marginal equipment to the session. Excellent players almost always bring excellent equipment. If at all possible, don't waste time on questionable players for any instrument.

If you're working with a band, you probably won't have control over who plays the instruments. In this case, work with the players to construct excellent musical parts. Also, spend some time preparing their gear for recording. Although these are excellent tracking tips, they are also the most efficient ways to provide great tracks that will efficiently work together during mixdown.

Kick Drum

The simple fact is that the recorded kick drum doesn't always sound that great. You need to decide on the appropriate kick sound for your production. The techniques prescribed in *Instrumental & Vocal Recording* and *Sequencing Samples & Loops* from *The Hal Leonard Recording Method* will help you record drum tracks that are easy to mix and blend. When the tracks have been recorded well, the mixing task is far simpler than when the tracks are unsatisfactory.

Sweet Spot

The kick-drum sound often needs a warm low end that is controlled and blended with the mix. Try this procedure to locate the sweet spot in the kick drum sound.

- Set up a boost in the low-frequency range of a parametric equalizer.
- Adjust the bandwidth to about a half octave.
- Sweep the boost in the low-frequency range while the kick track plays back. Continue until you locate the precise boost that accentuates the warm tome of the drum.

There is almost always one spot where the low-frequency boost makes the kick sound come alive.

Mids

As you've seen previously, a simple cut in the low midrange band (between 250 and 600 Hz) helps isolate both high and low frequencies. When this cut is combined with a boost in the low-frequency band (between 40 and 150 Hz), the kick sound quickly takes on a personality and character that is appealing and supportive to the mix.

Highs

The genre determines whether the kick drum should have a high-frequency attack boost. The kick sound is very influential to the overall feel of the mix. Certain songs demand that the kick blends in with the mix; others call for an aggressive kick sound with exaggerated highs and lows.

To accentuate the kick drum attack, boost the highs between 3 and 5 kHz. Use a bandwidth between one octave and a half octave. A narrow bandwidth boost runs the risk of sounding unrealistically exaggerated on certain types of monitor systems. A wide bandwidth boost tends to increase apparent leakage from cymbals and other drums.

Complement Bass Guitar

Avoid using the same EQ on the kick drum and bass guitar. As stated previously, create EQ characteristics on the kick and snare that work together, resulting in increased definition and power for each.

Snare Drum

Mixing the snare drum is sometimes very easy—all you need to do is turn up the snare, and everything comes together. Usually the snare drum track requires the perfect equalization to blend into the mix, supporting the groove while providing a solid backbone for the mix sound.

To blend the snare with the track, boost the frequencies between about 250 and 600 Hz and cut the highs slightly above about 5 kHz. To highlight the snare, boost the frequencies between 3 and 7 kHz and cut slightly between 300 and 500 Hz. In addition, eliminate unwanted leakage in the low frequencies by using a high-pass filter to reduce the frequencies below 150 Hz.

Live Toms

If you're mixing a live drum set and you've got the toms on a separate track or tracks, it's not usually a good idea to leave the tracks turned up to their normal settings all the time. The ringing of the tom heads and the leakage of the rest of the drums into the tom mics can severely decrease the close, punchy sound of the kick and snare mics.

Either gate the tom tracks or, if you have any automation available, listen through the entire song, noting where the tom fills are. Locate each fill and, in the automation system, turn the track up just in time to be heard and then fade the track back out in a natural way. This procedure eliminates the need for gates, which are usually difficult to set properly on tom tracks, and lets you blend the tom tracks in and out at a rate that's less distracting than the gate might be.

Many mixers have MIDI-automated mutes. These simply let you write the channel on and off into your sequence—a useful and convenient feature. When muting the tom tracks, make sure the track's sudden entrance and exit are unnoticeable.

Sometimes the leakage from the tom tracks helps blend the track together. Given the appropriate musical setting (usually when recording in the aggressive rock genre), the open mic helps add rawness and edge to the sound. It's common to even track the band in the same room, embracing the leakage in an attempt to create a unique sonic character.

Drum Set Overheads (Live)

Blend in the overhead mics just enough to fill in the sound of the kit and cymbals. Use a high-pass filter to cut the lows below about 150 Hz. The punch and lows of the set come from the close mics.

Overheads are primarily for transient definition on the cymbals and other percussion included in the drum kit. They also serve to blend the sound of the drum kit.

If there are two overheads, boost a different high frequency on each mic. I like to boost 10 or 12 kHz on one and about 13 to 15 kHz on the other.

Overheads are often compressed in an effort to blend the kit together and to maintain an aggressive and intimate sound. Depending on the genre, the overheads might be extremely compressed. Aggressive rock and pop recordings make frequent use of this technique.

.... Video Example 6-2
Building the Drum Set Sound

Drum Machines, Sound Modules, and Sample Libraries

Modern drum machines and sample libraries contain many classic synthesized drum sounds along with high-quality sampled sounds from several genres and eras. Most drum machines contain powerful sequencers, which are capable of providing musical nuance and idiomatic authenticity.

Although drum machines and sound modules typically provide excellent and very realistic sounds, the challenge is to present them in a musical way that adds to the overall mix power. Not many ingredients will degrade the quality of a production more than a poorly used drum sequencer.

Kick and Snare Drums

The kick and snare are typically panned to center, each with its own channel on the mixer. Giving these instruments separate mixer channels from the rest of the drums and percussion makes a big difference in the punch and impact of the mix. Sometimes the snare needs plenty of large-sounding reverb. Other times the snare doesn't need any reverberation. It's much better to have the flexibility to reverberate the snare alone, without applying reverb to all of the drum sounds at once. Center position is almost always the best place for these instruments. If the kick and snare are off to one side or panned apart, your mix won't seem to have a solid point of origin, and the low-frequency content of the kick could cause its side of the mix to read hotter on the stereo meters.

I often want a solid and punchy kick with a clean but not overly exaggerated slap. I'll boost the lows at 80 Hz, cut the mids between about 250 and 500 Hz, and leave the highs flat or possibly boost slightly between 3 and 5 kHz. The actual settings you use are dependent on the sound of the instrument and the sound you're trying to create.

I want the snare to be full and clean. Sometimes, I'll boost between 3 and 5 kHz by 2 or 3 dB just to help the clarity of the sound once the song starts coming together. And I might add a little bit of a plate reverb with about a one-second reverberation time to the snare. I'm assuming that you've already gone through the individual instrument sound chapters already and you have several basic sound-shaping techniques at your disposal.

Often, the rest of the kit—the cymbals, toms, and percussion—come from two outputs of the sound device. Connect those two outputs to the mixer and pan them hard left and right. Individual instrument panning must be done within the sound module. I'll bring up the drums starting with the kick and snare, rough in their levels and EQ, and then work in the rest of the drums. The panning of the cymbals, toms, and percussion is adjusted to achieve a balanced feel from left to right. From a control standpoint, it's always best to have every instrument on its own track, but it's not always necessary and is sometimes impractical.

Drum Machine Toms

Although it's less and less likely that a production includes analog tape, if you've printed the drum machine toms to tape, and especially if the tom tracks are an important and strong part of the mix, gate them or automate the tracks so that they are only active when the toms are sounding. Drum machine tracks are extremely easy to gate, and it's worth it to get rid of the tape noise between the tom hits. Remember to set the attack time as fast as possible and to adjust the release time for a smooth decay on the tom sound. In the digital domain, gating the drum machine toms isn't usually necessary unless you're using a vintage and noisy device. This is an important consideration because in modern recording, noise isn't much of an issue, but when it is present it needs to be controlled.

Pan the Cymbals for a Natural Sound

It isn't natural to hear one cymbal completely from one side and another cymbal completely from the other, so avoid this kind of panning.

It is natural to imagine the drum set occupying a particular zone in the mix. The drum set is usually in the center of a band, but it still has a little spread across the center zone. I've found that panning the cymbals between about 10:00 and 2:00 in the mix provides enough of a spread to hear separation, but not so much that the drums sound too wide.

Blending the Drum Machine Tracks

During mixdown, it is quickly apparent when the drum machine tracks provide a sterile and ultra-sanitary feel to the production. Some styles of music require a blended drum track, and the sterile drum machine tracks are unacceptable.

I've had excellent results with reamping—miking the drum machine tracks from speakers positioned in a sonically interesting room. Set up an excellent stereo mix of the drum machine tracks—use dynamic processing if you'd like, but don't apply reverberation effects. Place a pair of high-quality studio monitors in the location and room where you typically set the drums, and then set up a pair of condenser microphones in a stereo-miking configuration. Play back the drum machine tracks through the monitors and turn up the condenser mics in the mix.

Either use the room as a live ambient chamber and leave the mics set up for the entire mixdown process, or simply record the room sound to recorder tracks. If you record the sound of the drum machine playing back in the room, it will be much easier to recreate in the future if you need to remix the recording.

This very effective technique helps blend the drum machine tracks in a way that feels and sounds similar to a live drum set.

BASS GUITAR

Once the drums are roughed in, you can move on and add the bass guitar. Fine-tuning the drum sounds will have to wait until the mix is further along and you can hear how the sounds are combining.

You'll need to assess the bass guitar sound in your song. If it needs more lows, don't boost the same frequency that you boosted on the kick drum. Try boosting 150 Hz on the bass if you boosted 80 Hz on the kick, or vice versa. And, if you boosted 80 Hz on the kick, you're best off to cut 80 Hz on the bass, and if you boosted 150 Hz on the bass, you're best off to cut 150 Hz on the kick. This approach results in a more controlled low end.

If you need to boost highs in the bass for clarity, find a frequency that works, but don't use a frequency that's predominant in any of the percussion instruments. Also, the bass is almost always panned center. Low frequencies contain a lot of energy and can easily control the master mix level. If the bass is panned to one side, the entire mix level will be artificially hot on one side. This would be senseless because bass frequencies are omnidirectional; even if you had the bass panned to one side, the listener might not be able to tell anyway.

One of the biggest concerns in a mix is how the low frequencies fit together. If they accumulate, your mix will be muddy and boomy—in other words, it won't sound good. If you've been able to fit the pieces together well, your mix will sound full but very controlled and clean. Low frequencies are the most difficult to monitor accurately because many near-field reference monitors don't reproduce the frequencies that can cause most of the problems. For far-field monitors to work properly, they should be in a room that has a smooth, even frequency response.

When combining the bass and drums, remember that the kick drum and bass guitar rarely have reverb, though the snare and toms often do. Also the hi-hat, shaker, overheads, and tambourine hardly ever need reverb, while drum machine cymbals and some percussion instruments, such as congas, and some very sparse percussion parts can benefit from the appropriate reverberation sounds, often room ambiance.

Crafting a low-frequency sound that is supportive and not overwhelming is difficult. In many cases, an attempt to build a large and powerful sound in the low band results in a boomy sound and artificially strong mix levels. In addition, if your monitor system is incapable of providing an accurate picture of the low band, it is common for the novice recordist to create a mix that is incredibly boomy and unacceptable when played back on a system that incorporates subwoofers and, at the same time, thin, weak, and powerless when played back on an average monitor system or on an average car stereo. As I mentioned previously, it's important to fit the low-frequency mix components together like puzzle pieces, making sure that the equalization settings are complementary across the low band. This normally means that a boost at one frequency—100 Hz for example—indicates that another low-frequency component might have a cut at 100 Hz. This type of equalization will produce mixes that are balanced and powerful in the low-frequency range.

MIXING GUITARS

Guitars, whether electric or acoustic, are a very important part of most mixdown situations. Typically, acoustic guitar provides both tonality and fundamental rhythmic momentum. Electric guitar usually adds fills and guitar performance effects, or it might provide the primary rhythmic and tonal content. The tone and performance style of the guitar tracks are definitive. They must be appropriate for the genre and they must support the authentic character of the song.

Acoustic Guitar

The fundamental character of the acoustic guitar sound is defined during tracking. In the mixdown process, there are certain characteristics of the acoustic part that can be altered and some that can't.

Any misuse of dynamic processing, such as overly extreme compression during tracking, is difficult to repair during mixdown. Poor mic technique that includes excessive room ambience along with the guitar sound is also difficult or impossible to fix after the fact.

It is very important that the guitar tracks you record provide flexibility and ultimate control during mixdown. A simple acoustic track that has been recorded with one good condenser mic positioned for an intimate and full sound is virtually always easy to include in the mix. If you are working with a well-recorded acoustic guitar track in the mix, you can add dynamic and effects processors to control intimacy and the space around the guitar.

If you are tracking an acoustic guitar and are trying to include the room ambience, always record the ambience to its own tracks. Also, record a single close mic near the front of the sound hole or at the point that provides the close sound you want. As long as the ambience tracks are separate, you can always adjust the balance during mixdown. I'll often record the direct output from the built-in pickups on the acoustic to a separate track. Even though I almost always dislike the direct sound from an acoustic pickup, there is no reason not to record it, and you never quite know where the mix might take you. It might be the one thing that makes the sound come to life or you might be able to use it as an effect in a song section.

Dynamic Control

Any time the acoustic guitar is the primary rhythmic and tonal instrument, the proper use of compression and limiting helps blend it into the desired mix space.

Set the ratio control between 3:1 and 8:1, and then adjust the threshold control for a maximum gain reduction of about 6 dB. Set the attack time to its fastest position to blend the track into the mix, or adjust for a slower attack time to accentuate the attack of the pick plucking the string. Adjust the release time to a fast setting to control more transient information or to a longer release time for more global gain control.

It is not mandatory to compress the acoustic guitar in the mix. It depends on the guitar, the part, and the performer. If the performance is even and smooth and if the guitarist was playing with sensitivity in the recording environment, the track might sound best without compression. In limiting the dynamic range of the acoustic sound, there is potential for reducing the instrument's apparent size and sonic transparency. Assess each sound individually. There are certain mixes that are so dense that the acoustic guitar needs to be compressed, equalized, and positioned in a single mix position. However, there are also textures that leave room for the acoustic to occupy a wide dynamic range and increased sonic mix space. It's important to have an ample bag of mix tricks, but it's also important to be willing to let a track breathe during the mix in a more natural state.

EQ

To help the acoustic guitar stand out in the mix, create a slight boost between 3 and 7 kHz. Because this frequency range contains most of the clarity and presence of the acoustic guitar tone, a boost here has the effect of turning up the entire track. Frequently, the low-frequency portion of the acoustic guitar sound is nonessential to the mix, so it is a good idea to use a high-pass filter to eliminate the content below 100 or 200 Hz. Avoid creating a thin and weak acoustic guitar tone, but sweep the high-pass filter up from the low band just until you hear a thinning of the tone, and then drop it back down slightly to regain the full tone. The lows are filtered to make sure there are no unwanted or unnoticed thumps or bumps that inhabit the mix. They're also minimized to help eliminate competition between the lows on the acoustic guitar and the lows coming from the bass guitar and kick drum.

Effects

Acoustic guitar is a traditionally pure instrument, so effects such as chorus, flanger, and phase shifter should be used only when artistically and musically called for. Depending on the arrangement and orchestration, an electronic double might be appropriate. Try delay between 11 and about 35 ms. Pan the original track to one side and the delay to the other to widen the acoustic guitar sound without creating an obvious effect. Be sure to cross-reference the delay in mono. If the track diminishes in level or takes on a hollow sound when monitored in mono, adjust the delay time in small increments until the sound is smooth and natural. Next, listen to the track in stereo to verify that the delay effect still sounds impressive—if it sounds good in mono, it will virtually always sound good when switched to stereo. Although an electronic double is often very appropriate, an acoustic double is frequently preferable, but it still needs to be referenced in mono. If the guitarist is extremely precise and consistent, he or she might play the acoustic double so tightly with the original that phasing occurs between the two takes when switched to mono.

.... Video Example 6-3
Building the Acoustic Guitar Sound

Electric Guitar

Because electric guitar parts are driven by the instrument sound, the guitarist determines the sonic character as he or she develops the tones for a specific song. As with the acoustic guitar, it is usually preferable to deal with a clean and simple electric guitar track. Given a clean and simple electric track that includes dynamic processing and the perfect distortion sound, the size and scope of the guitar image can be easily shaped and molded.

Creating a Huge Sound

In the hard rock genre, guitar sounds are often supernaturally huge. In the pop rock and alternative rock genres, the guitar sound are frequently cleaner and more focused. The guitar sound is very telling about the genre. A Metallica guitar sound would be out of place in a Death Cab for Cutie mix. And a vintage Beatles guitar tone would be out of place in most Incubus recordings. There are several factors involved in creating a huge guitar sound.

- Natural distortion. If the distortion sound is small and buzzy, it is very difficult to achieve a massive guitar sound. If the distortion sound is warm and smooth, it is much easier to get an aggressive tone that sounds huge while still being smooth.
- Width. Whether in stereo or surround, the use of short delays (similar to what I previously covered with the acoustic guitar) to widen the sound of the guitar across the panorama is very effective.
- Tone. A very broad tone with extended high and low frequencies is the fundamental basis for the development of a huge sound. A thin and piecing tone can project well in a mix but it is difficult to transform into a huge sound.
- Depth. Long delays and reverberation can help a guitar to sound and feel like it's being listened to in a large room, but they don't guarantee that the actual guitar sound will be huge. Keep in mind that a single slapback delay defines the size of the room that the guitar is being placed in. Because sound travels roughly at the rate of one foot per millisecond, combining the guitar track with a 400-ms delay of the guitar will create the image that the guitar is being heard in a space that is 400 feet long.
- Dynamics control. Compressing a guitar track helps keep the track precisely in a consistent mix space. A fundamental consideration of most electric guitar sounds is the compression setting. It is very important to the intimacy of the guitar sound and it highly influences the way the player performs the part.
- Low tuning. Even though this must be done during tracking, it's good to remember that there are no rules stating that the electric guitar must be tuned to standard tuning. Try tuning the lower string or two down a whole

step or more. Next, build a musical part that takes advantage of the low tuning for a really larger-than-life sound.
- Add guitars. There is also no rule that says you can't add guitar tracks during mixdown. If you really need a low-tuned electric guitar track, go ahead and record it and then blend it into the mix.
- Monster sound. This technique sometimes works really well and other times it is just too much trouble. Copy the entire distorted guitar part to another track on the DAW and then transpose the entire track down an octave. Combine the newly transposed track with the original for a really big sound.

Creating a Focused Clean Electric Sound

The beauty of a clean electric guitar tone is in very dependent on the guitar and the guitarist. An excellent guitarist pays attention to tone and clarity and is capable of playing with precision and cleanliness. A novice or marginal guitarist often sounds like it was just luck that all the notes were fretted—if they were—and tone quality falls low on the list of considerations. Good guitarists do what it takes to get an instrument to speak clearly—they have high standards for what they expect from themselves and the sounds they create. A pure and clean tone relies on the guitarist a bit more than the distorted tone. Distortion, overdrive, and compression can all fill in a lot of gaps in a guitarists performance. Without those things, the clean sound relies on the musician's touch.

Even a sound that is slightly overdriven requires more from the guitarist. Also, the guitar makes an amazing difference in the tone. A Les Paul, Telecaster, Stratocaster, and so on each provide a unique tone and it's really quite difficult to shape one of those tones into another. The weight, construction, and scale of the instrument all add up to a characteristic sonic personality that's unique on multiple levels.

················· Video Example 6-4
Building the Electric Guitar Sound

Keyboards

Modern keyboards provide ample control to shape nearly any sound imaginable. Spend some time learning to adjust the MIDI parameters on your keyboard or sound module—it will result in better tracked sounds and a more streamlined mixdown process.

MIDI and Virtual Synths

When using a MIDI-driven or virtual instrument during mixdown, there is ultimate control to alter the timbre and envelope of the sound or even to simply choose another sound for the existing musical part. Modern keyboards and virtual synths are incredibly flexible, so tonal changes are usually easy to make on the fly. Vintage classic synths such as the Prophet 5, Juno 106, OBX, and Jupiter 8 have loads of personality and they sound big and full. And, some of those keyboards might or might not have even included MIDI, so changes during mixdown might need to made through regular EQ, effects, and dynamics adjustments.

Piano

Mixing piano is often more about defining the mix space than it is about radically changing the instrument sound. Piano should generally sound like piano, but either it needs to occupy a wide physical section of the mixing panorama or it needs to be positioned in a specific region with another important mix ingredient, such as acoustic guitar, panned across the panorama for the sake of the mix balance. Either way, the piano tone should be fairly natural—not too thin and aggressive, and not too smooth and mellow.

The stereo perspective on the piano should be natural-sounding and not too separated between right and left hands—highs and lows. Piano is frequently tracked with the mics a little too close to the strings, so the resulting sound is a little too differentiated between highs and lows. This problem can often be solved by simply panning the mics closer together around the center position or leaning left or right, but it is best to record a piano sound that it's well-balanced across the entire keyboard during the initial tracking session.

Synth and Pad Effects

Roll off the high frequencies above 3 kHz on these keyboard sounds to create a warm and smooth tone. The apparent volume of many synth effects and pads is very dependent on a boost or cut in the high-frequency band, so rather than turning the entire synth track up or down, it is often advantageous to simply adjust the highs.

The desired function of synth sounds is often to simply fill up the mix and to help everything blend into a cohesive musical entity. Be cautious, however, that the synth sound does not artificially boost the mix level by emitting low-frequency energy that is essentially inaudible.

Standard synthesizer sounds are frequently designed to sound great on the showroom floor—they exist to help sell units. However, the broad frequency content that sounds great when the synth is alone in a room is typically destructive to a dense musical production.

It is advisable to blend the synth sound with the mix and then to use a sweepable high-pass filter to get rid of unnecessary low-frequency information. Simply trim the low-frequency range until you actually hear the sound thin out when the mix is running, and then back the filter off slightly. Eliminating unnecessary low-frequency information helps remove confusion in the mix. If you are continually fighting to hear low-frequency instruments, it is likely that you have multiple ingredients competing for the low-frequency band. To create a clean and powerful mix, allocate frequency bands to specific mix ingredients. To blend a mix together, create increased overlapping in the frequency range of the mix tracks.

LEAD VOCAL

Typically, the lead vocal track requires special attention to maintain visibility and impact. The dynamic range exhibited by most vocal tracks creates the need for either constant level adjustment or automatic control through the use of compressors or limiters. The primary focal point of the mix is almost always the lead vocal. Because of this, it has to maintain a constant space in the mix. The style of the music generally determines exactly how loud the lead vocal should be in relation to the rest of the band; however, once that's been determined, the relationship must remain constant.

In a heavy R&B or rock song, the lead vocal is often buried into the mix a little. The result of this kind of balance is rhythmic drive and punchy drums. In addition, the bass and primary harmony instruments are accentuated. It's important to adjust the lead vocal level so that the lyrics are consistently understandable but it's also important to note that the actual level that's appropriate can be style-specific. In a country or commercial pop song, the lead vocal is usually predominant in the mix, allowing the lyric and emotion of the vocal performance to be easily heard and felt by the listener.

When the lead vocal is being mixed, there are many times when one word or syllable will need to be turned up or down, but sometimes the changes are more general. This is the point where you, as the mixer, need to have a copy of the lyrics. The more organized you can be, the quicker your mix will go. Listen through the entire song and mark the lyrics that need work. Then go back through and either note specific changes to perform during the mix process or, if you're utilizing automation, write the changes into the actual automation data.

There will probably be several changes to make during the mix, and the lead vocal will probably contain many of them. If you're working in an old-school fashion, mark the recorder counter numbers or SMPTE times on the lyric sheet at each verse, chorus, interlude, and bridge—this will help speed things up, no matter what. As you develop a list of vocal level changes, write them on the lyric sheet next to, above, or below the lyric closest to the move. Lead sheets are very convenient for keeping track of mix moves. If you're using a DAW, use Volume view on

Volume View Automation

Any modern DAW provides a track view that lets the user adjust the track level by simply raising and lowering an on-screen line. This is an excellent tool, used to visually fine-tune the track level.

Notice on the vocal track below that the volume line is very actively fine-tuning the level, creating a track that is more controlled and easier to fit in the mix.

Changes in the volume line (up and down) result in changes in volume (up and down).

the lead vocal track and draw in automation moves to adjust each note so it works well with the rest of the track.

Intonation

Prior to the digital workstation era, intonation problems were handled primarily in tracking. There was a constant battle between feel and intonation. I've spent a lot of time during vocal takes not breathing simply because I didn't want to do anything that could possibly mess up what seemed to be the perfect vocal take.

In the truly analog era, when everything felt great but one or two words in the lead vocal track were unacceptably out of tune, the part would need to be repaired or the decision had to be made that the musical impact outweighed the bad intonation.

Popular music must be compelling to the listener, emotionally powerful, and musically interesting—but it obviously doesn't always have to perfect. Modern production tools enable near perfection as a norm. Inspiration and musicality are still the responsibility of the artist and producer, but technical perfection is attainable from almost any recording. I have artists that I work with regularly who joke at the beginning of a project that all they really need to do is say "ahhhh" and then show up in three weeks to hear the finished album.

I'm constantly amazed by historical truths:
- Many of the hit pop recordings of the '50s, '60s, and '70s contain some extremely out-of-tune vocal tracks. It makes one wonder whether anybody who knew about intonation was even involved.
- Most of the classic big-band recordings of the '50s and '60s contain nearly flawless vocal tracks. It makes one think that the singers in that genre, during that time, were really very good vocalists.
- Much of the classic music from the '70s and '80s—prior to digital pitch manipulation—is phenomenally in tune and perfectly in time with a great feel from every instrument and voice. It makes one think that the musicians, producers, and engineers involved in these recordings were excellent craftsmen and that they cared enough about their craft to spend the time to get it right.

My musical background compels me to strive for perfect timing and meticulous intonation. I must consciously be aware that the emotional performance, especially from a vocalist, is what provides the power and intrigue for the average listener.

The beauty of working on music in the third millennium is that we can take advantage of technology to help enhance the emotional power. Whereas prior to digital pitch manipulation, I often had to tear a singer down and then build him or her back up again to capture an acceptable emotional and technical performance, today I let singers sing their hearts out until we capture a powerful emotional delivery. I'm relatively unconcerned with intonation. As long as we all feel the power of the performance, I can easily go back and fix intonation problems.

Antares developed Auto-Tune several years ago. In many ways, this software plug-in revolutionized the way vocals are recorded. The overuse of tuning plug-ins quickly becomes irritating, but their proper use can help bring vocal intonation into an acceptable range while retaining the natural and real feel from the artist.

Using the Tuning Plug-In

I do a lot of vocal recording and have been very pleased with the folks at Antares and their consistent efforts to update and improve their tuning plug-in, Auto-Tune. There are other tuning plug-ins currently on the market, but they all function in a similar manner.

During mixdown, you must evaluate the integrity of vocal intonation. If something needs to be fixed, this is the final stage of the process where it's possible.

Tuning plug-ins can be inserted into the vocal-track signal path and always ride the vocal pitch. Sometimes this technique works very well, especially when the track is mostly in tune with just a few notes that are sharp or flat.

Often singers lose their pitch perception during long notes as the tone fades off. Even though this characteristic is typically due to poor performance technique, it still might end up in the mix, and you might just need to deal with it. Tuning plug-ins do an amazing job of pulling these long notes back in tune.

Set the plug-in for an average tolerance and an average reaction time. Really, it's best if the tuner gently pulls the long notes back in tune, rather than immediately locking the pitch in place and holding it there rock-solid until the note ends. Tuning plug-ins are capable of providing synth-like pitch, where every note immediately locks in tune and stays there. Country music tends to overuse this concept. It's all a matter of personal taste in terms of how you tune your own vocals. Just be aware that vocal tuning can provide a very natural or a very unnatural sound.

Tuning plug-ins are always trying to pull the pitch of each note to the closest defined pitch. Therefore, if a track is too far out of tune, the notes might be pulled to the wrong pitch value. You might need to tune some of the notes manually, using whatever tuning utility you have, just to get the note close enough for the tuning software to pull it to the correct pitch.

I prefer to go through the vocal tracks and manually tune the major problem notes, and then, if I run a tuning plug-in, it's not working as hard as it would have been and the track has a more natural feel.

Diatonic or Chromatic Pitch Correction

Tuning plug-ins typically provide many types of scale options, including modal scales and many pitch systems foreign to American tonality. Many Eastern cultures are comfortable with a tonal system that is different from the typical European tempered tuning—these are well represented.

For most applications, select a chromatic or diatonic scale. When set to chromatic, the tuner pulls each note toward the closest of 12 half-steps in our tonal system. When set to diatonic, the tuner pulls each note toward the closest specified scale degree. If you have selected an A major scale, each note will be drawn to the closest note in the A major scale: A, B, C#, D, E, F#, or G#. If you have selected an A minor scale, each note will be drawn to the closest note in the A minor scale: A, B, C, D, E, F, or G. If you are certain that the vocal track doesn't use notes outside of a defined tonality, choose the appropriate diatonic scale. This helps the tuning plug-in provide greater accuracy within the musical context of your mix.

To Tune or Not to Tune

Sometimes it's the slight imperfections that draw the listener into the music. If you're mixing a blues album with a great blues singer, think twice before you simply insert a tuning plug-in into the signal path. The stylistically correct manipulation of pitch during many performances defines the power and emotion of many productions. The tension and release caused by a long note sliding in tune at the last moment is often inherent to the musical intent.

Sometimes, if the vocal track requires constant pitch manipulation, the plug-in becomes an irritant. The constant pitch changes can become obviously recognizable and the track begins to feel synthetic.

It doesn't take too long to work your way through the vocal track, spot-checking the pitch all the way through and adjusting only what needs to be adjusted. This approach helps produce authentic and natural pitch control and results in a better mix.

Compression

If the lead vocal track is very inconsistent in level, try running the track through a compressor. I suggest a fairly high compression ratio, between 7:1 and 10:1 with a fast attack time and a medium release time. Adjust the threshold for gain reduction on the loudest notes only; most of the track should show no gain reduction. Your purpose here is to simply even out the volume of the track without extreme compression.

If you're using analog tape, it's typically best to compress during tracking so you can keep the entire track farther away from the tape noise floor. In the digital domain, it's common to use little or no compression during tracking and then to compress for the desired effect during mixdown.

Many engineers don't like the sound of the compressor circuitry in action—the constant level control isn't always transparent. On the other hand, a compressor can help the vocal track blend into the mix better. In addition, depending on the genre, the increased sibilance and other vocal subtleties that are a result of extreme compression are often stylistically correct.

Generally speaking, the more musically dense your production, the more appropriate extreme compression is on the vocal tracks. Conversely, the more open your production, the less necessity for extreme compression.

Expander

Expanders are more frequently used in the analog domain in an effort to reduce the cumulative effect of tape noise from a multitrack mixdown. Because digital recordings are relatively noise-free and level control during mixdown is easy to control, you probably won't regularly use an expander.

However, tape noise between the lyric lines is often blatantly irritating—especially if you've boosted the highs for clarity. An expander is a convenient tool that helps get rid of all noise between the lyrics. Set the expander's threshold so that it turns down only when there is no vocal. Set the attack time to fast, the release time to medium, and the range to infinity.

Vocal EQ

If you used proper mic choice and technique to record the vocals, you might not need any EQ in the mix. If you need a little, it's safest to make subtle changes. If you boost or cut dramatically, it might sound okay on your mixing setup, but you'll be increasing the chances of creating a mix that could sound bad on some sound systems.

The basic vocal sound should be full, smooth, and easy to listen to. Don't create a sound that is edgy and harsh. There isn't much need for frequencies below 100 Hz because those are covered by the rhythm-section instruments, so it's usually best to roll off the lows below 100 or 150 Hz.

If there's a lack of clarity, try boosting slightly between 4 and 5 kHz.

Exciter

Another tool that will add clarity to the vocal without using EQ is an exciter. Be careful not to overuse the exciter or your vocal will sound harsh and edgy. If used in proper proportion, an exciter can add a pleasing clarity.

Simple Delay

A common technique for building a vocal sound includes the addition of a single slapback delay in time with the eighth note to help solidify the rhythmic feel. Listen to your mix and add a slapback delay that's in time with the eighth note. Notice that as you turn the delay up, the sound becomes richer and more sonically interesting. Be certain that the delay is 100 percent wet so there is no phasing problem between the direct track and the delay and notice how much more interesting the sound becomes. The single delay is typically panned to the center position along with the vocals. To widen the sound of the delay, while not changing the dry track, use a stereo delay with two separate times that match the eighth note or quarter note timing and shift them so they're between 7 and 23 milliseconds apart.

As your equipment list grows, try setting two or three aux buses up as sends to two or three different delays. This way they'll all be available at once, and you can pick and choose what to send to which delay and in what proportion. This technique requires restraint and musical taste to keep from overusing delay, but it's a convenient way to set up. When I set up for mixdown, I often set each delay to a different subdivision of the tempo; I usually use a quarter-note and eighth-note delay and sometimes a sixteenth-note or triplet delay.

> **Video Example 6-5**
> Building the Lead Vocal Sound

Add Backing Vocals

As you build the backing vocal sound, you must consider the musical and production style. Sometimes it's appropriate to double the backing vocals with a digital delay or chorus. Sometimes it's appropriate to use a reverberation time of about 2.6 seconds. Sometimes it's okay to use a one-second reverb. And sometimes it's appropriate to use one single backing-vocal track dry, just as it was recorded.

Background vocals often include the same kinds of effects as the lead vocal, but in a differing degree. Usually there's more effect on the backing vocals than the lead vocal. If the lead vocal has less reverb and delay, it'll sound closer and more intimate than the backing vocals, giving it a more prominent space in mix.

These choices are purely musical. For your songs to come across as authentic and believable, you or your producer must do some stylistic homework. Listen to some highly regarded recordings in the same style as your music; listen through the lyrics. Focus on the kick drum sound. Does it have reverb? Is it punchy in the low end? Does it have a present or exaggerated attack? Where is it panned in the mix? Go through this process with each instrument in the mix that you're evaluating.

Backing vocals don't usually need to be thick in the low end, so I'll roll the lows off between 100 and 150 Hz. A

Backing vocals should support the lead vocal without covering it. If the parts are well written, background vocals should nearly mix themselves. Well-written parts fill the holes between the lead vocal lines without distracting from the emotion and message of the lyrics; they also support the lead vocal on the key phrases of the verse or chorus while offering a musical and textural contrast. There's an art to writing good backing vocal parts that are easy to sing, make musical sense, and aren't corny.

Practice and diligence pay off quite well when it comes to these very important parts. If the drums, bass, lead vocal, and backing vocals are strong and mixed well, most of your work is done.

Compressing the Group

If you are mixing a group of backing vocals, try inserting a stereo compressor on the entire group. Develop a good blend of the backing vocals, pan them appropriately across the stereo panorama, and equalize each part for the best possible sound. When the group sounds good without compression, patch the stereo submix of the vocals through a high-quality stereo compressor.

A vocal group that is compressed together typically sounds much more blended and unified. Deciding whether or not to compress the vocal group is a creative decision that affects the musical feel. There are many applications in which the backing vocals should maintain a greater degree of transparency and individuality, so compression might not be appropriate. However, when you want to develop a backing vocal sound that is very tight, consistent, blended, and supportive, compression is very effective.

Intonation

A group of vocals that is perfectly in tune can be very powerful in the mix. However, part of the size dimension created by a large group of vocalists is derived from the slight imperfections in pitch and timing that naturally occur in a group of singers.

Avoid overusing tuning plug-ins on backing vocals. If you use settings that correct the vocal pitches quickly and keep them there, you could end up with tracks that have a phasing problem because they are so close to perfectly in tune. Extreme use of Auto-Tune, Melodyne, or other tuning plug-ins can actually decrease the apparent size of the backing vocal sound.

If you're presented with backing vocal tracks that are under pitch, do whatever is necessary to bring them up to the correct pitch range. Backing vocals that are flat decrease the energy and brightness of any mix.

Pitch corrections are most effective on individual tracks. Some tuning plug-ins aren't able to analyze a multiple-part group harmony and adjust the separate voices to correct pitch—they're ineffective on group harmonies recorded to a single track. However, a group unison track that rides out of tune can often be corrected. Choir groups often share the same pitch tendencies. For example, tenors frequently sing flat, and they all do it together. As long as the group rides flat together and they're recorded together to one track, the tuning plug-in will sense the discrepancy and repair it. Tuning plug-ins that can analyze and pitch-correct a multitimbral track have grown in sophistication. However, if you're inserting one of these plug-ins, be careful to avoid perfecting the parts too much. When used to an extreme, they can provide a sound that is clinically accurate but musically sterile.

> .... Video Example 6-6
> Building the Backing Vocal Sound

RHYTHMIC KEYBOARDS AND RHYTHM GUITARS

It's standard to pan the basic keyboard and guitar apart in the mix. Often these parts work well when panned to about 3:00 and 9:00. Because it's typical that the guitar and keys have been recorded with effects, there's often not much to do to get these parts to sound rich and full. If you've followed this series from the beginning, you should know several techniques to help shape the sounds of these instruments during tracking. If there's only one basic rhythmic chord part, it's often desirable to create a stereo sound through the use of a delay, chorus, or reverb.

Filling in the Holes with the Guitar or Keys

There's often one instrument that provides the bed—or constant pad—for the song, and another instrument that's a little less constant that can be used to fill some of the holes that might crop up.

This might be one case when the mixing engineer becomes the musical arranger. It could be best if an instrument is only included during certain sections of a song, even though the instrument was recorded throughout the entire song. The process of mixing involves musical decisions.

Deciding exactly what needs to be where is one of the most important parts of the final mix. If too many things are going on at once during a song, the listener can't effectively focus on anything. Frequently during a session, the basic tracks will be very exciting and punchy, and everyone in the studio will be able to feel the excitement and energy. Eventually, as more and more parts are added, everyone can feel that the music's punch and energy have been buried in a sea of well-intended musical fluff. That's not very exciting.

The old standby rule of thumb continues to pertain in music: keep it simple. The more musical parts you include, the harder it is to hear the music. When there is a rhythmic keyboard comping part and a rhythmic acoustic guitar part that have been recorded all the way through the song, I'll listen to the mix and decide which part should be playing and when. There might be a spot toward the end where both should be playing, but it's usually best to choose one of the two competing parts in a particular section and then maybe the other in the next similar section.

The fact is, sometimes in the middle of a session there is so much going on that the band or producer doesn't want to make a decision about which part should be playing at each point of the song, so everyone just plays from the beginning to the end. In the big picture, that's an inefficient way to work. It is most efficient to work with the musicians to craft a powerful and effective arrangement before laying down the tracks. It's usually possible to build something that flows well during mixdown, but there is a different energy that happens when the parts are more finely crafted during tracking. If the guitarist knows that everything breaks down to a single guitar, he or she will bring a little extra passion to the part. If the keyboardist knows that the entire song breaks down to just vocals and piano, he or she will play with a completely different mindset than if the part was supposed to fit with the rest of the band. Fortunately, modern technology and digital editing enable us to move things around to create motion and excitement where it doesn't exist organically, but that process is almost always time-consuming and not quite as powerful as a naturally inspired performance.

LEAD LINES AND SOLO PARTS

It's common to include a lead instrument part that adds fills and solo licks—depending on the genre, this is often a guitar, keyboard, trumpet, or sax. It often runs throughout the song filling holes and, essentially, adding spice and emotion while maintaining flow and interest. If you can get the player to play only what's needed on the lead track, your mixing job will be easier. Often, when the lead parts are recorded, the total scope of the song, arrangement, or orchestration hasn't been defined. In this case, I'll let the lead player fill all the holes and then pick and choose what to include in the mix. If you let the lead part fill all the holes between the lyrics, verses, or choruses, the element of surprise or contrast is lost.

There's an art to finding the appropriate spots to include the lead licks, but remember that at any point of the song there only needs to be one primary focal point. Lead parts are usually good to include in the intro, leading into a chorus, between verses and choruses, sometimes between lyric lines, and in the repeat choruses at the end of the song.

It's a good idea to record multiple takes of the lead and solo instrument tracks. On one hand, it's best if we capture the inspired performance that is absolutely perfect for the song—that's ideal. On the other hand, it is extremely valuable to have options stored on other takes of the track. In the same way we comp vocal tracks, we can comp solo tracks. If the first half of one take is great and the second half of another take is great, create a new comp track and combine them to the comped master solo track. In addition, since the chord progressions are consistent from verse to verse and chorus to chorus, having multiple takes recorded provides a lot of options for comping from one chorus to another or from one verse to another. Often, the fade out section loops the chorus over and over, so it provides many options—many of these end sections contain some of the most creative lines because the performer is testing out new ideas.

In the digital era, solo licks and fills are musical variables. As I mentioned previously, I often move a filler lick from the end of a song to the beginning of the song, or I'll find one very characteristic musical idea and repeat it several times throughout the mix. I'll also frequently combine the beginning of one lick with the end of the other. Sometimes a note or two needs to be tuned, lengthened, shortened, or shifted. As much as the purist in us all would like to think that every performance in a song was naturally inspired and delivered with perfection, the truth is that we do what we can to make the parts as stylistically excellent as possible. We have the technology to make everything perfect, but for certain styles and genres, perfection is appreciated through slight imperfections. In jazz, blues, rock, and country there are certain notes that can be "blue," meaning they never quite make it up to the pitch they're aiming for. Tuning all of the "blue" notes would result in a production that was stylistically incorrect and a bit corny. As an engineer and/or producer, it is your job to be familiar with the genre and to adjust any mix parameters within the range of authenticity.

Note: It's often good to put the same effects on the solo as the lead vocal. This adds continuity to the emotional flow and acoustical space of the song. Like the lead vocals, solos are almost always panned center to help keep the focus.

Many solo instruments contain a bright, and often edgy, sound. In an acoustic performance environment, this extra edge helps them soar above the rest of the group. This is also a useful characteristic in recorded music; however, be sure to check the instrumental solo level in your mix on multiple types of playback systems. It is likely that when you're monitoring on a large, full-range system, the instrumental solo level will sound just right. However, often the especially edgy solo sound is radically louder on a small speaker system that is deficient in low- and high-frequency reproduction. There is always a balance at which the solo sounds good on all systems but it can be unpredictable depending on the actual timbre of the solo instrument.

CHAPTER TEST

1. The _____ is frequently secondary to considerations about how the tracks all work together to form a complete mix.
    a. sonic character of an individual track
    b. relative volume of each track
    c. blended character of the mix
    d. ambient character of the mix

2. _____ causes the entire mix level to increase artificially.
    a. Turning all tracks up
    b. Adding reverberation
    c. Boosting the same frequency on several tracks at once
    d. All of the above

3. Which frequency range adds the most proportional level to the mix?
    a. Highs
    b. Mids
    c. Lower mids
    d. Lows

4. If you need to boost the low frequencies on the kick drum, bass guitar, and synth pad:
    a. pan them all to different pan positions from hard left to hard right
    b. delay each by a few milliseconds to establish a phase relationship that averages rather than accumulates level
    c. choose different frequencies to boost on each track
    d. All of the above
    e. Both b and c

5. When you need to fill out the kick drum and bass guitar tracks in the low frequency range, try boosting the kick slightly at 60 Hz and then boosting the bass guitar at 120 Hz. With this done:
    a. create a dip in the EQ curves of each of the two tracks to create a space for the boost in the other
    b. the cumulative mix level will be unaffected
    c. keep boosting discrete frequency bands on the other tracks in the production
    d. you should see a 3-dB boost in the overall mix level

6. If you find a problem frequency that needs to be eliminated:
    a. sweep a very narrow peak across the suspected problem area until the problem frequency is most noticeable, then change the boost to a cut
    b. turn the mix volume way down until all you can hear is the problem frequency
    c. create a boost on a parametric EQ and sweep it across the spectrum until it masks the problem frequency
    d Any of the above that work

7. Not many ingredients will degrade the quality of a production more than a poorly-used drum sequencer.
    a. True
    b. False

8. The kick drum and snare are typically panned:
    a. to the center position
    b. slightly apart but equidistant from center
    c. hard left and hard right
    d. to 10:00 and 2:00

9. When panning drum machine channels:
    a. it isn't natural to hear one cymbal completely from one side and another cymbal completely from the other, so avoid this kind of panning
    b. it is natural to imagine the drum set occupying a particular zone in the mix
    c. the drum set is usually in the center of a band, but it still has a little spread across the center zone
    d. panning the cymbals between about 10:00 and 2:00 in the mix provides enough of a spread to hear separation, but not so much that the drums sound too wide
    e. All of the above

Chapter 6 .... MIXING

10. To compensate for the sterile sound that a drum machine can produce:
    a. add long hall reverberation (more than 2-second decay time) to each channel
    b. send a mix of the drums to a high-quality playback system in an interesting acoustical environment, mike the speakers in a stereo distant-miking configuration, and blend the mics back into the mix
    c. invert the phase of three or four of the tracks
    d. Both a and c

11. An excellent drummer will almost always provide a very usable drum part, even on a substandard kit. On the other hand, even with the best of drums, a mediocre drummer almost always provides a mediocre drum track.
    a. True
    b. False

12. To get a full and clean kick drum sound:
    a. sweep a boost in the low frequencies to find the appealing warm low tone
    b. sweep a mid-frequency cut to eliminate uncomplimentary tone
    c. sweep a high-frequency boost to accentuate the attack
    d. All of the above
    e. Both a and c

13. To blend the snare with the track, boost the frequencies between about _____ and cut _____.
    a. 100 and 250 Hz, the mids between 700 and 900 Hz
    b. 3 and 4 kHz, below 150 Hz
    c. 250 and 600 Hz, the highs above about 5 kHz
    d. 1.5 and 2.5 kHz, the highs above 10 kHz

14. The ringing of the tom heads and the leakage of the rest of the drums into the tom mics can severely decrease the close, punchy sound of the kick and snare mics.
    a. True
    b. False

15. When mixing live drum tracks, leaving the open tom mics turned up throughout the song can help add rawness and edge to the sound that is appropriate for some genres, such as rock and jazz.
    a. True
    b. False

16. Drumset overheads:
    a. are primarily for transient definition on the cymbals and other percussion included in the drum kit
    b. serve to blend the sound of the drum kit
    c. should only be turned up when the crash or ride cymbals are played
    d. All of the above
    e. Both a and b

17. Drumset overheads should never be compressed because of the strong potential they present for pumping or breathing.
    a. True
    b. False

18. When compressing vocal tracks:
    a. the more musically dense your production, the more appropriate extreme compression is on the vocal tracks
    b. the more open your production, the less necessity for extreme compression.
    c. a compressor can help the vocal track blend into the mix better
    d. All of the above
    e. Both a and b

19. If the backing vocal parts are well written, they should nearly mix themselves.
    a. True
    b. False

20. As a rule, the more ingredients in the mix, the more interesting the overall texture and the more powerful the production.
    a. True
    b. False

Test answers are on page 298

Automation

CHAPTER 7

Mix automation systems are used to integrate computer functionality into the mixing process. In its simplest form, mix automation enables the recording of fader and mute changes into the computer's memory. After you've performed the move once, the automation system memorizes it, and from that time on the computer performs that move for you every time the mix plays. This is a big bonus when you're building a mix. Automation gives you the ability to make new level changes while you hear the old level changes. This is like giving you several more hands to use during the mix.

It is valuable to establish a base understanding and appreciation for the history and development of automation systems. Let's look at the progression from analog VCA-based automation systems to the modern digital automation workflow.

CHAPTER AT A GLANCE

Analog Mixer Automation Systems .. 163
VCA-Based Automation.................... 164
Automation Data Time Reference 164
Digital Mixer Automation Systems.... 165
Basic Automation Types.................... 166
Snapshot Automation 166
Dynamic Automation....................... 166
Automation Parameters 167
Mutes 169
Pan.. 169
Function of Fader Motors in
  the Digital Domain 170
Graphic Automation 170
Snapshot Automation.......................171
Operational Procedures 172
Saving 173
Undo and Redo 174
Building Automation........................176
Software Plug-Ins 178
Mix Procedure Using Automation..... 179
Inserts 179
Write Mutes 180
Documenting the Mix....................... 180
Outboard Gear Without Patch-
  Storage Capabilities 181
Locate Points and Markers 181
Copy Moves and Settings................. 182
Digital/Plug-In Equalization 182
Dynamic Control and Special
  Effects 183
Automation Data Storage Format 184
Audio Storage Formats 184
Hard Disk 184
DAT 185
CD or DVD Recorder 186
VU Mix Levels 186
Peak Level.. 187
Fades... 187
Summary 189

ANALOG MIXER AUTOMATION SYSTEMS

Automation systems provide automated control of channel levels and mutes, at the very least. Automation systems for analog mixers are very different from automation systems built into digital mixers. Whereas analog mixer automation is typically limited to writing and recalling fader and mute changes, a modern digital console writes and recalls every control on the mixer surface along with every parameter in every inserted plug-in and every control on every virtual instrument, and it can automate

the MIDI data parameters on any connected MIDI device. Most automation systems for analog consoles use one of two methods to control the mix:
- VCA-based automation
- Moving fader–based automation

VCA-Based Automation

VCA-based systems use a voltage-controlled amplifier to adjust levels. From the purist's view, any time an amplifier is inserted into the signal path for whatever reason, there is degradation of signal integrity and sonic character. Many VCA-based systems provide excellent results, and they are the least expensive of the systems, but they are the least sonically transparent type of automation. The VCA is the same type of amplifier circuit that is at the core of a typical compressor. It is simply an amplifier that turns up and down in response to the amount of signal it senses. In the case of a standard compressor, the VCA responds to the signal strength at the device input, turning down the signal that passes from input to output when the signal at the input exceeds the threshold. With VCA-based automation, the VCA is controlled by an external voltage source determined by fader position, unaffected by the strength of the signal at the channel input. Moving the fader up or down sends a variation in voltage to the VCA, which determines the up or down status of the voltage-controlled amplifier.

Moving-Fader Automation

The moving-fader automation system eliminates the need for a VCA by including a voltage-controlled motor on each channel fader. The motor physically moves the fader as you would if you had 56 hands and a mega-multitasking brain. A moving-fader automation package on an analog console maintains 100 percent of the sonic quality and character that exists without the automation system because the signal passes through the channel in exactly the same way as if the fader were being moved by hand. Think of moving-fader automation like several tiny voltage-controlled electric engines whose gears mesh with gears on the fader. Positive voltage moves the fader up and negative voltage moves the fader down.

Automation Data Time Reference

Any automation system needs a way to keep track of parameter changes, fader moves, knob twists, and so on. Some of the original automation systems printed data right onto a track of the multitrack. That data contained all the information about fader moves and mutes printed on tape at the instant of the change. The mix processor simply responded to real-time data changes as read off the tape.

Other automation systems refer each move to the continual flow of SMPTE time code. SMPTE is the standard time address reference. Digital recording systems that utilize a computer and software can follow SMPTE time code or, internally, they can refer to MIDI time code (MTC), which is the MIDI equivalent of SMPTE. The mix moves and changes are stored in the computer, and then data is transmitted at the precise time prescribed by the time-code reference. If channel 12 must move up 4 dB at SMPTE reference 01:22:33:15, the data change is transmitted at that precise time reference. In fact, most digital mixers let the user access the edit decision list for all mix data. This list accounts for each parameter change listed with the time-code reference. If a move happens too early, the operator can quickly enter the EDL and then correct the time-code reference by entering the correct value in the time-code field.

The premier automation system for analog consoles is the SSL Total Recall system. In addition to moving fader automation, this system actually takes a status reading of each knob on the console, including levels, mutes, equalization, aux settings, and so on. Whereas a digital mixer remembers and replays settings on every control, the Total Recall system only notes the status of each control as the basis of a mixing session. To recreate a mix, the engineer must, prior to beginning the remix, manually reset every control according to the onscreen video interface. In this modern era, the Total Recall system seems archaic, but it was a step in the right direction and helped the engineers of an era do a better job and more easily recreate a mix that they might have spent several hours or even days creating!

DIGITAL MIXER AUTOMATION SYSTEMS

Compared to automation systems that are commonly added to analog mixers, the capabilities of the automation systems on digital mixers are vast. Digital mixers routinely offer automation systems that record and replay the motion of every control on the mixer. Whereas analog automation systems control faders and mutes, digital mixers automate level, mute, pan, aux sends, effects parameters, routing, subgroups, and so on—virtually any control on the mixer.

A high-quality digital mixer provides a wonderful mixdown environment. The fact that every mix move is stored as you build the complete mix leads to intelligent settings based on exact comparisons to previously constructed textures.

BASIC AUTOMATION TYPES

Even though there is quite a difference between the capabilities of automation systems, there are several automation parameters, controls, settings, and features that apply to any automation system. Automation is divided into two basic types: snapshot and dynamic automation.

Snapshot Automation

Snapshot automation enables instant recall of the console configuration, including all parameter settings controlled through automation. The user has the option to select snapshots at any time, but continuous real-time fades and parameter changes are not supported. Fixed, or static, positions are recalled when a snapshot is selected. A snapshot is a singular global event. Although it can be used within a dynamic mix, it's usually best to keep it separate and select either dynamic or snapshot automation.

Dynamic Automation

Dynamic automation provides for real-time recording and playback of any automation-controlled parameters while referenced to time code. Data for fader moves, mutes, pan, EQ, and plug-ins can all be stored within memory and replayed at the correct time-code reference. The digital controllers then recreate the mix moves precisely as they were performed by the mix engineer. There are typically five modes of operation in dynamic automation: Auto Read, Absolute (or Auto Write, Update, or Replace), Auto Touch (or Auto Latch), Trim Levels, and Bypass (or Auto Off or Rehearse).

Dynamic automation is the most commonly used form of automation for building a strong and powerful mix. Quick control changes along with smooth musical transitions impact musical expression in the mixing domain. The following automation modes are typical of any system. The terms might change slightly between manufacturers, but the concepts are consistent.

AUTOMATION PARAMETERS

The terminology and specific controls that are accessed by automations systems are very consistent from platform to platform. Notably, vintage analog systems only control the root set of core parameters, but those same parameters are typically referenced in the same way whether used in an early 1980s VCA-based automation system or the most modern digital console or DAW.

Auto Read

Auto Read is playback mode. It reads any automation data that's been recorded. It's important to remember that automation data represents the time code–referenced status of controlled mix parameters. When a digital mixer reads automation data, the functions are mathematically calculated for the mix changes. The binary data is altered to represent the mix changes. In contrast, the analog mixer simply varies an analog control through which the analog signal passes. Digital mixing is a much more pure form of waveform manipulation because it doesn't use an analog signal path or amplifying circuits.

Absolute Mode/Auto Write/Update/Replace

This mode operates much like a multitrack recorder punching in. You must first select parameters to change or update; then, once the button is pressed to write or record automation, all selected parameters overwrite the existing settings for those parameters only. You can manually punch in and out; plus, most automation packages let the user change parameters and repeat the punch-in process while the mix is running. This is one of the primary mix-building procedures. Mixes often start with a single pass all the way through the song to establish data boundaries. Then the individual moves and intricacies are entered through this mode and Auto Touch mode.

Auto Touch/Auto Latch

Auto Touch mode is similar to Absolute mode. In Auto Touch, all data is in playback mode until a controller is touched or moved. Once the controller is touched, that particular parameter goes into record mode.

In some systems, the controller remains in record mode until it is manually turned off or time code stops. This method is often called Auto Latch because the record mode latches on until the user physically turns it off. Other systems that have conductive faders capable of sensing touch go in and out of record as the controller is touched and released. This is typically Auto Touch mode.

Trim Levels

Trim Levels mode retains all relative moves on a particular controller but adds or subtracts user-specified amounts of change from all moves in a specified region. If you'd simply like to turn up the entire track by 1 dB, adjust the parameter control by the appropriate amount on the mixer channel, then press Trim Levels. The mix-automation computer will add 1 dB to all levels on the selected track starting when the record/write button is pressed and time code is running.

When you adjust the fader for a 1-dB up or down trim, the entire track level changes by the same amount as long as you leave the fader in the same spot. However, the true functionality of the trim process is a merger of previously recorded data with new data being recorded. If the trim moves are active, the resulting levels will be the sum or difference of the original data and the new data.

To trim levels, controls—typically faders—must be set at the unity gain position. The unity position is essentially a controller position that the computer and user agree is a "zero change" position. Moving-fader systems often move a fader to unity gain position the instant the trim level button is pushed. This way, it's easy for the user to discern how far the level has changed from its original position, and it's easy to get back to unity for a smooth transition from trim to the previous status. Faders that don't automatically go to unity setting when the trim button is pushed simply assume that wherever they are at the time is unity. If this is the case with your automation system, get in the habit of setting the fader at unity gain (typically the 0 level setting close to the top of the fader throw) before entering trim mode. This provides the most reliable and easy method to trim levels up or down.

In the DAW, trim mode is frequently available and visible at the same time as the automation volume line. This is very useful because it lets the user adjust the level of the entire automated track or just a portion of it. By selecting the target area on the Trim Levels track, only the automation moves in the selected region are trimmed, either up or down.

Bypass/Auto Off/Rehearse

This mode stops all automation playback and recording. With the automation off, or bypassed, it's much easier to set up a basic mix from which to start. In addition, tracking is typically best done with the automation off to avoid any inadvertent automation writing. Automation can be bypassed for the entire mixer or for individual channels.

Rehearse mode is very similar to Bypass or Auto Off mode in that automation data is not recorded. In Rehearse, however, the write button will switch the status from automation playback to record-ready, reading the selected controller at its current manual status. This is a great way to test your settings before actually printing them as automation data. Once you're sure the moves are close, switch to Absolute or Auto Touch mode and record the mix changes.

Mutes

Mute status is written like other automation data except that it's not updated or trimmed—it's simply rewritten. Some automation systems deal with mutes differently. The most convenient systems continuously monitor the mute status; if the user makes a change, it's registered and the data proceeds normally from that point. Other systems regard the mute as a relative change. If the mute status is on, the next status is off. Once the user makes a change in mute status, the rest of the mutes in the song might be changed. Some early automation packages were not user-friendly and had features that seemed to be poorly thought out. Most modern systems are relatively intuitive, with operating procedures that have been developed and refined in the field.

Pan

When pan automation is selected alone, all other moves are ignored. In a practical light, most panning remains consistent. An occasional change is necessary, especially if one track contains two or more instruments. It's usually most effective to record the basic pan data along with the first-pass automation data throughout the entire song. Then, when the mix details are forming, punch in any pan changes at the desired locations. In practice, including too many sweeping variations in pan position is distracting. Although it seems like fun at the time, it usually calls attention to itself rather than supporting the emotional impact of the music being mixed.

Function of Fader Motors in the Digital Domain

Moving faders on a digital mixer—faders that play along with the mix—serve primarily as automation tools. They provide the user with a visual reference to the status of each fader. For example, when the engineer touches the fader in Auto Touch mode, the data is seamlessly transitioned from the computer status to the user status. If you don't move faders, it's difficult to punch an automation move in without creating a jump in level that might distract from the mix. Many systems don't have physically moving faders. Instead, they utilize onscreen faders that the user can match with the physical fader. There's typically an onscreen fader representing the computer playback fader and another colored fader showing the manual fader status. The user simply matches the computer fader with the manual fader before punching into record, avoiding any unwanted level jumps. Moving faders are more intuitive to use, but the onscreen process is also very efficient.

Aside from assisting the intuitive nature of mixing automation, moving faders are functionally unnecessary. They don't have any effect on the audio quality; they only indicate the status of digital data. No audio actually passes through fader circuitry because there is no audio circuitry, only controller data that indicates a mathematical variation in the binary data stream.

Also—and this can't be discounted, considering the nature of the music business—moving faders are fun to watch. They provide a "wow" factor that might turn a client's head and make you some money. The original Euphonix CSII digitally-controlled analog console confirmed for me that digitally controlled audio was the only way to fly. However, the thing that all the clients thought was really cool was "Vegas" mode. The board scrolled quickly through all its lights—and it had a lot of them. It was very impressive, especially with the studio lights turned down. Since that early entry in the new-technology console realm, many other manufacturers have included this flashy but limited-value function.

Graphic Automation

Modern automation systems provide a graphic automation view. This view provides access to all of the available mix parameters on each mixer channel, including inserted plug-ins and other external devices that are MIDI-addressable and connected via MIDI to the system interface.

Graphic automation (sometimes called the "mix editor") is a very powerful tool, especially for precise changes through complete musical sections. In addition to providing the most precise way to make intricate mix adjustments, this view also frequently lets the user make large global changes to one or more mix channels at a time. Even though these tasks are simple to accomplish in the mix editor, they're often cumbersome and not quantifiable in the typical mix automation screen.

Snapshot Automation

Snapshots are typically saved as specific numbers between 0 and 99 or 0 and 999, and so on. The data that's stored with the snapshot number represents the global status of the mixer at the time of the save. Every controllable parameter is part of the snapshot. Snapshots are very convenient for tracking. Once you've found a great-sounding set of EQ and processor settings for a drum set that you'll be recording during the course of several days, simply save the snapshot of all set-

Graphic Automation

Graphic automation lets the user change any mix automation parameter with great accuracy and without needing to run the mix again. Simply find the mix parameter that needs to be changed and either enter the desired value or drag the line to the correct location. Screens like the one below offer an easy-to-use graphical interface, where parameter settings can be changed by reshaping, resizing, and repositioning. This is a very valuable DAW feature. It's important to note that several parameters are adjustable with this graphic tool, from volume to pan, mute, sends, effects parameters, dynamics parameters, and so on. Graphic automation is very powerful. It provides controls that allow an operator to can craft amazingly precise mixes.

tings. This way, each time you need to re-mike the kit, you'll have a good starting point. All the settings you slaved over on day one will instantly return for your tweaking pleasure.

Snapshots also serve as an excellent means of comparing mix concepts. Set up a guitar-heavy mix and call it snapshot 1. Then, set up keyboard-heavy mix and call it snapshot 2. Finally, try a percussion-heavy mix. Then, scroll through the snapshots as the song plays back. The difference in emotional impact is obvious when you compare the mix approaches in this real-time way. You'll soon recognize the sound you've been looking for.

Snapshots can be integrated into the dynamic mix, but use this technique with caution. Once the dynamic mix sees a snapshot number, it automatically switches to that snapshot as if someone had actually pushed the snapshot number. For example, if the mixer is told on the chorus to switch to snapshot 10 but you've since changed snapshot 10—or it somehow got lost in the ether—the mix might be ruined at that point.

Also, because a snapshot represents a complete global change in mixer status, there's more of a chance that switching to a snapshot will cause an audible pop or click. Instantly changing the status of all the controls frequently results in an audio change that's drastic enough to be noticeable, which will sound amateurish.

You can use snapshots very simply and effectively to create subtle changes between sections. They provide you with the opportunity to step through the duration of a mix and select scenes tailored for each musical section. In some cases, this simple scrolling concept provides plenty of control and personalization for the entire mix. Simply create a snapshot for each musical section, and then select each scene at the appropriate time while the mix plays.

OPERATIONAL PROCEDURES

There are certain routines and procedures that help increase the efficiency of the mixdown process. Although automation systems dramatically increase the creative capabilities in mixdown, certain considerations, which are non-issues when you're not utilizing automation, become very important.

Saving

I've said it before and I'll say it again: whenever you are dealing with any computer, whether for sequencing, digital audio recording, video recording, or automating a mixdown, save frequently. I make it part of my regular procedure. I save very often unless I'm really in a zone and I forget for 10 or 15 minutes. Most newer DAWs include an auto-save option. This feature can be a lifesaver in case of an untimely crash, although some recordists like to disengage the auto-save feature so they can decide when to keep the current mix status and when not to. However, with the readily available Undo and Save As features that typically provide for multiple levels of Undo (multiple steps backward through your mix changes), I recommend using auto-save. If you have a mix you really like, you should save it as a separate file for safekeeping or print it to whatever mixdown storage medium you've selected—before it gets away. Then you can go off on a completely different tangent with the mix, free from anxiety. Developing a new mix approach is stimulating and fun if you know you have a great version already in the can.

Save often!

Develop a Naming Protocol

The names you choose for your DAW session files are important. In the moment, right after a mix has been printed or a new session template has been developed, "Session 2" might seem like an appropriate filename. We think we'll somehow remember the unique characteristics of Session 2, even through the myriad of details and tasks that occur during tracking or mixing—we won't. After some time has passed, a well-named session file is a valuable commodity. It is true that every file is date-stamped and that the best mix is usually the most recent mix, but that's not always the case.

Here are some suggestions for naming protocol.

- Underscore or hyphen—or not. Technical computer file names frequently use underscores between words instead of spaces. This procedure is a carry-over from dated operating systems that don't/didn't allow spaces. In the modern DAW, it isn't necessary to conform to this procedure, but that doesn't necessarily mean we shouldn't. If you'll be uploading and downloading files to an FTP server, you'll soon find that spaces in titles are replaced with "%20." This is an annoyance when the title is copied for reference. When letting someone else know the location of a file, *"By the Light of the Silvery Moon"* in the *"Bill*

Gibsons Music" folder on www.billgibsonmusic.com becomes ftp3.billgibsonmusic.com/inbox/Bill%20Gibsons%20Music/By%20the%20Light%20of%20the%20Silvery%20Moon. Using underscores rather than spaces results in a much cleaner address copy from an FTP site: ftp3.billgibsonmusic.com/inbox/Bill_Gibsons_Music/By_the_Light_of_the_Silvery_Moon.

- A string of words separated by underscores is selected as one word—double click anywhere in the title or phrase separated by underscores and the entire phrase or title is selected. Hyphens and back slashes, however, break the double-click selection. So, copying the file names on either side of the hyphen is simple in "*Bill_Gibsons_Music-By_the_Light_of_the_Silvery_Moon.*" Just double-click anywhere in "*Bill_Gibsons_Music*" to select and copy it or anywhere in "*By_the_Light_of_the_Silvery_Moon*" to select and copy it. This might seem like a small point, but it can be very beneficial to the momentum of your daily workflow.
- Use dates and times in your titles. Keep these short. Even though the files are time-stamped, these tags are easiest to recognize when you simply want to identify the most current mix or track. "*Jump_City-9_23_2012-1015AM*" is instantly differentiated from "*Jump_City-9_24_2012-0237PM.*"
- Use simple descriptions in your titles. This can't get out of control because there is a limit on the number of characters used in the title, but you'll thank yourself if you provide some clues about the unique differences in each mix or session. "*Jump_City-9_23_2012-1015AM-vox_up_2dB*" is very useful.
- Select a file and use the Get Info command (Cmd+I on Mac and Ctrl+I on PC) to open the information window. Add a description to the Notes or Comments field.
- Some characters are illegal for use in file names. Using numerals, letters, hyphens, and underscores in any file name is acceptable. Commas, forward and back slashes, colons, question marks, asterisks, double quotes, semicolons, bullets, ampersands, and so on are illegal for some operating systems.
- Mac, Windows, and Unix operating systems all permit long file names of up to 256 characters, typically including the extension.

Undo and Redo

As the transition from analog to digital recording progressed, it was obvious that the Undo and Redo commands were extremely valuable. When recording with the

Saving and Naming

It's extremely important to save often. Although most modern DAWs are more stable than they were a number of years ago, crashes still happen. And, they usually happen after a long string of edits and changes. For some unexplained reason, the worst computer-related problems seem to happen just at the point where the user is in a groove and thinking only about wonderful creativity and musical magic. If a crash causes the loss of an hour of your creativity, it could take many hours to repair or replace that loss. Utilize the auto-save feature in your DAW to avoid losing your work. If the auto-save parameter is set to save your work every five minutes, you'll be assured that any losses will be minimal.

Use manual Save As... commands to build a list of alternate mixes or tracking setups. Once you build a session to a functional point, save it as "Mix 1," "Set 1," or whatever terminology is most appropriate, and then immediately save as "Mix 2," "Set 2," and so on. Build and mold Mix 2 to the point where it could be complete or to a point that you'd like to be able to access at a later time. Once you've reached a status that could be a final mix, add brief descriptive terms to the end of the file name so it's easy to tell what the differences are between mixes or sessions. It can also be a good idea to include dates in the file names, but be careful not to use illegal characters when naming the files. Even if your OS allows for unusual filename characters, there is a likelihood that you or someone else might someday want to open your files on a different platform.

modern DAW, there are very few moves or changes that can't be undone or, once they're undone, redone. This safety net establishes a workflow that can be fearless. Trying something aggressive, new, or just plain crazy is acceptable because everything can easily be reverted using the Undo command.

Undo and Redo are available in virtually all modes and most DAWs offer multiple levels of Undo and Redo. So, if you find yourself up against a brick wall of dissatisfaction, simply keep pressing Undo until you find your way back to an acceptable status and, if you go too far back, press Redo to work forward again.

Check the application's Preferences window to control the actual number of available levels of Undo/Redo—in some instances, the DAW is set to track almost every move in the session and allows unlimited levels of Undo/Redo.

Building Automation

There are several valid approaches to creating a mix with automation. The right method is the one that results in the musical and emotional impact you feel is best for your music. Any suggestions about mix procedures are just that: suggestions. Try several approaches until you find one that matches your musical and working style.

Often, after all the tracking is completed, the mix process begins. The mix is built from scratch. All the blends and textures are recreated and meshed together from the ground up. Sometimes this is the best approach because it gives the mix engineer a chance to step back and reevaluate all of the mix ingredients. Upon scrutiny, the parts might be panned, equalized, and processed in a completely different way from the original intent. That might be very good for the music, or it might destroy the fire and spontaneity of the original performance.

Some engineers prefer to build the mix as they go, from the first note of the first tracking session. I've had the following happen to me multiple times: the basic tracks feel great when they're recorded. The mix and balance have life and energy. Then, at the next session, the life doesn't seem to fully return. Moreover, the same thing happens at the following session.

This process doesn't have to happen many times for you to realize a change in procedure is needed. If you have a digital mixer with automation, try automating the mix from the first session on. Capture the life of the original session by saving the mix so it can be completely recalled at a later date. Anything that's not automated should be documented and saved with the master files so write down any external effects-processor settings and keep them with the session documentation. If the external processors are equipped with MIDI, connect them to the system interface to facilitate recall and automation during the mix process.

If you work in this way, you'll find that the mix builds as you go through the creative process. Those beefy drum sounds you got on day one of tracking become part of the song, and everything builds around them. The guitar pan that inspired the keyboard sound is simply part of the song's fabric. It doesn't need to be recreated during mixdown because it remains an integral part of the song's growth.

Working this way is only possible with modern technology. Affordable plug-ins and modern external devices provide the home-studio owner access to tools that are very capable of producing professional-quality mixes, and these tools fit easily into an efficient and streamlined workflow—they've had an amazing impact

Inserts to the Digital Console

Any serious digital console needs to provide insert capability. One of the many appeals of a digital console is its ability to combine digital accuracy with classic analog sound. Inserts provide an analog patch point for the efficient inclusion of outboard gear.

Most classic outboard gear lacks any type of automatic control features, such as MIDI or mLan. However, many high-quality analog devices provide MIDI and mLan controls that can be included in the sequence automation system. Whenever an external device is used with a digital mixer, the challenge is to include it in a way that can be restored at a later date. Without MIDI or mLan, be sure to document each parameter setting and mix change, keeping the documentation with the project archives.

The best approach, when using external processing, is to connect via MIDI or other communication protocol to the DAW providing the multitrack inputs to the digital or automated analog console. Use the sequencing capabilities in the DAW to record settings and parameter changes throughout the production.

on modern production techniques. As you combine techniques and technological mix procedures with musical passion, you'll find the work style that works best for you. The methods will most assuredly vary from song to song. Different music should be treated according to its need, not technology's, so address each musical piece on its own merit and build your mixes accordingly.

SOFTWARE PLUG-INS

Gates, compressors, limiters, expanders, delays, reverbs, and special effects commonly reside within the digital mixer or DAW. The audio quality of the "stock" onboard effects is very good, especially as sample rates and word sizes increase. Plug-ins have become central to modern production. In fact, most of the industry leaders in hardware effects processors also offer software-based versions of their hardware. These plug-ins are compatible with the virtually all of the industry's leading digital audio workstations, from Pro Tools to Digital Performer, and Studio One to Cubase.

Plug-ins provide a simple means to customize a digital setup for your needs. The user gets to pick the emphasis of the mixer's feature set. If everyone bought the mixer du jour and was locked into all the same effects and dynamics, individuality and personality would soon fade from their recordings.

Plug-ins utilize the built-in computer or control-surface architecture. Whereas the digital mixer is a computer-based data router with several converters, a plug-in uses the power of the computer to create different processing effects. If a particular plug-in requires extra processing power or if it extends the capacity of the mixer with more inputs, outputs, or processing power, you can easily insert a card into one of the computer's expansion slots.

Plug-ins fit into the recording software's automation scheme. The user simply enters automation mode on the plug-in channel, and all moves performed within the channel, including those of the plug-in, are recorded and played back on subsequent passes. Actual functionality depends on the software and the plug-in.

Manufacturers who take advantage of the incredibly cost-efficient way to distribute their products utilize the existing computer functions and architecture included in the digital recording/mixing system. Therefore, hardware costs are minimal or nonexistent, and their products are distributed as data on an inex-

Chapter 7 .... AUTOMATION

pensive storage medium. Many manufacturers even minimize their printing costs, sending a minimal startup manual with the product, and then referencing "read me" files on the software disc or technical support sites on the Internet. And for the ultimate in quick and easy delivery, it can all be had online as a download with no postage or disks or manuals.

What does all this do for the end user? It just gets us more, better, quicker, cheaper. That's all! For a more in-depth study of plug-ins, refer to *Recording Software & Plug-Ins* from *The Hal Leonard Recording Method*.

MIX PROCEDURE USING AUTOMATION

Digitally controlled automation adds a completely different dimension to mixing. It gives the mix engineer incredible flexibility and creative freedom as well as providing for a custom-designed work environment. Much of the outboard equipment that used to be patched into the mixer is now internal. Less patching is not only convenient, but also, with digital processors, the sonic clarity is much more consistent. Dirty contacts and sloppily wired patch bays are often the mix engineer's worst nightmare. With the advent of plug-ins, the digital mixing system is very easy to customize. It can be made as powerful as you can afford to make it.

Inserts

Any good digital mixer or interface contains inserts. There have been so many great analog devices developed through the years that it would be unthinkable not to provide a means of including them in a system. Inserts on a digital mixer or interface provide the same function as they do on an analog mixer. Each digital mixer manipulates audio as data. However, audio from a microphone or line source enters the mixer in its analog form. The signal is converted from analog waveforms to digital data once it has passed the gain-trim stage. The insert is positioned just prior to conversion.

While the signal is still in analog form, it is sent from the insert output to the processing device. Then, the signal flows from the output of the processing device back to the insert's input. Immediately after the signal enters the mixer's signal path, it's converted to digital data for further treatment, shaping, and mixing.

Mixing & Mastering...by BILL GIBSON

Devices, whether analog or digital, should be considered as important as any musical instrument. The sound of a vintage mic through a classic tube compressor can be as sweet and inspiring as the sound of a Les Paul lyrically wailing through a Marshall half-stack. In addition, the sound of a complex and carefully shaped digital reverb can be as stimulating and intriguing as the ambience in a natural concert hall. None of these instruments or devices should be held in higher esteem than another. They are simply tools to help you create better music—music that evokes passion and emotion.

Write Mutes

The first step in most automated mixing sessions is to write all the channel mutes or, depending on the system, simply turning the mix channels down in the absence of signal. The mute function is typically separate from the level function, so frequently levels can be written after the mutes have been carefully placed. Each system is a little different but the bottom line is that you should be sure the tracks are off when there is no audio signal present.

On any given track, it's best to leave the mutes on unless there's audio on the track that's part of the mix. This procedure helps minimize unwanted sounds in the mix that might originate as electrical clicks, electronic blips, or dweeblike titters.

Careful muting eliminates any noise that might come from analog sources at the input—effects processors that have been inserted, headphone leakage, drum-mic leakage, or extraneous noises on vocal tracks. This technique helps create a feeling of intimacy and closeness, whether there's one track playing or forty.

Once the mutes are all written, it's time to build a mix.

DOCUMENTING THE MIX

Any time you include an outboard processor, it's important to document all the settings. In the likely case that you need to reconstruct the mix later, you'll be very glad you did. If you're using devices with presets, simply store the preset in the sequence, or, if you didn't use a sequence, create one for archiving device settings. Almost all MIDI devices allow for patch storage and retrieval at the very least and many allow for full automation of all parameters. Keep the archive with all your mix files.

Outboard Gear Without Patch-Storage Capabilities

If you've used several analog devices with no facility for patch storage or retrieval, write down the settings for each knob or parameter. Be as precise as possible. If you're repeatedly using a device, make a template for it with all knobs, numbers, and switches. This will help speed up the record-keeping process. Try contacting the manufacturer at their website; they might already have a perfectly drawn template for you to download and print out.

It might seem like a bother to archive and document all your settings and sounds, but it's the only way to guarantee easy reconstruction of the mix. Even at that, it still takes a lot of tweaking to recapture the feel of the original mix when analog devices are included.

Locate Points and Markers

Modern digital devices function together in a nearly seamless manner, providing a work environment that is amazingly efficient, fast, and creatively freeing. Locate points and markers are fundamental to an efficient workflow. Most systems provide for numeric or named locations throughout a recording. Each locate point or marker is tagged to a specific time-code reference. The user simply types in a number and presses the locate button or makes a selection on the Marker list to jump instantly to the reference time and location in the recording. All devices then chase to the referenced time-code point and join in perfect sync. The digital mixer or DAW also plays along with the recording devices, with all moves and automated changes referenced to the running time code. In fact, most digital mixers, DAWs, and control surfaces have transport controls built in for ultimate ease of use in the recording process.

Text descriptions of each locate point are most convenient because instead of trying to remember what happens at each numbered mark, the locations can be labelled with descriptive terms such as "Verse 1," "Chorus 2," "Bridge," "Solo," and so on.

Using these text-driven locate points streamlines the mix process. There is no need to repeatedly search for the proper point in a song. Once you label each section, your location problems are solved. Most systems let the user click the onscreen text, enter the location number, or type in the first few letters of the section name to move the mixer and all recording devices to the correct song position.

COPY MOVES AND SETTINGS

Digital mix automation facilitates application of the same kind of cut, copy, and paste functions found in any word processor. If you like the mix settings in one portion of a musical work, simply copy them to another similar section. Even if they don't work perfectly, they'll probably be close enough to provide a good starting point.

DIGITAL/PLUG-IN EQUALIZATION

Equalization in the digital-mixing domain offers great flexibility, convenience, and ease of use. Visually, the best an analog EQ can offer is graphic sliders. In comparison, digital onscreen equalizers let users see the actual curves they're shaping. Concepts such as bandwidth, frequency, and extreme cuts and boosts are self-explanatory. Equalization curves like this are not only straightforward to set up and use, they can be stored for future use or copied to different channels in the same mix.

Most digital equalizers offer a way to compare changes from previous EQ settings. A simple bypass function lets the user switch between a flat (not equalized) signal to the current settings. Always check the signal in bypass mode so you can verify the effect of the equalization. Sometimes we play with equalization too much. Later, when we hear the original sound in bypass mode, it's easy to hear that it contained more interest and life than the equalized sound.

Many systems let the user set a couple of EQ settings, and then switch back and forth between them. This is a convenient way to check the musical effect of a particular setting and to try the effects of two extremely different equalization approaches. Some systems let the user morph between two settings at a user-selected speed. These changes are stored in automation data, so a special section can be switched smoothly to the proper EQ and then switched smoothly back to the original EQ later in the song.

There are often portions of a track in which the sound takes on an unpleasing character for a brief moment. Without sophisticated automation, the operator typically has to let the part go in the interest of time. It's also possible that, lacking extra hands or feeling overwhelmed by too many mind-boggling moves, the operator might choose to figuratively sweep the glitch under the rug.

You have the capability through digital automation to fix a momentary problem by simply automating as you equalize the problem spot. With repair techniques such as this available, it's possible to keep perfecting the mix and arrangement until they are the best they can be. Time and patience become the primary limitations.

DYNAMIC CONTROL AND SPECIAL EFFECTS

Digital compression, limiting, expanding, gating, and special-effects devices use most of the same parameters and controls found on their analog counterparts. In fact, many software-based dynamic- and effects-control screens look like classic equipment, complete with onscreen VU meters, knobs, switches, and buttons.

The appropriate amount of dynamic control and the types of special effects used are dependent on a few factors, including:

- Genre
- Current trends
- Musical taste
- Creativity

It is most important that creative freedom is honored. Given trends and genre considerations, the most important rule is that there are no rules. There are recommendations based on experiences and accepted current procedures, but you should allow yourself the latitude to experiment and follow a vision through to completion. Then be open to the possibility that it might not really work well. Even if the path has a disappointing end, you'll learn something about mixing and your musical instincts in the quest.

AUTOMATION DATA STORAGE FORMAT

Using a digital mixer is a little different than using a DAW. The DAW contains all automation data, which seamlessly follows the session files. On the other hand, when using a digital mixer, the mix data must be backed up to an external data storage device. This is usually a very simple process, not unlike any other computer file saving procedure. To store the mixed master, when using a digital mixer, either record it digitally from the mixer output to a separate computer-based DAW or record it directly onto two or more tracks of the digital device that's playing back the tracks.

Most modern automation systems provide for data storage to your format of choice. Although virtually any system that stores data will suffice in the short term, be sure to save your data in a format—or multiple formats—that are likely to be around for years. Occasionally a new format hits the market with the promise of breaking new ground, offering enticing functionality. I have a closet full of such drives and I have to keep them around even though they don't really connect to any system I have running right now. If I need the data from them, I must set up an old computer system—I have several just for such occasions.

If possible, back up to a format like DVD±R that promises to be around for a while.

AUDIO STORAGE FORMATS

Once the mix is perfected, print it to a usable format. Any digital storage medium with suitable size can store the digital data that comprises the mixed audio. Print the mix to hard disk, CD, DVD, Blu-ray, or any other suitable storage device or medium.

Hard Disk

Some systems provide a means to digitally bounce the mix, along with all its mix adjustments and parameters, directly to the hard drive. This method provides for a clean data transfer. Once the mix is on the hard drive, it can be stored accurately on any digital storage medium, such as CD, DVD, or other optical cartridge. One of the truest means of storage for playback utilizes transfer of data directly from the hard disk to the playback medium. Avoiding the transfer to DAT or analog tape is typically preferred, unless the user specifically prefers the sound and accuracy of high-quality analog tape.

Printing the mix within the recorder system also provides a simple means of saving a high-resolution audio format such as DVD-Audio or SACD directly from your DAW without the need for an expensive stand-alone recorder.

DAT

Digital audio tape (DAT) was the format of choice for years but its popularity has dwindled with the increased popularity of DAWs and standalone CD recorders. DAT offers all the sonic benefits of digital recording but the standard DAT recorder is limited to 48-, 44.1-, and 32-kHz sample rates. With the increased importance of high-definition samples with increased bit depth, DAT isn't able to accommodate most recordists' needs. In addition, the error correction scheme used in this format can produce inaccuracies and anomalies that degrade the audio quality, especially through multiple generations.

When DAT was originally introduced, it was advertised as the end to all noise problems. Supposedly, it wasn't necessary to maximize levels because even at lower levels DAT was far superior to analog tape. Having been plagued by analog tape noise, most engineers basked happily in the silence between notes and at the end of a fade out. Then, upon scrutiny, it became apparent that something wasn't exactly right. Analog tape offered warmth, clarity, accuracy, and a feeling that wasn't quite there in DATs. Hence the beginning of the big debate: Is analog better than digital, or is digital better than analog? Analog is theatrically more accurate but it has limitation imposed by tape formulations, head gap width, and so on—and it's noisy. The digital recording process keeps getting better with the growth and expansion of technology. As I indicate previously in this series, in *Recording Software & Plug-Ins*, a 192 kHz, 24-bit sample is very close to providing sonic accuracy that matches the human ability to perceive spatial positioning. As sample rates and bit depths increase along with computer speed and power, digital recording should take over completely as the across-the-board method of choice for all recordists. However, there is still charm in the magnetic recording process—it'll be hard to let go of the feel and smell of tape and the washing–machine sized tape recorder/heat generator.

CD or DVD Recorder

Hardware CD and DVD recorders offer a convenient way to record to a commercial medium. The disadvantage of the typical CD recorder is that it is locked into the 44.1-kHz, 16-bit digital data flow. Some CD and DVD recorders allow syncing of the digital word clock to an external source. Using this feature, CDs and DVDs are capable of storing audio in sync with the external word clock in excess of 44.1 kHz.

The most appealing feature that the CD recorder offers is its immediacy. Simply record a mix straight to the CD recorder, finalize the CD, and take it with you to play in your car or home stereo. Most DAW interfaces provide a digital output that can connect to the CD recorder's digital input, so the transfer is clean and accurate. Granted, it is almost as easy with a modern DAW to bounce a mix, import it to iTunes, Toast, or some other disk burning application, and then burn a CD for the same purpose. However, the CD recorder streamlines that process a bit.

VU MIX LEVELS

When using a standard VU meter, levels should hang around 0 VU, with the strongest part of the song registering up to +1 or +2 VU—the weakest part shouldn't usually go below about -5 VU. For a song that is going to be heard on radio or TV, you need to keep the mix as close to 0 VU as possible so the quiet parts aren't lost or distractingly inaudible.

When you're recording a symphony, piano, or other wide-dynamic-range source, it can be very difficult to keep levels around 0 VU; with these types of sources, that wouldn't be natural-sounding or easy to listen to. If you're mixing to a digital two-track and your music will be heard primarily on CD or other digital format, there's plenty of room for including a wide dynamic range; in this context a wide dynamic range can be fantastic. Some of my favorite symphony recordings include passages that are barely audible, even on CD, followed immediately by very strong full ensemble passages.

However, most of what the normal recordist works with is commercial in nature and should maintain a constant and strong mix level. In contemporary music, contrast is usually most effective when demonstrated by changes in orchestration rather than changes in ensemble volume. Taking a full group and cutting immediately to a single acoustic guitar is often very effective and a great dynamic change, even though the mix levels might stay constant.

PEAK LEVEL

Digital devices monitor signal levels from silence to peak levels. The most important factor involved with setting digital levels is avoidance of overloads (OL), also called peaks. Digital recordings are accurate up to the peak level, also called "Full Scale," because the meter is at full level without peaking. A recording that uses the full digital level without overloading takes advantage of the full available amplitude resolution. The sample rate stays the same no matter how hot the signal level is, but recording unnecessarily cold levels reduces the effective bit-depth resolution.

The peak signal level of -18 dBFS equates to an average level of 0 VU. Recording with peak levels hovering between about -18 and -12 dBFS allows sufficient headroom and keeps the levels under control. If every track of a multitrack session hovered up toward 0 dBFS, there is a strong likelihood that the mix buss would be overdriven. One of the strong rationalizations for recording 24-bit audio in any session is the existence of a dramatic increase of vertical resolution steps relative to 16-bit recordings. This lets the engineer record with slightly more conservative levels while still realizing an increase in sample accuracy. As a reminder, 16-bit samples provide 65,536 vertical resolution steps, but in comparison, a 24-bit sample provides 16,777,216 steps.

FADES

The majority of recordings end in a simple fade out. The fade is a good way to end a song while sustaining the energy and emotion of the choruses or end section. Sometimes an ending adds too much finality and resolve; it detracts from the continuity and flow of an entire album. Other times endings are the perfect resolution of the song, album, or section of the album.

Seven to fifteen seconds is the typical range of fade lengths. If the fade is too short, the end seems even more abrupt than an actual ending. If it's too long, the

Mixing & Mastering .... by BILL GIBSON

Digital Levels

Digital recording devices measure peak signal levels. The meters that are used to measure signal levels on digital devices respond very quickly and indicate peaks and transients, unlike the standard VU meters that measure average signal levels. The most important aspect of digital recording is avoiding overloads, but typical levels should hover between -12 and -18 dBFS.

Digital levels and meters are referenced by a few different terms. Meters that measure digital level are called Peak Program Meters (PPM). The signal strength they measure are referred to as decibels full scale (dBFS).

0 VU= -18 dBFS

0 dBFS=Full digital level

continuity of an album can be lost or, if the tune is heard in a car or other noisy environment, most of the fade will be covered up, creating the feel of a huge gap between songs.

Fades should begin right after the beginning of a musical phrase and must be smooth and even throughout the length of the fade. Don't get excited toward the end and duck out too quickly. And, don't try to feather the last bit out so smoothly that the average listener won't be able to hear the last four or five seconds of the fade.

I like to time the fade so there's an interesting fill or lick just before the end. This gives the listener the feeling that something is going on after the fade. If the listener imagines that the band keeps playing, the emotion and energy of the mix should continue even though the song is over.

If there are lyrics during the fade, try to finish the phrase just after a key lyric, such as the last word of the chorus or a crucial vocal fill lick. Don't cut an idea off with the end of the fade. End between ideas.

For a fade to begin naturally, start the fade after the beginning of a musical section. Often the length of the fade is determined by the length of the musical section happening during the fade.

The fades in Audio Examples 7-1 through 7-4 are for time only, so you'll get the feel of each fade length.

Audio Example 7-1 demonstrates a seven-second fade.

Audio Example 7-1
Seven-Second Fade

Audio Example 7-2 demonstrates a 10-second fade.

Audio Example 7-2
Ten-Second Fade

Audio Example 7-3 demonstrates a 15-second fade.

Audio Example 7-3
Fifteen-Second Fade

Audio Example 7-4 demonstrates a five-second fade.

Audio Example 7-4
Five-Second Fade

SUMMARY

The debate will continue over which format is better as long as there are options. The nature of the creative mind is to push the limits—to create the very best version of art. If the recordist and the artist pour their passions into a musical work, they'll always care about the form of delivery to the public. I enjoy the debate process, the experimental process, and the creative development of art through technology.

Listen to your work on as many systems as you can and mix it in as many formats as you can gain access to. There are definitely differences; one format might be the perfect choice for one song while another format excels for another. Your decisions are most valid for your music.

Mixing in the third millennium brings seemingly countless options. The question at nearly every economic recording level is no longer, "How can I possibly get a musical and professional sound with the few tools I have?" Now the question has become, "How can I ever use all these professional-sounding tools to get a musical sound?"

Chapter 7 .... AUTOMATION

CHAPTER TEST

1. Automation:
   a. is a means of integrating a computer system into your mixing process
   b. enables you to, at the very least, record fader and mute changes into the computer's memory
   c. gives you the ability to make new level changes while you hear the old level changes
   d. is like giving you several more hands to use during the mix
   e. All of the above

2. In the realm of analog mixers, which automation system hold less potential for signal degradation?
   a. VCA-based
   b. Moving fader

3. VCA stands for:
   a. variable circuit amplifier
   b. variable controlled amplifier
   c. voltage circuit amplifier
   d. voltage controlled amplifier

4. A moving-fader automation package on an analog console maintains _____ of the sonic quality and character that exists without the automation system.
   a. 98 percent
   b. 80 percent
   c. 100 percent
   d. 50 percent

5. Mix automation systems refer each move to:
   a. the continual flow of SMPTE time code
   b. MTC
   c. data from an automation data control track that is printed to tape
   d. Any of the above depending on the system design

6. Whereas analog automation systems control faders and mutes, digital mixers automate level, mute, pan, aux sends, effects parameters, routing,

s, and so on—virtually any control on the mixer.
   a. True
   b. False

7. _____ enables instant recall of the console configuration, including all parameter settings controlled through automation.
   a. Snapshot automation
   b. Dynamic automations
   c. Real-time automation
   d. SMPTE

8. _____ provides for real-time recording and playback of any automation-controlled parameters while referenced to time code.
   a. Snapshot automation
   b. Dynamic automations
   c. Real-time automation
   d. SMPTE

9. In automation systems, _____ is playback mode. It reads any automation data that's been recorded.
   a. Update/Absolute
   b. Auto Touch
   c. Trim Levels
   d. Auto Read

10. In _____ mode, once the button is pressed to write or record automation, all selected parameters overwrite the existing settings for those parameters only.
    a. Update/Absolute
    b. Auto Touch
    c. Trim Levels
    d. Auto Read

11. In _____ mode, all data is in playback mode until a controller is touched or moved. Once the controller is touched, that particular parameter goes into record mode.
    a. Update/Absolute
    b. Auto Touch
    c. Trim Levels
    d. Auto Read

12. _____ mode retains all relative moves on a particular controller but adds or subtracts user-specified amounts of change from all moves in a specified region
    a. Update/Absolute
    b. Auto Touch
    c. Trim Levels
    d. Auto Read

13. _____ lets the user change any mix automation parameter with great accuracy and without needing to run the mix again.
    a. MIDI automatic
    b. The mix editor
    c. A real-time automation system
    d. A pencil editor

14. The first step in most automated mixing sessions is to:
    a. turn the mix channels down in the absence of signal
    b. write all the channel mutes
    c. start building the reverberation sounds
    d. Both a and b

15. When building a mix, careful muting eliminates:
    a. any noise that might come from analog sources at the input
    b. noise from effects processors that have been inserted
    c. headphone leakage
    d. drum mic leakage or extraneous noises on vocal and acoustic instrument tracks
    e. All of the above

16. Any time you include an outboard processor in a mix:
    a. it's important to document all the settings
    b. be sure to set the VCAs correctly
    c. you'll get a more unique sound
    d. All of the above

17. Organizationally during the mixing process, _____ are the key to working efficiently.
    a. yellow legal pads and pencils
    b. interns and second engineers
    c. locate points and markers
    d. track sheets

18. Digital compression, limiting, expanding, gating, and special-effects devices use most of the same parameters and controls found on their analog counterparts.
    a. True
    b. False

19. The typical fade out is _____ long.
    a. 3 seconds
    b. 5 seconds
    c. between 12 and 21 seconds
    d. between 7 and 15 seconds

20. Fades should begin _____ and must be smooth and even throughout the length of the fade.
    a. at the end of a musical phrase
    b. in the middle of a musical phrase
    c. right after the beginning of a musical phrase
    d. Either a or b

Test answers are on page 299

Pulling It Together

CHAPTER 8

This chapter covers practical applications of the mixdown techniques discussed in this edition of *The Hal Leonard Recording Method*. It is one thing to know and explain a technique—it is another thing to be able to actually accomplish and master a technique. Practice the procedures and routines that I present. Apply them to your own musical productions and constantly evaluate the results. Listen in your studio, your car, your friend's car, on your sound system at the gig, on your laptop, through headphones, or wherever you think your music might be heard.

The examples we'll examine include two different types of genres. It doesn't matter much if your music is radically different from these examples. The techniques I describe are classic in nature. They apply well to many musical situations and they are used heavily in many styles of musical productions.

CHAPTER AT A GLANCE

Predetermine the Mix Density	193
Develop Your Own Sonic Signature	195
Blending the Drums and Bass	196
Blending Electric Guitars	197
Blending Acoustic Guitars	197
Simple Acoustic Production	198
Acoustic Guitar with the Band	198
Creating the Lead Vocal Sound	199
Intelligibility	199
Clarity	199
Consistent Audibility	200
Dominance of the Appropriate Mix Space	200
Perfectly Controlling Ambience	200
Appropriate Vocal Balance with the Instrumentation	201
Procedures for Creating a Good Lead Vocal Sound	202
Compression	202
Equalization	203
Effects	204
Blending Backing Vocals	205
Level Control	205
Equalization	206
Find the Melody	206
Watch Out for the High Parts	207
Thin the Thick and Thicken the Thin	207
Don't Over-Bass the Bass	207
Panning	208
Compression/Limiting	209
Emphasize the Important Ingredients	209
Eliminate Unimportant Ingredients	210
Include High, Mid, and Low Frequencies	210
High Frequencies in the Mix	210
Midrange Frequencies in the Mix	211
Low Frequencies in the Mix	211
Classic Recordings: How'd They Do That?	211
Surround Mixing	216
Layout	218
Mixdown Formats	219
Surround Master Track Assignments	221
Stereo Compatibility	222

PREDETERMINE THE MIX DENSITY

Decide on the mix density before you start the mix—this is especially important for the inexperienced mix engineer. Mix density can be easily understood visually. The pictures in the following illustration demonstrate image density from low to high.

A subject or two against a white backdrop represents low density. An image filled with several active and dominant images represents high density.

Correlate your mix to a visual image. The essence of image density begins with the production phase; however, as the mix engineer, you hold the power to transform mix density through your implementation of level, dynamics, panning, and effects.

There is an amazing difference in mix density between the latest Diana Krall or Norah Jones release and a release from Minor Threat, Black Flag, or Rancid. Every type of music serves a particular listening audience. If you're mixing in any genre you must become an informed listener before you can mix—there's no way

Mix Density

The photos in this illustration provide a frame of reference for mix density. Create a visual image for your mix intentions. Let that image guide your decisions. Listen to several pieces of music and imagine a photographic density for what you hear.

around it. If you're a country-western fan, your rap or R&B mixes just might end up sounding a little countrified if you don't spend some serious one-on-one time with your iPod and recordings that are like the music you're mixing.

There are many excellent and very successful mix engineers who regularly mix a variety of musical styles. At a certain point, most experienced and talented people develop an appreciation for musical diversity. It's not too difficult to understand the creative requirements prescribed by most musical genres. If you capture and appreciate the energy, passion, tonality, and density of the music, you can be effective as a mix engineer for any music genre.

There is a school of thought that dictates you must be of an authentic mindset to portray the music of a specific segment of society or state of mind. There might be some validity to that ideology from the purist's standpoint, but it's not supported by the reality of most successful commercial producers and engineers.

DEVELOP YOUR OWN SONIC SIGNATURE

I like drums. I play drums, guitar, and some keys, but drums are at the root of my musical soul. Even when I'm playing guitar or keys, I'm very aware of how the parts sit in the rhythmic groove. I love how all the parts fit together rhythmically and I love how slight variations in their rhythmic feel change the emotion and passion conveyed by the music. This essence of groove affects everything I do as a musician, engineer, and producer.

The fact that I like drums means I pay close attention to drum sounds and rhythmic grooves. Therefore, I end up with good drum sounds and authentic and accurate rhythmic interpretations. When rap music was relatively new, I mixed a lot of local Seattle rap projects. I developed a reputation as a guy who liked to build big fat drum tracks. That characteristic became part of my sonic signature, plainly stamped on most of the projects I produce and mix.

Your soul might respond deeply to distorted electric guitar, acoustic guitar, grand piano, Afro-Cuban percussion, or fiddles. A certain part of that preference will influence all you do. Most of the time, the fact that your soul resonates to music in any way provides a frame of reference for you to understand and emulate other musical facets. It's most important that you find a driving force for your creativity—the source of that driving force is least important.

BLENDING THE DRUMS AND BASS

First, take a look at blending the drums and percussion with the bass guitar. The drum sound is so fundamental to the sonic signature of any production that I could never overstate the importance of mixing and blending the sounds of the drum kit in a musically effective, stylistically correct, and powerful way. One reliable method of establishing the drum sound is to build from the bottom up. Start with the kick and add the snare, overheads, and toms.

························· **Audio Example 8-1**
Build the Drum Sound

The exact kick sound you build is very genre-dependent. Some genres depend on the kick sound for the tonal foundation of the mix, in which case there should be substantial low-frequency content and not many conflicting low midrange frequencies. In these types of mixes the bass guitar typically contains more low mid and highs frequencies, but not as many deep lows, diminishing or eliminating any tonal conflict with the kick sound.

Listen to Audio Example 8-2. Pay close attention as I adjust the kick-drum tone from a deep and rich sound to a very pointed midrange sound.

························· **Audio Example 8-2**
Kick Tone

Now listen as I build the drum-set sound and integrate a compatible bass-guitar sound.

························· **Audio Example 8-3**
Building the Drum and Bass Mix

························· **Video Example 8-1**
Building the Drum and Bass Mix

BLENDING ELECTRIC GUITARS

Sometimes the best guitar sounds are clean and simple. Other times several guitar sounds combine to make one massive sound. Listen to the two different types of guitar sounds in the following Audio Examples. Each is very appropriate for the type of music it serves.

When blending multiple electric guitars to form one sound, evaluate each part for its strengths and weaknesses, and then highlight the best aspects of each. If one part has a smooth high-frequency content that's easy to listen to and fairly unspectacular lows and mids, try a high-pass filter and filter out everything other than the highs. This then would obviously need to be combined with the lows and mids from other tracks. Using this concept, you can create unique and powerful sounds that add to your production.

In the following Audio Examples, I'll demonstrate and specify each sound and how I equalize, pan, and blend the sounds together.

First is a guitar track from a band I produced called Glimpse. We spent quite a bit of time miking cabinets and combining different sounds. We had several amps available (Marshall, Mesa, Matchless, Fender, Line 6, and so on) and eventually, throughout the project, we used them all. We also combined the live amps with some of the Line 6 direct outputs of several modeled amplifiers.

.... Audio Example 8-4
Several Amps Combined to One Sound

Second is a guitar track from a solo artist I produced, Faith Ecklund. This is still a great guitar sound, but we simply used a single guitar track, processed and blended for a big sound.

.... Audio Example 8-5
One Guitar Track Blended into the Mix

BLENDING ACOUSTIC GUITARS

When faced with production decisions, the temptation is usually to build a bigger sound by adding more and more instruments. Often, the more tracks you add, the smaller your mix sounds. In fact, many tracks fighting for the listener's attention typically result in diffusion, rather than a concentration of focus.

A simpler production and mixing approach often creates a more impressive sound than a complex and busy approach.

Simple Acoustic Production

The following song, from Jamie Dieveney's first solo album, could have been produced as a dynamic ballad with a full band and lots of overdubs. Instead, we decided to build an acoustic guitar–oriented sound. It includes one basic acoustic part with a second acoustic track for musical fills.

Blending acoustic guitars is more complicated than just getting each guitar to sound impressive by itself. Consider the overall picture. Emphasize the strengths of each guitar and be sure the parts work together and don't distract from each other. Create complementing equalization on each guitar—in the frequency range where one part is emphasized, the other part should be de-emphasized.

We also brought in some light percussion and eventually a smooth electric-guitar solo. Notice how the mix still sounds impressive and the acoustic guitars provide a production signature that is unique and effective. In this Audio Example, I'll tell you how I've adjusted the EQ, pan, and processing to create an impressive sound.

............................Audio Example 8-6

Simple Acoustic Production

Acoustic Guitar with the Band

It is often very effective to include the acoustic guitar in a larger-scale production. The bright transients of the steel-string acoustic guitar provide an excellent contrast to a distorted, aggressive electric-guitar sound.

The following song starts off with an intimate acoustic guitar and solo voice. The title of the song, "I Never Knew Love Before," begs for intimacy at first—this simple texture fits the emotion of the first part of the song very well. As the song builds and becomes very passionate, so do the production texture and energy.

When the acoustic track occurs along with the electric track, it must be blended perfectly. If the acoustic guitar is too loud in relation to the electric guitar, neither sound is optimized, and vice versa. The louder acoustic track typically detracts from the power and energy of the electric track. If the electric track is too loud in relation to the acoustic track, there's no real need for the acoustic. Blend both tracks perfectly to achieve the energy and power that's appropriate for your production.

Listen to the effect provided by this acoustic track as it integrates into the complete production.

.... **Audio Example 8-7**
Acoustic Guitar Blended with the Band

CREATING THE LEAD VOCAL SOUND

There is not one definitive vocal sound that works for every mixdown application. The style and character of the music determine the style and character of the lead vocal sound. Keep in mind that there are always exceptions to any rule, especially in any creative endeavor—there are, however, some characteristic traits that define a well-shaped lead vocal sound. Try to achieve these objectives in the development of your lead vocal sounds.

Intelligibility

Most musical styles demand that the lead vocal offers lyrics that are understandable. This doesn't necessarily mean they must be substantially louder than the rest of the mix, but they should be strong enough to be intelligible. Certain aggressive rock and alternative styles lend more credibility to the conveyance of emotion than the projection of lyrics. In these cases, the lyrics might only be understood when you read them in the product insert. This is neither good nor bad—it just is.

Clarity

Other than in specific aggressive genres, the lead vocal should be clear and clean. You can achieve clarity and intelligibility through the proper use of equalization and compression. However, a lead vocal track that has been recorded using the right microphone and excellent technique is easy to blend and shape into the mix, while retaining ample clarity and intelligibility.

Consistent Audibility

No matter what the genre, it's important that the lead vocal be consistently audible. It is distracting when the vocal disappears in the mix and, even if the lyrics can't be understood, the feeling provided by the vocal performance must be felt.

Dominance of the Appropriate Mix Space

The vocal must dominate the stylistically correct mix space throughout the production. Depending on the density of the production, that mix space might be ample or negligible.

Norah Jones typically uses a small rhythm section. The musical ingredients are crafted by excellent musicians to leave lots of room for space around the vocal sound. There is a lot of space for her vocal sound.

U2 leaves a lot of room for Bono to be heard and understood. They're a very authentic band with little pretense and clutter in their live or recorded productions.

50 Cent is about the energy and the vibe. There is an equal importance placed on the vocals and the groove. Rap music has really come a long way since its inception. It has, at the same time, become much more commercialized and much more diverse. It crosses cultural, ethnic, and social barriers.

Alternative, hard rock, and punk bands leave a very narrow mix space for vocals. Often the band track is so aggressive and punchy that there is little space left for the lead vocal, so extreme dynamic control is required to ensure that the vocals set perfectly in the mix and never stray, regardless of whether the singer increases or decreases vocal or lyrical intensity.

PERFECTLY CONTROLLING AMBIENCE

The ambient content of every mix and the way the ambience is distributed throughout the mix panorama set the stage for the music. Some music cries out for intimacy and closeness—other music begs to be bathed in stadium-like reflections. Neither choice is bad unless it doesn't serve the lyrics, instrumentation, and artistic intent.

As a rule, most mixes function well when one instrument, voice, or sound defines the close perspective and another instrument, voice, or sound defines the distant perspective. Typically, placing all mix ingredients in the identical ambient environment results in a mix that is indistinct in many ways.

Imagine listening to a live performance. Even though all musical ingredients coexist in the identical ambient environment, there is almost always a difference in the specific directionality of each instrument or in the amount of reinforcement through the sound system.

The crowd causes a variation in reflections across the frequency spectrum, so some sounds that create reflections absorbed by the audience seem close. Other sounds that create reflections consisting of frequencies that are relatively unaffected by the audience seem more distant.

APPROPRIATE VOCAL BALANCE WITH THE INSTRUMENTATION

It is obviously important that the balance between all tracks is appropriate. One of the best ways to judge balances between mix ingredients is to listen to the mix at radically differing volumes and on radically different systems.

It is truly amazing how different the mix sounds at different volume settings. At loud volumes, the sounds compress as your ears change their characteristic response. When a mix sounds full and balanced at 110 dB SPL, it is very likely that it is unbalanced at 70 dB SPL. On the other hand, when a mix sounds good, full, and balanced at 70 dB SPL, it is very likely that it will sound great at 110 dB SPL. Mixing first at a very low level not only saves wear and tear on your ears, but it also usually results in mixes that sound consistently good at various levels and on various types of playback systems.

Stylistic concerns dictate the exact balance between the lead vocal and the rest of the tracks. However, most lead vocal tracks should demonstrate the characteristics just listed. A typical pop lead vocal is nestled in the track so that the groove is powerful and dominant, yet in many styles the lead vocal is dominant, clean, and in the forefront of the mix.

PROCEDURES FOR CREATING A GOOD LEAD VOCAL SOUND

There are certain consistent procedures that help create a polished, commercial-sounding lead vocal track. Try these suggestions and build a sound that works for your music. Remember these are just suggestions—they're effective and are a good place to start when you are developing a good lead vocal sound.

Compression

Compression is optional from the purist's standpoint. Inserting any extra device in the signal path increases the risk of degrading the audio quality. The purist would ride the level manually in automation rather than let a processor perform the task automatically. It is true that the elimination of compression in the signal path results in a more transparent and pure sonic quality.

A first-rate example of minimal compression on an excellent recording can be heard on the Norah Jones album, *Come Away with Me*. This album is very well recorded and produced. Husky Huskolds did a masterful job recording excellent sounds and blending them in a mix so they can be heard and felt in their complete essence. The mixes are easy to listen to, and the lead vocal is pure and natural.

Practically speaking, for most commercial popular productions, the orchestration is thick and aggressive, leaving a minimal mix space for the lead vocal track. Any word or vocal sound that dips under the level of the track is lost. Therefore, compression is a crucial ingredient in a commercial pop mix. The amount of compression varies depending on the music, but some aggressive rock and dance music utilizes extreme compression on the lead vocal to keep it squarely in the forefront of the mix at all times.

Most of the time, a ratio between 3:1 and 7:1 works well. The greater the severity in gain reduction, the more important it is that the attack time is short. If the attack time is too slow and the gain reduction is too extreme, the result is overly exaggerated sibilant sounds.

An example of extreme compression on the lead vocal can be heard on Switchfoot's "Meant to Live." Notice how the lead vocal stays right in front of the band track, yet the band always sounds full and punchy. A track like this is severely compressed. The ratio setting is still typically between 3:1 and 7:1, but the threshold is adjusted so that the processor is nearly always acting on the voice.

There should be several times when the gain is not being reduced, but there might be 9 to 12 dB of gain reduction much of the time. Set the release time at about 0.5 seconds so that the processor releases the gain reduction in time for the tracks to turn back up to reveal the ends of the words along with the vocal inflections and nuances. Adjust the release time while listening to playback. The processor should reduce gain and release it back to its original level in a way that sounds smooth and musical.

Extreme compression demands the use of a very high-quality compressor. Vintage devices such as the Universal Audio 1176 and the Teletronix LA-2A are excellent tools that are capable of extreme compression while retaining a transparent and musical feel. Empirical Labs, Manley, Focusrite, Grace, Tubetech, Summit Audio, Avalon, Drawmer, dbx, and several other manufacturers make excellent compression devices. Many of these devices are based on the vacuum tube, and most are relatively expensive. The Distressor, by Empirical Labs, is commonly used to keep the lead and backing vocals in a narrow dynamic range. This device compresses in a very musical way, while maintaining a full and natural sound. Extreme compression from the Distressor still sounds strong and full. Most of these high-quality compressors are capable of excellent results whether the lead vocal track requires gentle or extreme compression.

A low-quality compressor sounds very thin and weak when set for extreme action. If you want your recordings to sound full and clean while maintaining a natural, powerful sound, invest in high-quality compressors. In the long run, it is much less expensive to buy more expensive, high-quality devices that will last you throughout your recording career than to purchase inexpensive devices. Sub-par equipment rarely produces completely satisfactory results. It is frustrating to use and it eventually ends up buried in a box of outdated gear or on eBay, selling for a small fraction of what you paid for it.

Equalization

High-quality vintage and new equalizers are like high-quality compressors. They just sound a lot better than the less-expensive models. Equalizers such as the Focusrite Red series, almost anything made by Neve, and SSL have a characteristic sound that is recognizable once you've used them in a mixdown. To call the essence that they add to the signal path "coloration" isn't completely accurate. They add a "sound." The Focusrite Red EQ adds warmth and size. The Neve equalizers typically add a smooth, silky feel. The SSL signal path adds an aggressive edge most of the time. Obviously, the severity of the effect depends on the strength of the input signal and the device settings.

Many lead vocal recordings are recorded using a mic with a cardioid pickup pattern in order to decrease ambient room sound and to increase intimacy. Often, this technique results in a thick vocal sound that needs to be cleaned up during mixdown. Decrease a bandwidth between one and two octaves wide, centered on a frequency between 300 and 600 Hz, by a few dB to clean up a muddy vocal. It's also a great idea to use a high-pass filter to roll off below 100 Hz or so. These lower frequencies aren't very important to most vocal sounds—reducing them helps clean up the vocal sound and ensure against unwanted rumble and other noises that might have leaked onto the vocal track.

High-frequency treatment of the lead vocal is very production-driven. Some vocal tracks, especially tracks recorded from a distance of a foot or so on a bright-sounding large-diaphragm condenser mic, are plenty bright and don't require much equalization. Often, especially when the lead vocal is thick-sounding to start with, a high-frequency boost helps emphasize the intelligibility and clarity of the vocals. Boosting a peak that is about one octave wide, centered between 3 and 7 kHz, is usually very useful—it adds understandability and presence to a track that might otherwise be buried in the mix texture. Sometimes, boosting a shelf above 8 or 9 kHz by a couple dB adds just enough clarity and air to the lead vocal sound that it fits perfectly on top of the mix.

Listen to the following lead vocal track as I compress, equalize, and blend it into the mix.

Video Example 8-2
Mixing the Lead Vocal

Effects

From year to year, trends change regarding the appropriate effects treatment of lead vocals. Use your insight into the trends in the genre you're producing to build the specific sound that works for your music.

Often, we look for effects that increase the blend and size of the lead vocal track. Most inexperienced recordists instinctively add reverberation to the lead vocal to increase the size of the vocal image. Typically, a dramatic amount reverberation results in a muddy and indistinct mix sound. When used in subtle amounts, reverberation adds a blending quality without an obvious buildup of reflections.

To create the effect of performing in a large room, use a slapback delay between 200 and 400 ms. A single slapback delay mimics the acoustic reflection from the opposing room surface. This reflection cues the brain as to the room size and its implied dimensions. A slapback increases the implication that the performance takes place in a large space. In addition, the single delay is much cleaner-sounding than reverberation alone. Set the delay in time with an eighth or quarter note to help solidify the groove and to create a cleaner mix.

If you use reverberation on the lead vocal, try setting the predelay in time with the eighth or sixteenth note. This separates the reverberation from the dry attack of each note, therefore retaining the intimacy of the sound while adding the dimensional size that is characteristic of reverberation.

The rule of thumb indicates that the lead vocal track has less effect applied to it than the backing vocal tracks. This helps reinforce the image that the lead vocalist is singing closer to the listener with the backing vocals farther back in the room sound.

BLENDING BACKING VOCALS

It is very important that the backing vocals are edited meticulously to eliminate sloppy entrances and releases. Also, be sure that all distracting intonation problems have been repaired.

Blending backing vocals can be accomplished primarily through equalization, panning, compression/limiting, and level control.

A single backing-vocal track is treated in a very similar way to the lead vocal. Typically, single backing tracks should blend easily with the lead vocal sound; however, the backing vocal track is typically wetter than the lead track.

To create a backing vocal sound that retains individuality for all parts, process them separately and re-blend them with the primary mix faders.

Level Control

It seems obvious that level control is integral to blending backing vocals but, at first, many recordists don't understand how meticulous this process should be.

The temptation to simply set the overall backing-vocal track levels and let them ride throughout the production is strong. However, to achieve an excellent blend throughout the production, the mix engineer must listen carefully to all backing-vocal segments. If a voice or two sticks out of the group in a distracting way at any point, adjust the individual levels to compensate in the automation system—or make careful notes about their locations for a manual mix.

When I'm mixing backing vocals, even though I might be using mixer automation, I prefer to blend the basic levels within the DAW software. Most recording software features include a graphics-based mix edit window, in which level changes are drawn in by dragging a volume line up or down. Set the mix edit window so that all backing vocal tracks are visible. As you listen to the vocals, use the visual graphic interface to quickly draw in level adjustments. This is a fast way to build an excellent blend throughout the production. Be meticulous in this process, listening through the entire arrangement several times and adjusting the blend so it is smooth and cohesive.

Equalization

Equalization is fundamental to the blending process. Evaluate each frequency range and make adjustments to build a smooth, easy-to-listen-to blend. Avoid boosting or cutting all vocal tracks at the same frequency. Create compatible EQ curves that work together. If every track is boosted at the same frequency range, there's a good chance the group will sound edgy and harsh, especially when heard on a system that happens to be extra sensitive at the boosted frequencies.

If you're blending a traditional SATB vocal group, distribute the emphasized frequencies among the various vocal ranges—use your ears and your head to decide which frequencies to boost on which parts. Simple logic indicates that a good choice might be to boost the highs on the sopranos, upper mids on the altos, lower mids on the baritones, and lows on the basses. Sometimes this approach is appropriate, but there are other musical considerations that will help guide you to the proper choices.

Find the Melody

First, if the group is by itself and includes the melody, there's a good chance that you should boost the presence range on whatever part is the melody. This will help the melody stand out in the blend and increase the understandability of the group. Most listeners need a little help discerning the melody in a wall of vocal blend, so adding a little presence to this part, between 4 and 7 kHz, creates a more effortless listening experience.

Watch Out for the High Parts

Often, the upper vocal parts are the most edgy and penetrating. If you're building a blended vocal sound, it's often a good idea to decrease the highs (above 6 to 9 kHz) in the soprano part. The nature of the vocal range is usually enough to enable domination of the vocal sound without needing an abundant amount of upper frequencies.

Thin the Thick and Thicken the Thin

Baritone and sometimes alto singers can sound a little thick in midrange content. A thick sound can stand out in a blended vocal as much as an edgy and harsh sound. A slight cut between 200 and 600 Hz along with the application of a high-pass filter that trims the lows below about 100 Hz can eliminate a poor vocal blend on these parts.

High vocal parts often sound thin and edgy, whether a high soprano or high tenor. Depending on the actual vocal timbre, these parts often stick out and lack any blending quality. To blend edgy-sounding vocals, use a shelving equalizer and turn down the high frequencies above about 5 kHz or use a bell curve EQ and sweep an octave-wide cut between 2.5 and 8 kHz to mellow the tone. Sometimes, these sounds blend better after boosting an octave-wide band somewhere between 200 and 500 Hz—sweep a slight boost until the sound blends well with the other vocal tracks.

Don't Over-Bass the Bass

I mix a lot of vocal tracks, many in the a cappella group niche. Part of the challenge in this type of music is developing a bass voice sound that creates a mix with low end that rivals a full band mix. I have found some great ways to create a huge bass voice sound; however, always keep in mind that huge is good, but boomy and obnoxious is bad.

Avoid creating a bass voice blend that is super-infused with bass frequencies because you'll lose intelligibility and decrease the blend with the other voices. Create a bass sound that is full, but not overly full, in the low end. Compression and limiting are very helpful in the quest to keep the bass voice tracks full and present. Also, if the bass voice is acting as the sole low-frequency instrument, try supporting the bass vocal sound with a very mellow low-synth sound. Be sure the synth part is played precisely with the vocal and that there is no telltale edge that gives away the fact that you've reinforced the sound. I've had good results supporting vocal tracks with pizzicato string samples, simple sine waves, and mellow guitar sounds.

Panning

Panning any track helps you hide or reveal that track or other tracks. It is standard procedure to record several tracks of each vocal part, or at least of each vocal group, and then blend them all together into one cohesive unit during mixdown. If you want to reveal tracks in a stereo mix, hard pan them to the right or left. If you want to hide or blend a track or tracks, move them away from hard right and left.

Listen while you pan between the right and left limits and the center position—it's easy to hear the track duck in and out of the limelight. Careful pan positioning and level control enable you to change each track from a feature to a support role. Keep in mind that once you find the pan location where the track is hidden, or blended, into the group, it is only hidden because it has been positioned directly behind an existing mix ingredient. If you increase the level of the blended track, you might end up hiding the ingredient behind which the track was previously hiding.

If your production only has one voice per harmony part (typically just two or three tracks) and you want to make them sound like a larger group, try blending the voices and panning them hard left. Next, using an aux bus, send the blended voices to a delay. Adjust the delay time between 11 and 23 ms and return the delay signal to a main mix channel, panning the delayed voices hard right. This technique creates a consistent delay time between left and right, so it's important to verify that the vocals still sound good in mono. Adjust the exact delay time for the best mono sound—when you switch back to stereo or surround the group will still sound large and impressive.

Compression/Limiting

To create a backing vocal sound in which all the parts blend into one impressive texture, try this limiting procedure.

- Set up a balanced stereo mix of the vocal group in an auxiliary bus or any available mix bus other than the primary mix faders.
- Send the stereo vocal group mix to a stereo limiter.
- Route or patch the limiter's output back into two tracks of the primary mix fader's bus.
- Decrease the limiter threshold so that the vocal group begins to sound more blended and cohesive. As the vocal group is increasingly limited, individual parts that stood out before begin to blend into the vocal texture. This technique is very commonly used on group backing vocals—it helps them function as a single mix ingredient rather than as several vocal tracks occurring at once.

It is also very effective to compress the group rather than limiting. Limiting helps blend the group into a tight, in-your-face, aggressive sound. Compression helps blend the group into a more musical and transparent sound.

.... Video Example 8-3

Adding the Vocals to the Mix

EMPHASIZE THE IMPORTANT INGREDIENTS

In any mix, don't make the listener guess what the important part is at any time. If an instrumental line is taking over the focal point from the vocals, turn it up so it's obvious what just happened. A sure sign of an amateur mix is an empty hole between the chorus and verse. Draw the listener into the mix. If you leave them uninvolved with your music for even a second, something else will grab their attention—even if it's just a stray thought. At that point, they've "lost that lovin' feelin'" that your musical mix should be providing.

ELIMINATE UNIMPORTANT INGREDIENTS

Avoid mix ingredients that just rattle around in the background with no real purpose. The recording process is so controlled that we sometimes think a musical ingredient will add interest and power to the mix if it's just blended in correctly. On occasion this is true, but usually if you're trying too hard to fit a track into the mix, you're much better off to eliminate it altogether.

Print separate mixes with questionable parts eliminated. Listen to them outside the control room, in your car, in your living room, and so on. You'll likely find that the mix is more powerful without the track present. As a rule, if a mix ingredient has to be set to a low level in the mix, it's unnecessary—if it's contributing to the musical impact of the mix it is worthy of turning up in the mix.

Conflicting parts that distract from the main focus must be removed in most cases. Layering sounds on a single musical part helps shape a sound and create interest, but there shouldn't be too many actual musical lines or rhythms happening at once or the mix will seem chaotic.

INCLUDE HIGH, MID, AND LOW FREQUENCIES

A mix that offers a solid blend of the audible frequency spectrum is typically very impressive and will sound good on a wide variety of systems. If your mix is too edgy (highs), boomy (lows), or honky (mids), it will sound bad on a wide variety of systems.

High Frequencies in the Mix

It's important that your mixes include the entire spectrum of highs, mids, and lows. If you've created a blended rock or rap mix with live drums, distorted guitars, and an aggressive lead vocal, you might have overlooked the frequencies above 4 or 5 kHz. Sometimes this might be musically appropriate, but usually your mixes will be more powerful if you've included content throughout the audible spectrum.

Percussion instruments, percussion samples, and steel-string acoustic guitars offer access to the upper frequencies that are difficult to include with any abundance in other tracks, such as electric guitar, bass, and vocals. Simply boost the frequencies above 9 or 10 kHz on these types of percussive instruments to create a mix that has clean and pleasant highs.

Midrange Frequencies in the Mix

Sometimes the inexperienced mix engineer gets so caught up in creating a clean high end and a thumping low end that the midrange frequencies disappear. Although this "disco smile" type of sound was popular in the disco era, modern mixes are typically fairly well balanced in their broad-range frequency content.

Midrange frequencies are an important part of a blended mix—they provide a full and powerful ingredient that blends in a commercially appealing and musically polished way.

Low Frequencies in the Mix

In the era of analog recorders and vinyl albums, mix engineers were very cautious about the amount of appropriate sub-bass frequencies they included in a mix. The definition of "appropriate low frequencies" has changed with the growth of the digital era.

Vinyl records could only contain so much music—the actual time for each side depended on the size of the grooves. Bass frequencies created wide grooves in the vinyl—too much bass and sub-bass level resulted in a severe decrease in the available time on each side of the album.

Digital recordings include capacity for the entire audible spectrum in every digital word, so a mix with all sub-bass takes the same amount of disc space as a mix with all highs.

Modern mixes are typically full and powerful in sub-bass content—happy day. Now it is desirable to include the full audible spectrum as long as the sub-bass doesn't dominate the mix level, causing your mixes to sound quiet compared to other commercial releases.

CLASSIC RECORDINGS: HOW'D THEY DO THAT?

I am intentionally putting forth theories on how these different sounds were achieved on classic recordings—they're suggestions on how one might go about imitating the specific sounds heard on various hits. In many cases, only the producer or engineer would hope to know exactly how the sounds were recorded or mixed—and then only when referencing the session notes and track sheets.

Because most recordists operate on a relatively limited budget, there is great instructive value in deducing the method of each recording and suggesting equipment and techniques that are capable of emulating the sonic quality of that recording.

Mic choice and equipment selection are fundamentally crucial to any sound, but during mixdown every piece of gear in every signal chain determines the essence of each ingredient. I'll focus on specifics in each recording and offer experience-based conclusions about how you could reconstruct the sounds in your studio.

Eric Clapton: "Tears in Heaven"

This live recording contains some inherent issues that are present in many live recordings. High-quality studio microphones do not function well in a live performance application. Because of their sensitivity they generally cause a lot of feedback problems. Therefore, as with this live recording, standard live sound reinforcement mics are used. These mics typically provide a presence peak between 4 and 8 kHz, which is good for live sound reinforcement but a little edgy in a recording application.

Listen to Eric's vocal sounds and notice their high-frequency presence. This sound is the essence of the Shure SM58. However, in mixdown it sounds like they've included high-quality vintage dynamics processing. The wispy air in the lead vocal is characteristic of the Universal Audio 1176 or even possibly the built-in compressors on the SSL consoles. Incorporating a Neve EQ along with a current high-quality vocal processor like those offered by Avalon or Focusrite could also create this sound.

"Tears in Heaven" is an excellent example of a well-developed arrangement. It sounds deceptively simple, but if you assess the activity of the instruments, it soon becomes obvious that there are several simple mix ingredients that enter and exit in a way that supports the musical momentum and flow.

Incubus: "Have You Ever"

This track is aggressive with lots of layered electric guitars. Notice the distorted bass guitar. This bass has a very active sound, and the distortion is reminiscent of the '80s buzz distortions—this could also be an overdriven Mesa Triple Rectifier head.

It sounds like they have layered a few types of distorted electric guitar along with a relatively clean (slightly overdriven) electric sound. My guess is that they used a few different guitars to create the basic layered guitar part; however, the overall sound is big and clean and doesn't necessarily sound like a Les Paul or a Strat, which often indicates that a PRS guitar was used for the primary track.

Notice that the kick drum sound is very flat with little low-frequency content and a very pointed attack around 4 or 5 kHz. This small kick sound precisely indicates the beat placement while leaving ample room for the bass guitar and electric guitars to sound very big and fat in the low end.

The lead vocal track is heavily compressed. The high frequencies sound a lot like a vintage U67, and the compression sounds like the Empirical Labs Distressor being pushed very hard. If you're into plug-ins, try the Universal Audio suite of vintage plug-ins. These tools are capable of mimicking these high amounts of compression while still retaining life and body in the sound (much like their hardware predecessors).

Nelly: "Hot in Here"

The kick drum and bass guitar are like one sound on this track. I don't think either happens without the other. This provides a solid and very clean foundation for this tune. The kick drum sounds like a sample that includes the leakage from the drum kit—notice the air around the kick sound.

The lead vocal sound can be achieved a couple ways. To create this sound electronically, combine the original lead track with between a 17- and 23-ms delay of the lead track. This creates the effect of two people singing. In this case there is a slight variation of the delay, which can easily be recreated by setting up the LFO on the delay to gradually sweep (about one cycle per second) throughout a shallow range. The LFO constantly changes the delay relationship, resulting in a live double feel.

This sound could also be a simple double of the lead by Nelly himself. This effect is powerful and usually requires careful editing on the engineer's part to create a double that is in tune and still retains a high degree of intelligibility. There are several instances when the two parts are slightly out of tune—this could be performance-related or a result of the LFO sweep.

It really sounds like there is a combination of electronic and live doubling. Rap music makes great use of lyric doubling to highlight the key lyrics, and that is happening a lot in this song. Notice that the female vocal is also doubled.

This entire mix is very dry, which adds substantially to the in-your-face punch of this mix. However, if you listen closely, you should be able to hear a very dark and understated reverberation underneath the mix. It sounds like it is applied primarily to the lead vocal in such a way that it subliminally suggests size and importance.

Nelly Furtado: "I'm Like a Bird"

Nelly Furtado's vocal sound is very dry here. This is a classic tube sound, exhibiting an analog ring that almost sounds like a microphonic tube in the mic or preamp. This sound can also be achieved using the Antares Mic Modeler and driving the simulated tube circuitry hard. Tube distortion like this provides a unique presence in the lead vocal sound and tends to warm up an edgy vocal sound.

This sounds like a vintage microphone that is less refined than an excellent Neumann U47 but still very vintage-sounding. The signal path all seems very vintage. The poor man's answer to this might include an Audio-Technica tube microphone through a Joe Meek preamp, but I'm not sure either would provide the headroom to get this kind of sound.

Some of the new technology processors, such as those made by Avalon and Manley, are capable of creating this type of sound also. The equalization on the lead vocal seems minimal—this sounds mostly like the right mic through the right gear rather than a lot of EQ hocus pocus.

Steely Dan: "Josie"

Steely Dan is a classic and somewhat timeless musical entity. They have always produced ultra-high-quality music. The interesting thing about their current material is that it sounds a lot like their older material and it still receives high accolades for its musical and technical brilliance.

"Josie" is a classic Steely Dan song. The drum sounds are dry and upfront in the mix. The kick drum is relatively thin in the low end with a fairly flat sound and an attack peak around 4 kHz. This type of kick sound cuts through the mix while leaving room for the low frequencies from the bass and guitars.

The snare drum is a classic snare sound miked with a mic on the top and bottom heads. The snares are clean, bright, and more present than the sound created by a typical single-mic setup. If you set up a mic on the top and bottom of the snare drum, be sure to invert the phase of the bottom mic so that the mics work together rather than against each other.

The entire band track is very dry on this song and yet the vocals are very processed with plenty of effects. Notice that the lead vocal uses a slapback delay in time with the eighth note. It also sounds like a Lexicon reverb (either a 224 or a 480) on the Gold Plate setting with about a two-second decay time and a predelay that's roughly in time with the sixteenth note—this might also be the EMT plate (250 or 252). The technical specifications of this vocal sound are easy to set up, even on an inexpensive effects processor, but the quality of these expensive reverberation devices is hard to match.

The lead vocal is very compressed and the brightness of the sound could indicate a nice Neumann U87 or possibly a U67 through a Universal Audio 1176 compressor. To match this smoothness without paying the high price for the real vintage gear, try an Audio-Technica 4047 through a dbx tube compressor/limiter. The sound of the 4047 is very clean and smooth, much like the U67 or a U47, and the dbx tube sound adds to the vintage feel.

The backing vocals are very compressed, and it sounds like the entire group was compressed together as a stereo submix because the individual parts don't stick out at all and the vocal texture is very unified and compact.

Faith Hill: "The Lucky One"

This is a very aggressive country mix. There is extreme compression on almost everything. This snare drum sound is the definitive compressed snare sound. Notice how the attack is very dominant and yet the body of the snare is immediately compressed. You can hear the compressor release on each snare drum hit as the level increases through the drum sound. This snare sound also exhibits the characteristic timbre of combined top and bottom mics.

Faith Hill's vocal sound is very sibilant and very compressed. The "S" sounds are almost annoyingly present. These types of Ss are common from singers with perfectly straight teeth and a perfect bite. The silky sound of the sibilance indicates a very warm and smooth mic with plenty of brightness. The Neumann U47 could sound like this, but so could several of the new technology mics, such as those from Sony or AKG. This sounds like a vintage mic with a lot of updates.

Notice the bright high end on the acoustic guitar. It sounds like this part has a very specific place and purpose in this mix. A part like this sounds bad alone, but in the mix context it adds color and texture.

The backing vocals sound like a multi-track recording of two or three vocalists throughout the production. It is amazing how large a group of one, two, or three singers can sound in the world of unlimited track availability.

Even though there is a fairly constant wash of B3, pad, and distorted electric guitars through most of the song, this mix provides an excellent example of the concept of maintaining a focal point throughout a production. Notice how there is an instrumental fill, even if somewhat subtle, between virtually every vocal phrase. This technique helps the arrangement build, and it also helps the listener maintain interest throughout the song. Also notice how the texture varies with each musical section. The verses thin out, the choruses build, and the bridge provides an excellent contrast to both the verse and chorus.

SURROUND MIXING

Mixing in surround-sound format is an evolving art form. When it was first introduced there were arguments in the audio community about its viability as a commercial format—then it became a commercial format. There were arguments about the best functionality for the center, rear, and sub channels—then there were excellent mixes produced using them for differing functions. Eventually everyone settled into the conclusion that anything is possible as long as it supports and increases the impact and power of the music.

There are two fundamental surround-mixing approaches that produce excellent results.

1. The traditional music-listening perspective positions the listener in front of the performers—the room adds natural reflections and reverberation. This added dimension, surrounding the listener with an ambient bath, is very difficult to simulate with a stereo mix, yet it is a simple task when mixing in surround.

Chapter 8 .... PULLING IT TOGETHER

Surround Configurations

The popular surround formats are 5.1, 7.1, and 6.1. This illustration demonstrates the standard speaker positions for each format. Since low frequencies are omnidirectional, the actual position of the subwoofer is not as important as the simple fact that it should be in the same room as the rest of the speakers.

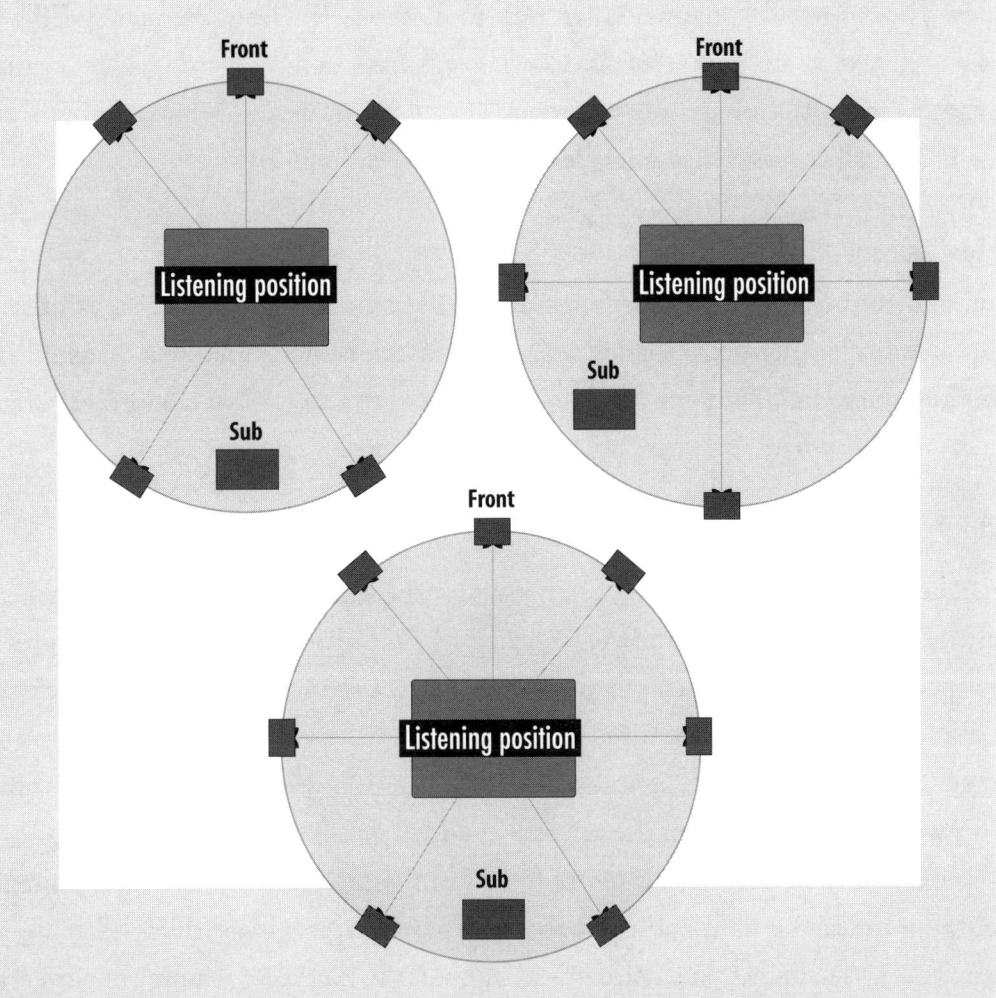

2. The musician's perspective positions the listener in the middle of the musical performers. The sensation of being surrounded by the musical ingredients is very powerful and compelling, yet even for an experienced musician this type of mix can lack a cohesive musical feel—it's not a natural way to experience music, although it can be a fun way to experience a surround mix.

Layout

The most popular surround format is 5.1 surround. Although 7.1 is a surround standard, almost all commercially released surround mixes are in 5.1.

5.1 surround systems consist of three front speakers (left, center, right), two rear speakers (left rear and right rear), and a subwoofer.

The subwoofer channel is referred to as the LFE (Low Frequency Effects) channel and is intended for occasional sub-bass sounds, such as explosions, crashes, and eruptions in movie scenes as well as musical sub-bass content. The LFE channel covers the frequencies between 25 and 120 Hz.

Front Left and Right Channels

In a surround mix, the front left and right channels perform a very similar, if not identical, function to the left and right channels in a stereo mix. Most of the instruments, backing vocals, and often the lead vocal tracks reside in these channels—this is where the primary mix image is created.

The Center Channel

The center surround channel is often used for the lead vocal and solo instruments, although not always. For those entrenched in the history of stereo sound, the center position is almost distractingly blatant when used for the lead vocal. Because most of the effects used in modern recording are stereo or surround, the placement of the vocal in the center position alone can isolate it from the rest of the mix in a way that detracts from the musical feeling.

Try positioning the lead parts (solo, lead vocal, fills, and so on) simultaneously in the center, left, and right channels. This helps spread the focal presence across a wider image and helps these ingredients blend in a more musical way. Some mix engineers avoid the center channel altogether.

Rear Channels

Using the rear channels for ambience and room sounds creates a natural, realistic listening experience. Simply adding the dimension of the back of the room to any mix increases its size dramatically.

As soon as you place mix ingredients, such as individual instruments or voice, in the rear channels, you risk creating a distraction to the musical intent rather than an enhancement. Positioning a specific track in the rear channels alone will cause quite a distraction if it is only on one side. Create a balanced image in the rear speakers by always matching a timbre on one side with a similar timbre on the other side. For example, a percussive sound in the rear left channel should be balanced with a percussive sound in the rear right channel.

The LFE (Subwoofer) Channel

Most experienced mix engineers prefer to intentionally place specific instruments in the LFE channel, although the surround protocol uses a bass management system that redirects automatically frequencies below 80 Hz from all tracks to the sub channel.

If you're not absolutely sure that your subwoofer is precisely and accurately calibrated, letting this automatic bass management system direct the low frequencies to the sub channel is the safest way to mix. It ensures that you won't create playback disasters by including too much of a specific instrument in the LFE channel. However, precise assignments to the LFE channel can result in some very powerful and musical mixes.

Keep in mind that the LFE channel filters all frequencies above 120 Hz, so any mid- and high-frequency definition must come from the other five speakers. Typically, all tracks exist in the front and rear channels, with certain tracks also assigned to the LFE channel for impact and power.

Mixdown Formats

You can use any recorder with enough tracks to record your surround mixes. The most important consideration is whether your intended mastering engineer can play back your mixdown format. When you begin mixing a surround project, call the mastering engineer where your mixes will become commercially ready and verify that they can play your mixes.

The following sections describe a few standard mixdown formats that most mastering houses can readily accommodate.

Tascam DA-88

The Tascam family of modular digital multitracks, although becoming uncommon, became the recording standard in the '90s film industry, so almost all mastering facilities are set up to easily create surround masters from this format.

The downfall of all the MDMs is that they are functionally limited to a 48-kHz sample rate, and only a few are capable of word sizes greater than 20 bits—they don't offer room for growth into high-definition audio formats.

Alesis ADAT

The Alesis ADAT single-handedly provided the impetus that drove the digital revolution. Due to their larger tape format (S-VHS) and slower shuttle times, they lost the battle for the film industry to Tascam, although they were embraced by the music recording industry.

These machines, especially the XT20 series, provide a valid surround mixing platform, although, like the DA-88 family, they are limited to a 48-kHz sample rate and 20-bit words.

One- or Two-Inch Analog Tape

Eight-track analog tape recorders offer an excellent mix format, especially for music. However, in the film-surround audio world, analog machines are relatively slow to use and somewhat imprecise in their sync to image. And, the incredible dynamic range of most movies can quickly reveal any analog tape noise.

Computer (Internal Bounce)

If you are mixing completely within the computer environment, the cleanest and most efficient mix format is the Bounce to Disc feature, residing in your DAW software. Create your mixdown at the highest audio resolution possible, and then simply bounce all audio data into a surround audio file. The efficiency of this bouncing system depends on the power, speed, and efficiency of your computer. Additional processing cards can help make an internal bounce of surround files a viable option, but some engineers hold that this method results in less than satisfying sound quality.

Once the bounce is completed, software is readily available that will conform the surround mix to DVD playback standards, so you can almost instantly reference the mix on your own home audio surround system.

Computer Through a Line Mixer

Whether mixing stereo or surround, there is a growing opinion that playing the mix through an external line mixer into another recorder produces a more open and higher-fidelity final mix. The theory assumes that there is less strain on the computer's processor if it is only playing back the mix than if it is bouncing it through the assigned outputs and summing it to the final mix files.

Many power users have adopted a high-quality line mixer or analog console to run their mixes through on a regular basis. Some even prefer to use the DAW as a playback device only, applying effects, dynamics, and EQ in the analog domain, either through the line mixer or through a classic well-respected analog console from a manufacturer such as Neve, Solid State Logic, API, or Trident.

Computer Connected to a Media Network

Powerful computers connected via gigabit Ethernet work closely together in many ways as if they were a single computer. Many modern DAWs and media software manufacturers are utilizing distributed processing across a network of powerful computers. This feature is available as part of the Unix OS, which the core of Apple's OS X. It is available for developers to implement and it provides an amazing opportunity to take advantage of modern processing speed and power.

Surround Master Track Assignments

There are a few different track-assignment standards when creating your surround mix master. Most surround mixes conform to a standard track assignment that is emerging as the norm, although as long as you clearly note the layout of your surround master, a good mastering engineer will easily reconfigure your assignments. The film-sound industry has traditionally conformed to a separate standard, and DTS protocol has conformed to another.

Refer to the following illustration for comparisons of the current popular surround master track assignment formats and refer to Chapter 3 for a more in-depth look at surround configurations.

Surround Channel Assignments

Below are the currently popular channel assignment choices for three different surround applications.

Format	Channels	1	2	3	4	5	6
	Emerging Standard	L	R	C	LFE	LR	RR
	Film Style	LF	C	RF	LR	RR	LFE
	DTS 5.1	LF	RF	LR	RR	C	LFE

Stereo Compatibility

The DVD-Audio spec and the Dolby Digital encoder include an automatic downmix algorithm that renders a stereo combination of the surround mix tracks. This is a convenient feature, although it is unpredictable. If you really care about the stereo mix, create your own stereo mix and include it on the commercial DVD instead of the automatic downmix.

CHAPTER TEST

1. Before you begin the mix, decide on the _____.
   a. mix density
   b. length of the mix
   c. basic reverberation sounds
   d. the vocal sound

2. It helps in the mixdown process:
   a. to add a lot of reverberation so the mix sounds professional
   b. to monitor at about 110 dB
   c. get everyone's opinion as the mixing begins
   d. to correlate your mix to a visual image

3. There really aren't any successful mix engineers who do a great job mixing multiple genres.
   a. True
   b. False

4. As an initial consideration, the _____ are (is) fundamentally important to the sonic signature of any production.
   a. quality of the effects used
   b. backing vocals
   c. quality of the mic cables used
   d. drum sound

5. When blending multiple electric guitars to form one sound:
   a. layer full-bandwidth sounds to get a really full sound
   b. evaluate each part for its strengths and weaknesses, and then highlight the best aspects of each
   c. add plenty of reverberation to fill out the sound
   d. All of the above

6. A _____ production and mixing approach often creates a more impressive sound than _____.
   a. complex, a simple approach
   b. layered, a simplistic approach
   c. simple, a complex and busy approach
   d. modern, a more vintage approach

7. To combine multiple acoustic guitar sounds in an impressive way, find the one frequency that makes the guitar sound stand out and boost it on all the guitar parts.
   a. True
   b. False

8. The exact kick drum sound you build is:
   a. pretty much the same in all productions because a good sound doesn't depend on the genre
   b. depends on the type of effects being used
   c. very genre-dependent
   d. Both a and b

9. The _____ of the music determines the style and character of the lead vocal sound.
   a. style
   b. character
   c. tonal center
   d. All of the above
   e. Both a and b

10. Most musical styles demand that the lead vocal _____.
    a. blends into the rest of the mix without sticking out too much
    b. lyrics are understandable
    c. is full-sounding with an abundance of the frequency band centered on or near 150 Hz
    d. All of the above

11. A lead vocal track that has been recorded using the right microphone and excellent technique is easy to blend and shape into the mix, while retaining ample clarity and intelligibility.
    a. True
    b. False

12. Most mixes function well when one instrument, voice, or sound _____ and another instrument, voice, or sound _____.
    a. builds tension, provides release
    b. increases in intensity through the production, decreases in intensity throughout the production
    c. defines the close perspective, defines the distant perspective
    d. is boosted between 1 and 4 kHz, is boosted between 6 and 12 kHz

13. A typical ratio setting for vocal compression is:
    a. 12:1
    b. between 3:1 and 7:1
    c. 1.5:1
    d. anything above 10:1

14. Extreme vocal compression:
    a. is commonly used in the rock genre
    b. tends to minimize breath sound and vocal nuances
    c. demands the use of a very high-quality compressor
    d. All of the above
    e. Both a and c

15. Many lead vocal recordings are recorded using a mic with a _____ in order to decrease ambient room sound and to increase intimacy.
    a. cardioid pickup pattern
    b. wind screen
    c. bass roll-off
    d. omnidirectional pickup pattern

16. A dramatic amount of reverberation results in:
    a. a large and impressive sound
    b. a muddy and indistinct mix sound
    c. a nicely blended production
    d. great drum sounds

17. Using _____ on the entire backing vocal group results in a very blended group sound.
    a. a limiter
    b. room reverberation
    c. ambience
    d. extreme EQ

18. A sure sign of an amateur mix is an empty hole with no focal point between the chorus and verse.
    a. True
    b. False

19. In the digital realm, a mix with all sub-bass takes up more disc space than a mix with all highs.
    a. True
    b. False

20. In a surround mix, the subwoofer channel is referred to as the _____ channel and is intended for occasional sub-bass sounds.
    a. LFE
    b. Low Frequency Effects
    c. power alley
    d. OMF
    e. Both a and b

Getting Ready to Master

CHAPTER 9

If you've completed mixing all ten or so songs for your album, it's time to get everything into a form that the mastering engineer or duplication facility can work with. Before moving forward, let's define a few terms that are frequently confused or misused.

- **Multitrack master:** This is the master recording that contains all of the individual tracks in the project, from kick drum to hi-hat, vocals to guitar, strings to brass, and so on. This multitrack master, recorded by the tracking engineer, is the source for the mixdown process, in which balances, pans, effects, edits, and enhancement occurs.

- **Mixed master:** Recorded by the mix engineer, this is the final result of the mixdown process. The mixed master is typically stereo, but increasingly likely to be in any of a few surround formats depending on the target audience or presentation environment.

- **Mastered album:** This is the final result of the mastering process. The album master is used as the source for duplication, replication, or vinyl master cutting. It includes all of the mastering engineer's changes, which can include equalization, limiting, level matching between songs, or any other global changes the mastering engineer feels warranted to perform. The mastered album is the final word and, once agreed to by the producer, artist, and so on, there should be no further changes to the songs, mixes, or sounds.

CHAPTER AT A GLANCE

Preparing the Analog Master 227
Tools for Razorblade Editing............. 228
Procedure for Razorblade Editing 230
Preparing the Digital Master............ 235
Selecting the Edit Point 235
Shortening, Lengthening, and
 Replacing 236
Sequencing the Album/Song Order . 236
Spacing between Songs 237
Save It for the Mastering Engineer... 237
Timing Issues for Tape and Vinyl 238
Stereo Master Preparation
 Considerations 239
Technical Notes 240
Reference Tones 242
Surround Considerations 242
Lossy Versus Lossless 243

The way that the masters should be prepared is dependent on a few important factors:

- **Mixed master format**: Although the vast majority of musical projects are delivered in a digital format, analog mixes still offer a sonic advantage over many digital formats and for many kinds of recordings. Though the relevance of analog recording is diminishing, there are still many engineers and producers who favor it, so it is important to be aware of delivery expectations for an analog master.

- **Target media**: Target media for the consumer has come from cylinders to 78s to vinyl 33 1/3 records to cassettes to CDs to SACDs to DVD-Audio discs. Source recorders have come from mono to stereo to four-track to eight-track to 16-track to 24-track to multiple 24-tracks to ADAT to DA-88 to digital tape-based multitrack to the modern DAW, with its essentially unlimited capacity for tracks, features, and signal processing. Obviously, the audio industry is constantly working toward the next best recording technology; however, our current target media options are not always an improvement! I think that we will be making great improvements in our more recent media delivery formats in the near future. But, considering that SACD, DVD-Audio, and high-definition downloads are so sonically amazing, it is interesting (and somewhat troubling) that the most commonly heard versions of the average modern musical release are downloaded 128 kbps MP3s—some demographic groups actually prefer the sound of an MP3 to the sound of another HD format! It is also very important to consider that many projects become popular through their release on YouTube and to take into account its relatively low-fi audio quality. The engineer must adjust delivery standards depending on whether the project will be replicated, duplicated, cut to vinyl, printed to cassette, or distributed as a download-only product.

Master delivery standards for several possible target media formats require the mix engineer to provide a completely sequenced and timed album master. When this is the case, the album should be in order, complete with adjusted spacing between the songs.

PREPARING THE ANALOG MASTER

Editing is very important in the professional audio world; it requires a lot of practice whether you're actually cutting and splicing tape with a razorblade or using the newest digital editor. Razorblade editing has, for the time being, become an art of the past, but many excellent engineers prefer to mix down to an analog tape format, such as half-inch stereo or one-inch eight-track surround. You might find yourself required to perform these kinds of edits.

It's important to be prepared for a few potential scenarios, including a completely analog workflow from multitrack to consumer, a completely digital workflow, or any possible combinations of analog and digital media.

Both the analog and digital master require editing of some sort to prepare for the mastering process. The mixed analog master is edited for these reasons:

- To put the songs in the correct order.
- To adjust spacing between songs.
- To remove or reposition a section or sections of a song. The "album" version of a song might need to be edited down to a more commercial version. Cutting a five-minute song down to three-and-a-half-minutes is quite common.
- To reuse a section at another time in the song. Sometimes one chorus section will be good and one will be bad. You could end up copying the good chorus section and using it in place of the bad one. This is also common with single phrases, lines, or lyrics. These tasks are simple in the digital domain but they require practice and experience to perform seamlessly in the analog domain.
- To lengthen a song. When you've been disciplined in your recording procedures and have produced a perfect three-and-a-half-minute song, someone is bound to request the "dance" mix that should be six minutes or longer. In this case, you'll need to grab bits of your song, remix them in several different ways, and then reassemble the pieces into something much longer than the original piece of music.

In the digital domain, edits are made casually and carelessly because there is no danger of damaging the master recording. Conversely, in the analog domain, edits are typically performed on the mixed master tape because generation losses that result each time a tape is copied are unacceptable. If the master is damaged beyond repair, the mix must be recorded again. If you've made extensive use of automation, it's not that difficult to recreate a mix. However, if you've spent hours

Razorblade Editing Tools

The tools used in the razorblade editing process seem very primal in comparison to modern digital editing tools. In many ways these tools equate to rubbing two sticks together or striking flint on a rock to start a fire. However, excellent results are obtainable when performing this classic procedure.

To perform razorblade edits you must have:

- Razorblades
- A splicing block to lay the tape into for exact cutting
- Specially designed plastic or paper leader tape
- Specially designed adhesive tape
- A white grease pencil (China Marker)

capturing a real-time manual mix, destroying the master recording is potentially devastating.

Many new recordists may never need to know anything about razorblade editing. However, the deeper you get into the recording industry, the greater the likelihood that you'll use this excellent mixing and tracking medium, so it bears mentioning.

Tools for Razorblade Editing

Besides an excellent mixdown recorder that has edit capabilities, the tools required for razorblade editing are primal. In the digital era, it's a little baffling to think of essentially destroying the master and then taping it back together, but that's what you do with razorblade editing.

Edit-Capable Mix Recorder

Any professional analog tape recorder will provide editing capability. Once you cut the tape, you must be able to play the tape through the regular tape path with the take-up reel disengaged. In this configuration, the tape plays up to the point where you need to make the next cut, with the tape spilling into a bin, on the floor, or into the trash instead of winding on the take-up reel. This way, you still hear the tape play back normally, so it's easy to locate the next edit point.

Demagnetized Razorblades

You'll need a sharp razorblade to cut the analog tape. A standard single-edged razorblade works fine, but the serious and meticulous purist will purchase surgical-steel blades. I've used surgical steel and I've used regular razorblades that you purchase at the local market. It didn't affect the sound of the edit, so I just keep a couple boxes of single-edge razorblades on hand.

The most important technical factor involved in razorblade use is demagnetization. You must demagnetize razorblades that are used for editing. The fact that you're using analog tape, which is really not much more than rust on plastic, requires only the proper magnetization from the record head. Using a magnetized razorblade causes an unwanted pop at the edit point. If you're using an analog tape machine you should have a head demagnetizer around anyway, so use it to demagnetize your razorblades. Use it in the exact same manner that you do when you demagnetize the tape path.

Grease Pencil

Mark the backside of the tape—the part that points away from the head assembly—with a white grease pencil. The easiest grease pencil to find is a China Marker at the local stationary store or computer supply store. The Sanford peel-off markers are perfect for this task. As the grease wears down, simply peel back another layer of the pencil to expose more writing surface.

The white grease mark is easy to see and non-destructive to the recording or splicing tape.

Splicing Tape

Once the cuts are made and it's time to repair the tape, use splicing tape designed specifically for connecting analog tape together. Never use any other type of adhesive tape. Splicing tape is strong, holds the edit together for a long time, and utilizes a glue formulation that resists bleeding out of the edit. Any sticky material will quickly cause oxide build up around, on, and in the head gap. This will reduce fidelity of both the record and playback heads.

Any professional tape supplier will have the right splicing tape for you. The splicing tape can be the same width as the analog tape; just trim off an inch or so of the splicing tape and lay it lengthwise across the edit. I prefer to use one-inch splicing tape, laying it across the edit and then trimming the excess off the sides. Using one-inch splicing tape works well on all analog tape widths, from eighth-inch to two-inch tape.

Splicing Block

The splicing block contains a groove that is precisely a fraction narrower than the analog tape. The tape lies in the splicing block and is held in place by friction. There are typically three different angles on the splicing block: 90 degrees, 45 degrees, and 30 degrees. The most commonly used edit angle is the 45-degree cut. This spreads the edit out over a larger area than the 90-degree cut, yet it provides a relatively tight edit—it is typically less likely to pop or click as the edit passes the playback-head gap than the 90-degree cut.

Use the 90-degree cut for extremely tight edit points that require instant texture changes that occur simultaneously across the left-right spectrum. Use the 30-degree edit to create a smooth edit that feathers across the in and out points while holding the least potential for a pop at the edit.

Procedure for Razorblade Editing

There are several important considerations in the razorblade editing process. Once you have your tools together, it's time to jump in and practice editing. It's best to practice on material that is unimportant. Record any material from a commercially released CD and start cutting it up.

Approximately Mark the In and Out Points

The first step in the edit process is finding the segment of tape you want to remove or move. Play the tape and take note of the tape counter in and out points for the edit. Review your intentional edit segment to verify its accuracy.

Next, with the tape counter numbers noted, play the tape. As the tape runs past the edit points, press the grease pencil on the playback head so a long mark is made on the tape across the edit in and out points. Depending on the tape speed, it doesn't take much to leave a grease mark several inches long, so just mark the tape across the intended edit point for a fraction of a second or so.

The Effect of Tape Speed on the Edit Process

Keep in mind that analog tape runs at different speeds depending on your fidelity needs. For excellent mix fidelity, choose a tape speed of at least 15 ips. The typically accepted standard for high-fidelity stereo analog master tapes takes advantage of half-inch tape running at 30 ips. Some mix engineers prefer to use half-inch tape running at 15 ips for projects that contain more low-frequency punch and less-pristine transient detail. In other words, a lot of rock mix engineers prefer the low-frequency punch they get when they mix to half-inch tape at 15 ips—other styles that exhibit finer sonic detail benefit from the increased fidelity of half-inch tape at 30 ips.

Tape speed affects the editing process greatly. The faster the tape is moving, the larger the window for an acceptable edit. If you consider 30 ips, there might be a half-inch window where the tape could be cut while still creating a clean edit and without interrupting the rhythmic feel. At 15 ips that window decreases to a quarter-inch, and at 7-1/2 ips the window decreases further to an eighth of an inch. It's easier to edit tape that's been recorded at faster tape speeds.

Select the Exact Edit Points

Once the edit in and out points are roughly marked, play them again and identify the exact edit points. To locate the exact edit point, stop the tape and press the edit button. This will release the supply and take up reel brakes so the tape can be manually jogged back and forth to locate the precise edit point. Listen for transients when manually shuttling the tape. If, for example, you're editing to a snare drum hit, play the tape until you hear the snare hit and immediately press stop. Then, press the edit button and manually shuttle the tape backward. The first sound you hear should be the sound of the snare drum hit. Mark just to the left of the hit.

Be sure the machine is in playback mode so that you know the tape is playing back from the playback head. Most professional analog tape recorders contain three heads: the erase head (furthest left), the record head (middle), and the playback head (furthest right). When you mark the tape, make the mark at the center of the playback head, which is where the head gap is sensing the variations in magnetized tape that produce the playback audio.

There are several considerations that will help you select acceptable edit points. The technique used is similar for music and voice edits. The perfect edit occurs in an audio void, where a moment of complete silence provides an opportunity for a transparent edit. If you edit in a silent hole, you must make a clean cut and you must make a seamless repair. In addition, your razorblade must be demagnetized so there is no magnetic pop at the edit point.

Especially when editing music, there might not be a perfect void in which to place the edit. Look for these characteristics to make intelligent edit-point choices:

- A clean hole. It is always preferable, although not always practical, to edit in a clean hole. This guarantees that there won't be a texture change at the edit point and typically that the edit will go unnoticed.
- A transient attack that is exposed. A great place to edit is on a snare drum hit. The transient attack is easy to hear as the tape slowly shuttles back and forth across the playback head. Mark the tape just before the snare hit at the edit in point and then put the machine in edit mode and run up to the out point. Mark the out point just before the snare hit at the corresponding out point. As long as there are no large ambience changes, these edits are almost always transparent.
- No big changes in ambience. You must find edit points that are the same texture and ambience at the in and out points. Even if the edits are clean and in perfect time, any notable differences in the ambience level at the in and out points will probably be very noticeable, resulting in an unacceptable edit.
- Similar production texture. If you are cutting from the first verse to the second verse, for example, be sure that the edit doesn't reveal a change in the production texture. It is common for each musical section to change in texture, even if slightly, from the beginning to the end of the song. Sometimes the texture thickens and other times it breaks down. Be sure that you're listening for consistent or compatible production textures at the in and out points.
- No instruments sustaining over the edit. Sometimes it seems like the edit will work fine, but once you make the cut you quickly notice that there was a piano chord, a crash cymbal, or the like that immediately appears or disappears at the edit point.
- Hidden transient beats in the groove. If you have an active and percussive groove, look for an exposed offbeat to edit. The hi-hat is a good instrument to listen for when searching for edit in and out points. Beats such as the second sixteenth note of beat three are the types of edit points that are com-

pletely transparent. With all other considerations in order, to create invisible edits choose rhythmic offbeats for edit placements.

Cutting Technique

Be sure that you've located in and out edit points that are both rhythmically and texturally identical. Mark the precise in and out points with the grease pencil and review the edits by locating and manually jogging across the in and out points. Cut at the in point. It is very important that each cut is clean and smooth. Ragged cuts tend to create a click or pop at the edit point. Precise, exacting cuts and taping create edits that are virtually imperceptible. Using a sharp razorblade that has been demagnetized is mandatory whenever performing razorblade edits.

- Lay the tape into the splicing block with the edit mark centered over the desired cut angle.
- Place one finger of your weak hand to the left of the mark and one to the right.
- Hold the tape in place with a slight pulling action to keep the tape tension snug.
- Use a sharp blade to ensure that very little pressure is required to make the cut. The blade should easily and quickly make a smooth straight cut across the tape. If the blade is dull, it will make a jagged cut and will likely stretch the tape down into the cutting guide, causing a rough edit that will probably click or pop on playback.
- Cut through the tape and into the guide on the splice block.

Find and Cut at the Out Edit Point

There are typically several feet of tape between the out edit point and the new in edit point. This excess is typically spilled into a container as the tape is played up to the next edit point. Use a clean and dry container for this purpose. A waste container is a good choice but use a dedicated, clean, dry container—not a dirty trash bin. It is likely that there will be an incident in which you'll need to remove part of the tape from the trash container to repair a mistake—it is never fun to see the tape you need laying in a puddle of soda in the trash. If you plan on performing razorblade edits regularly, find the perfect size and shape trash can, never put trash in it, and label it "Edit Bin."

- Place the recorder in edit mode and spill any excess tape into a bin until you reach the edit point.
- Manually shuttle the tape across the playback head to verify that the mark is correctly positioned at the gap of the playback head.
- Make a cut at the in point.

Complete the Edit

This is the point where precise, clean cuts become very important. Once the edit is complete it should be smooth and clean. Although it will be visible it should be so smooth that it is barely visible and almost imperceptible to the touch.

- Place both pieces of tape in the edit block and slide them together so that the ends touch without overlapping, and with the edit over the solid surface to either side of the angled cutting guides.
- Pull of a length of tape sufficient to cover the width of the tape plus between half an inch and an inch on either side of the edit.
- Place the length of splicing tape lightly on one corner of the razorblade. This provides a steady and visible way to guide the splicing tape into the splicing block groove.
- Press the splicing tape onto the recording tape. Press straight down over the edit with your finger to make sure the edit is taped together.
- Use a pencil eraser or the back of your fingernail to firmly press the splicing tape into place.
- Hold the recording tape on either side of the edit, outside the ends of the splicing block, and snap the tape up out of the block all at once. This will ensure the least damage to the tape. Do not grab the tape on one side of the edit and pull it up through the length of the splicing block because this will cause damage to the tape edges and risk adversely affecting the recording's integrity.
- Visually inspect the edit to verify that there is no space between the tape ends and that there is no overlap.

PREPARING THE DIGITAL MASTER

Digital hard-disk editing revolutionized the production of music. Whether in the multitrack or mixdown domain, the flexibility and creative freedom provided by digital editing can't be denied. Within a production, musical ingredients are quickly and easily moved, replaced, exchanged, and processed in countless possible ways.

Preparing the completed album for mastering is much simpler using modern digital editing tools than it ever was in the days of mandatory razorblade edits. The recording community quickly embraced the non-destructive aspect of digital editing along with the speed and accuracy it provides.

The beautiful Undo command is a bonus. In the analog era, the closest thing to Undo was, "Oh crap! I hope I can tape that back together the way it was!"

Selecting the Edit Point

Selecting the digital edit point is a much more casual process than selecting the analog tape edit point. The primary concern in the selection of a digital edit is that the time and tempo remain constant. Once the timing is correct and the rhythmic groove remains constant through the edit, it's a simple procedure to use the edit slip tool. This tool leaves the material on either side of the edit anchored but slides the edit point. With this technique, simply slide the edit point until the edit is smooth, natural, and sonically invisible. It just doesn't get much simpler than that.

Crossfades

Using the razorblade tool and the edit slip tool along with crossfades, virtually any edit can be adjusted to work well. If you need to edit between sections that have a textural change, try the crossfade tool. Set up a crossfade that's long enough to give the effect of one texture naturally fading out while the new texture takes over.

Take Chances

When I razorblade-edit analog tape, I'm very careful. I choose the edit points carefully and I plot the edit out in my head before I commit. I'm usually well enough prepared that the edit goes smoothly and almost always works great.

When I'm using a digital editor I think of some of the same considerations, but everything moves much faster. I guess at the correct edit point, put the pieces together, adjust for the correct groove, and shift the edit point until no one would ever even guess there was an edit present.

Shortening, Lengthening, and Replacing

The beauty of the digital revolution is that the multitrack master is as flexible as the mixed master, so many of the section changes and alternative versions are constructed during the mixdown process. It could be that the majority of the alternative versions are structured before mixdown happens.

If framing all of the alternative versions has been left for the mixing process, just take your time and piece the sections together. If you are mixing to the multitrack recorder or if you've mixed to a DAW synchronized to the multitrack with the identical tempo selected, everything becomes much simpler. If you have placed markers at the different musical sections and if the beats line up with the tempo map, selecting the edit points is simple. Also, copying and pasting sections is ridiculously easy. Select a section, copy it, and then insert it between two points, delete it, or repeat it.

.... Video Example 9-1
Performing Edits

SEQUENCING THE ALBUM/SONG ORDER

If you've printed several mixes of your songs, you'll need to select the mix of each song that's perfect for your album, and then you'll have to decide on an order for the songs. Song order is an important part of the flow and impact of any album. With the right song order, a listener can be pulled through the entire album with ease. If the order is wrong, listeners might be lulled to sleep or end up so emotionally jostled that they're left with a bad feeling about the album.

The actual order is typically determined by the style and personality of the artist. Many albums include the third song on side one as the title song. Sometimes the title song is the first song. Sometimes the title of the album doesn't come from a song, but from the intellectual theme of the album. These are artistic choices that reflect the personality of the artist.

Spacing between Songs

Adjust spacing between songs according to the energy and pace demanded by the energy of the music. A standard space between songs is four seconds. When you're dealing with fade outs, begin the four-second space from where the mix totally loses its presence, which might be sooner than the point at which silence occurs. Generally, the more contrast between songs, the longer the gap between the songs. Some songs need to be very tightly spaced.

Avoid automatically setting a 2- or 4-second space between songs. Listen to the transitions and note the spot where it feels like the next song should start. I've sequenced a lot of albums with several people in the studio and it is uncanny how much agreement there is when the perfect timing is discovered. Most people get the same "right there" instinctive reaction to when the next song should begin.

Save It for the Mastering Engineer

Because almost all modern mastering engineers print their mastered songs to a DAW or digital mastering application, it has become typical that spacings between songs and fade outs are established and created during the mastering process. In fact the fade out performed at the mastering stage is cleaner and fades more naturally to complete silence than the fade performed during mixdown—especially if the mixdown format is analog tape.

If you want the mastering engineer to perform the fades and set the spacing between songs, take excellent notes. Note the SMPTE reference where the fade starts and ends. This way, the mastering engineer can quickly perform the fade as you envisioned it.

Mark the Fade on the Analog Tape

When given analog masters, most mastering engineers actually mark the entire length of the fade. As the mix plays back, hold a grease pencil up against the playback head from the beginning of the fade to the end. This procedure doesn't take much time, but it ensures that the fade will start and stop at a consistent moment in time.

TIMING ISSUES FOR TAPE AND VINYL

If your project is going to be printed to CD or any of a number of other digital formats, there is one order of songs to consider and one musical and emotional flow. However, if your project is going to vinyl or cassette, organize two separate sides that have their own flow, emotion, and life. Typically, each side of a vinyl or cassette-tape album should feel like one entertainment entity.

Cassette tape hasn't really been a viable format in the modern era but—OMG—it's experiencing a bit of a renaissance with some audio enthusiasts! Most engineers and producers were thrilled to see the cassette era fade away. Tape hiss was a terrible distraction, tape jams were obnoxious, the thin tape stretched and damaged easily—it has indeed become very difficult to keep track of what's trendy, cool, popular, groovy, cherry, hip, boss, randy …

When preparing and sequencing masters for cassette or reel-to-reel masters it's very important to consider the comparative lengths of side A and side B. Side A should be slightly longer than side B. If side A is longer, the cassette can be listened to completely with minimal time gap as the playback direction reverses at the end of side A. If there is dead space it should be at the end of side B.

If your project is being distributed on vinyl, you must consider time limitations that are more restrictive than on a CD, DVD, or even cassette. Although by today's standards most albums contain 10 to 15 songs and the total album length is typically between 50 and 70 minutes, vinyl albums are limited to a maximum of about 22 minutes per side. Most vinyl albums contain between 17 and 22 minutes on each side.

The actual amount of audio that can be stored on vinyl depends on the content. If the audio has substantial low-frequency content throughout, the amount of storage potential decreases. Low frequencies require wider grooves on the vinyl surface to reproduce accurately, so consistently strong low-frequency content in the mix decreases the amount of music that can be stored on a vinyl record.

A great mastering engineer can do wonders to create a vinyl album that sounds incredible and doesn't tend to skip, while including as much music as possible. Vinyl albums are increasingly popular with the dance and hi-fi audio crowds, and vinyl mastering continues to exist as an art form. So, even if you might think that it's useless to note the special considerations of cassettes and vinyl records, there could be a time where this information is of great value. The fact that you know something about it could help you stand out in the crowd of people who want to be active recording professionals.

STEREO MASTER PREPARATION CONSIDERATIONS

The mastering engineer needs to receive more from the mix engineer than just a CD in a box. As the mix engineer you should provide all of the technical data you can.

First of all, document the location of every song—take meticulous notes. Most mastering engineers transfer all songs to a digital workstation; therefore, it is less important today than it used to be to have everything timed and spaced on the master. It's possible that each song will be on a different reel and possibly in a different format.

- Make a detailed list of the songs on the album and note the desired spacing between each song.
- Mark the specific location of each song.
- If you're using digital masters, note the track number or the time-code location. Note the song in and out points. If the mastering engineer is performing the fade, note the time-code reference of the beginning and end of the fade.
- If you're using analog masters, put leader tape between each song and note the song number on the reel. Even though it might seem obvious what you mean when indicating the third song on reel four, use a Sharpie and write the song title, take number, and date on the leader tape. Label the song on the leader just before the master recording. I also prefer to use an arrow to point in the direction of the correct take. Do everything you can to eliminate any possible confusion about which take is the correct one.

I prefer to take the mixes into a mastering session already in order and ready to go on one or two master reels. When using analog tape, use two 14-inch reels to store all of the mixes in album order. Simply compile the chosen mixes from all of the master reels by splicing the leaders together between songs. Even though this step is unnecessary by today's standards, it is convenient and it eliminates more opportunities for confusion.

If you're using digital masters, avoid making copies to take into a mastering session. You should make backups of every mix, but for the actual mastering session use the original digital master. Even though, in theory, the digital clone should be identical to the source recording, it's a fact that each digital copy holds the potential to increase the error ratio and threatens to degrade the sonic purity of the master recording.

Technical Notes

Provide a printout of all pertinent technical data for the mastering engineer. Along with the specific location of each song, provide the following information.

- Mixdown recorder. Whether you provide a digital or analog master, make a note for the mastering engineer indicating the mix recorder used to record the masters. A good mastering engineer should be able to adjust his or her analog playback machine to match the mix recorder by adjusting the playback electronics in reference to the tones provided by the mix engineer. However, if you've provided a digital master it is doubly important that you provide the manufacturer and model number of the mix recorder
- Tape type and operating level (analog). Whenever you're using analog tape, it's important that you indicate the tape manufacturer and specific formulation. Even though mastering engineers set the playback levels of their equipment according to the reference tones you provide, it's important to note the tape type and operating level.
- Leader marked (analog). Always write the song title, recording date, take number, and an arrow pointing toward the indicated song on the leader between songs. A Sharpie writes permanently on either paper or plastic leader, and it dries quickly without smearing as the tape rewinds, fast-forwards, or plays back.
- Time-code references for in and out points. When the mixes are stored on any digital format or any analog format with SMPTE reference striped on the tape, note the time-code reading of all in and out points as well as the beginnings and endings of any fades to be performed during mastering. Even if your digital format lets you add program numbers at the beginning of each mix, note all SMPTE references just in case there is an incompatibility between the program numbers written on your mix recorder and the mastering engineer's playback machine.

Chapter 9 .... GETTING READY TO MASTER

Mastering Documentation

Whether you're mastering for yourself or hiring a seasoned professional, be very organized heading into the mastering session. Know precisely where each mix is located, document it, and preconceive the course of events during the session.

If you have several analog tapes, label them all and have them ready in the order that you'll need them. If you have the mixes stored on various CDs, DVDs, hard drives, DAT tapes, ADATs, or any other format, gather all formats together and label everything precisely.

Proper documentation throughout the mastering process is fundamental to a successful experience. Once the mastering is completed and the media is prepared for duplication or replication, create a complete list of songs with accurate titles, song lengths, and any pertinent technical information. This form is comprehensive and is generated automatically by the master burning software. In addition to this information, be sure to mark the exact spots where peak levels occur and where you suspect the occurrence of any level overages.

- ✦ Program numbers. If your digital format provides program-number capabilities, use them. This is by far the quickest and easiest way to find the right mix.
- ✦ Peaks. Take note of all peak levels and questionable overs—note the specific time code location of each. Even if there are no questionable peaks and the maximum level of the mix is below 0 dBFS, note all maximum level readings. This is very helpful information for the mastering engineer and results in a faster mastering process and potentially a better-sounding final product.

Reference Tones

Analog mixed masters require a series of reference tones at the beginning of each reel. Because tape recorder alignment and equalization is such an important consideration, and because tape formulations are not always consistent from batch to batch, and just because of the wandering character of analog circuits, there needs to be some benchmark that equates the condition of the mixdown tape recorder with the mastering playback tape machine. Reference tones generated from the mixdown console into the analog recorder must be recorded on all tracks of the same tape as the master mixes, typically at the beginning of the reel (heads) but sometimes at the end (tails). Typical reference tones are 1 kHz, 10 kHz, and 100 Hz, all at 0 VU. These are very important for the duplication facility to recognize the settings of your analog equipment.

When the mastering engineer plays the mixed masters back on his or her analog machine, playback equalization will be adjusted so the mixed master 0 VU settings playback at 0 VU on the mastering playback machine. All professional recorders have provision to adjust the playback level, in relation to the 1 kHz tone; high-frequency playback level, in relation to the 10 kHz tone; and the low-frequency playback level, in relation to the 100 Hz tone. Once the mastering tape recorder plays back all three reference tones at 0 VU, it can be trusted that the mixes will be accurately represented in the mastering process.

Because of the stable and accurate nature of the modern digital recorder, reference tones are unnecessary. Most mastering engineers search the source material for overs and 0 dBFS peaks. Mastering changes and processing are performed in relation to these peaks rather than playback levels from designated tones.

SURROUND CONSIDERATIONS

As video becomes intermingled with audio and the program lengths approach and exceed one hour, disc space becomes a real concern. Consider the audio content alone from an hour-long program. If the program uses stereo audio in .aiff format, an hour uses about 650 MB. However, because most video audio is distributed in 5.1 surround, the same hour program uses three times as much data (almost 2 GB). A single-layer, single-sided DVD holds about 4.7 GB, so it's impractical to occupy 2 GB with audio.

Standard DVD-Video surround uses a Dolbly AC-3 compression protocol that limits the sample rate and bit depth to 48 kHz/24-bit with a maximum bit rate of 448 kbps. DTS protocol provides for higher-quality compressed audio of 96 kHz/24-bit with a maximum bit rate of 1536 kbps.

Lossy Versus Lossless

Audio compression schemes come in two basic forms: lossy and lossless. Compression architecture analyzes the audio content and gets rid of perceived useless information.

Lossy compression systems consider the material that's removed dispensable. Once it's gone, it's lost for good. MP3 and AAC are lossy compression schemes.

The lossless systems, such the Apple Lossless codec and the Free Lossless Audio Codec (FLAC), compress the audio files to roughly half of their original size, and in theory expand to a direct clone of the original file.

Lossy compression schemes, such as MP3 and AAC, typically compress the file to about one-tenth of its original non-compressed AIFF or WAV size (depending on the user-specified settings).

CHAPTER TEST

1. The mix engineer is typically responsible for providing an album master that:
   a. has the songs in the correct order
   b. has the proper spacing between the songs
   c. has each song in its final mixed and edited form
   d. All of the above

2. To use an analog recorder for editing tape, it must be able to:
   a. punch in and out
   b. lock to SMPTE
   c. play the tape through the regular tape path with the take-up reel disengaged
   d. freewheel

3. You must _____ razorblades that are used for editing.
   a. sanitize
   b. wash
   c. synchronize
   d. demagnetize

4. _____ is really not much more than rust coated plastic.
   a. Oxidation
   b. Analog tape
   c. A head demagnetizer
   d. A DVD-R

5. Any sticky tape substance, such as Scotch transparent tape, will work fine for razorblade editing—as long as it holds the tape together, it's alright.
   a. True
   b. False

6. Analog tape recorded at 7 1/2 ips is much easier to edit than tape recorded at 30 ips.
   a. True
   b. False

7. Digital edits are more time consuming than simply cutting and splicing the analog tape.
   a. True
   b. False

8. _____ can make the difference between an album that is enjoyable, all the way through, and one that loses the listener's attention quickly.
   a. Song order
   b. Harmonic activity
   c. Lyrical content
   d. Key changes

9. A standard space between songs on an album is:
   a. half of one second
   b. two seconds
   c. four seconds
   d. six seconds

10. When you're setting the space between songs of an album and you're dealing with fade outs, begin the space from where the mix totally loses its presence, which might be sooner than the point at which silence occurs.
    a. True
    b. False

11. When creating a master for cassette duplication:
    a. side B should be longer than side A
    b. be sure both sides are the exact same length
    c. side A should be longer than side B
    d. if there's a blank space at the end of one side it should be at the end of side A
    e. Both a and d

Chapter 9 .... GETTING READY TO MASTER

12. When creating a master for a vinyl pressing:
    a. there should be no more than 15 songs per side
    b. each side should contain between 17 and 22 minutes of audio
    c. the amount of music that will comfortably fit on each side depends on the frequency content of the mixes
    d. All of the above
    e. Both b and c

13. Even though virtually all mastering engineers transfer all songs to a digital workstation, it's still very important that everything is timed and spaced on the master.
    a. True
    b. False

14. When using analog tape as a master:
    a. insert leader tape between each take
    b. use a Sharpie to write the song title, take number, and date on the leader tape
    c. label the song on the leader just before the master recording
    d. draw an arrow on the leader, pointing in the correct direction for the tape to play back
    e. All of the above

15. When using digital masters, make backups of every mix, but for the actual mastering session use the original digital master.
    a. True
    b. False

16. _____ throughout the mastering process is fundamental to a successful experience.
    a. Contagious joy
    b. A positive attitude
    c. Proper documentation
    d. Strict disciplinarianism

17. When documenting the analog or digital master tape:
    a. note the SMPTE reference for both the in and out of each song
    b. be sure to note the peak levels and their SMPTE time reference
    c. always write the lead vocalist's name on the document
    d. All of the above
    e. Both a and b

18. In documenting the mix, even if there are no questionable peaks and the maximum level of the mix is below 0 dBFS, make a note of all maximum level readings.
    a. True
    b. False

19. AIFF audio in the 5.1 surround format occupies about _____ times as much media space as a mix in stereo AIFF format.
    a. two
    b. three
    c. four
    d. six

20. A single-layer, single-sided DVD holds about _____ of data.
    a. 4.7 GB
    b. 17 GB
    c. 2.4 GB
    d. 650 MB

Test answers are on page 299

Mastering

CHAPTER AT A GLANCE

To Master or Not to Master............ 248
Acoustic Considerations 250
Monitoring 252
Digital Versus Analog...................... 253
Mastering to Error-Correcting
  Recorders 254
Digital Modeling............................. 256
Cabling Considerations 256
Assembling the Album.................... 262
Equalizing.. 263
Noise Reduction 265
Real-Time Analyzer (RTA)................ 266
Levels... 269
Image Enhancement
  and Reverberation....................... 272
Limiting: How to Sound Loud 274
De-Essing 276
The CD-Mastering Environment 278
A Systematic Approach to the
  Mastering Process 286
Summary 286

Mastering involves the final preparation of the musical program for duplication. The reason the latest pop hit sounds punchier and more commanding than an amateur mix has much to do with the original mix, but it also has a lot to do with the mastering process. Several changes in the material can be made at this stage or, if everything is already perfect, no changes at all may be made. Mastering entails many technical decisions combined with many subjective choices based on the musical taste and experience of the mastering engineer.

The mastering engineer listens for consistent levels from song to song. If a song or two is slightly louder or softer than the rest, levels can be matched.

This is also the point at which global equalization might take place. If one song sounds weak in low-frequency content, for example, the mastering engineer selects the low frequency to boost, which helps the deficient song match the others in overall sound. These equalization moves typically affect the entire mix identically on both channels of the stereo mix.

Limiting and compression are commonly used during mastering. A hard limiter lets the engineer add decibels to the overall mix level. If the limiter registers a 6-dB reduction in gain during the mix and the levels are optimized to re-achieve a maximum signal level, the mix has been made 6 dB louder in comparison to its pre-limiting status. That's typically very good, since commercial music is often evaluated by the listener by how loud it sounds in a broadcast, dance, or environmental application. When a song is effectively louder, it is typically perceived as stronger and more appealing than the songs heard before or after it.

The mastering engineer also takes into consideration the flow of the album. A good engineer creates a flow where the songs actually grow slightly in level. This pulls the listener more effectively through the album. If the songs grow in perceived volume throughout the album, even if it's nearly imperceptible, the listener follows the musical progress from beginning to end more comfortably.

Techniques for the creation of continuity and flow aren't limited to level control alone. The mastering engineer might apply a little more limiting toward the end of the album, which could make an apparently constant level sound as if it's increasing—the songs at the end will seem louder even though their peak levels are the same as on the early songs.

Spacing between songs can also be decided during mastering. Most songs flow best with two to four seconds between them. However, there should be continuity and flow considerations that drive the decisions on spacing between songs. If a very slow song follows a very fast song, it's typically a good idea to leave a little more space after the slow song just to let the listener settle down. On the other hand, some songs want to fade directly into another.

When adjusting spacing between songs, listen to the transitions to verify how comfortably they flow. Even if you don't quite know why, you'll be able to discern much about the effectiveness of the transition from one song to the next.

TO MASTER OR NOT TO MASTER

With today's technology, anybody can prepare his or her musical product for duplication. You can send a master that will serve as the production master for your final product. You can compress, limit, equalize, effect, shorten, lengthen, space, and insert subcodes and indexes, all from the comfort of your bedroom studio. However, should you? What's the advantage to doing your own mastering at home? What's the advantage to sending your work out be mastered by someone else in another facility? How can you develop the skills needed to do a good job of mastering?

Should You Do Your Own Mastering?

I believe the answer to that question is entirely subject to the goal of the project. If you're recording your best buddy's band, they just want a product they can sell at their gigs, and they're down-and-out broke, go ahead and master the album yourself. However, do it in a way that is instructive. Research the best way to work with the equipment and software you're using. Research the art of mastering. Try different versions of your work and, above all, compare your work to the real world.

You are more likely to effectively master your own projects once you have experienced a mastering session with an experienced professional. Pay close attention to the changes made to your work by the mastering engineer. They'll reveal any consistent deficiencies. Carry the new insights you've gained back to your tracking and mixing sessions and do everything you can to build mixes that are closer to the final post-mastering status. The closer your mixes are to commercial-ready, the better they'll sound after mastering. If your mixes require dramatic and radical changes by the mastering engineer, he or she by necessity works to recover and salvage the project. It's much better when mastering time is spent looking for ways to make a stellar mix shine just a little more than when it is spent trying to bring a sub-par sound up to an acceptable sound.

What's the Advantage to Doing Your Own Mastering at Home?

The obvious answer is cost. For the price of some mastering software, you can create your own production masters, ready for duplication. The more important advantage to mastering at home is education. At any level, it's advantageous to learn mastering terminology, techniques, and possibilities. After you've mastered a few of your own projects, you'll not only have a better idea of what the mastering process entails, you'll look at the entire recording process differently. You'll set levels, equalize, use effects, and probably arrange and orchestrate differently. You'll operate according to insider information; you'll see the final picture more easily, even from the first recording of the first note. After completing several projects from the recording of note one to the mastering of the last track, you'll find that your tapes need less and less mastering. They'll be closer to perfect than they ever would have been if you hadn't experienced the mastering process yourself.

The Advantage to Hiring an Experienced Mastering Engineer

Competitive edge! When you record music that you feel strongly about and think is competitive, you owe it to the music to get a second opinion. Mastering engineers are the recordist's link to the real world. Once your project is complete and mixed, it's comforting to hire an engineer who has mastered successful albums that you think sound good. It gives your hard work a better chance to be held as worthy, relative to its competitors. I've sat through several mastering sessions with a handful of the best mastering engineers in the business, and even though I've learned a lot through the process, I still prefer to hire someone else to master.

If you want to pursue mastering as a passion or vocation, or if you just want to get good at it for your own use on your music, go for it. But how can you develop the skills you need to do a good job of mastering? Every good mastering engineer has an excellent set of monitors that are efficient throughout the audible frequency range. They also have accurate and stable monitoring environments. Their studios sound good and there isn't a lot of change in them throughout the months and years. Because this is the final stage before product production, be very fussy about the details. All components and cables should be the very best possible quality, and the wiring and implementation of all equipment should be meticulous and professionally done. Practice! Listen to everything you can get your hands on in the environment where you'll be mastering. Anything you master should sound great when compared to your favorite albums. It doesn't have to sound the same, but it still should sound very good.

ACOUSTIC CONSIDERATIONS

One of the essential factors in successful mastering is a finely tuned, finely designed listening environment. If your control room has inherent acoustic problems, everything you mix in it will have frequency problems. Acoustic problems are consistent, so they can usually be repaired during mastering. If your studio has a deficiency at 150 Hz and 600 Hz, you're probably putting too much or too little of these frequencies into every mix you complete. This typically makes the mixes sound bad in the car or in your friend's living room, for example. One of the primary values of a mastering engineer lies in compensating for bad mixing rooms.

No matter what gear you've amassed, if certain acoustic considerations haven't been addressed you're going to have a rough time getting world-class sounds. When you make decisions about mastering, the final sonic molding of your valuable music, you must make those decisions based on an accurate listening environment.

Somehow your studio must be broken up acoustically. At home, most of us operate in a bedroom-sized recording room that acts as a studio, control room, machine room, mastering suite, storage room, maintenance room, office, and possibly bedroom. The disadvantage to this setup is that you can't spread out into areas that are optimized for a specific purpose. The advantage is that you probably have a lot of stuff in your studio—stuff that absorbs, reflects, and diffuses sound waves.

Although you might have a lot of furniture and gear in your studio, additional help should be considered. Shaping the space around your recording equipment is clearly advantageous, especially in a room that is acoustically live. Live acoustics are good when they've been designed to enhance the acoustic properties of a voice or an instrument. When acoustics are randomly active, they are potentially destructive and must be controlled.

Physical structures within the acoustic space provide the best confusion of otherwise detrimental waves. Although soft surfaces dampen high frequencies, the low-mid and low frequencies (below about 300 Hz), which can be most damaging to sound, must be trapped, diffused, or reflected to ensure a smooth, even frequency response.

When absorption panels are hung on the studio walls and tools such as the Acoustic Sciences Tube Trap or baffles are used to confuse standing waves, the sounds you record are easier to mix and the mixes you construct possess sonic integrity. All of the sudden, your recordings sound more like the hits you hear on professional recordings. To overlook these considerations is to create a troublesome situation for your tracking, mixing, and mastering sessions. Address these issues so your music can have the best possible chance of impacting the listener with the power and emotion you know it deserves.

MONITORING

Be sure that your monitor environment is trustworthy and dependable. One of the things I love about mastering with the very best mastering engineers is that they confirm day after day that their systems are dependable. They listen to a lot of great music on their systems every day and base their mastering decisions on a reliable listening environment and solid experience. If you're doing your own mastering, begin the process by listening to several excellent recordings on your system. This process will help you discern what a truly great project sounds like in your own environment.

Speakers

Monitors are fundamental to the mastering process. If you plan to master your own music, select high-quality monitors that are accurate and consistent. Good, highly respected, self-powered near-field monitors are usually the best choice. Self-powered monitors are most consistent over several hours of use. Because the amplifiers and crossovers are at the speaker, they receive a line-level signal. Typically, the mixer's control room output plugs directly into each monitor. In this setup, the signal is then sent at line level to the crossover to be split into carefully selected frequency ranges. Once the signal is split, each frequency range is sent to its own amplifier—the amp sees the line-level signal and efficiently sends it to the speaker. Self-powered monitors contain amplifiers designed and adjusted to perform optimally with each component—and they sound good.

Non-powered monitors receive an amplified signal at the speaker input. The problem with this setup is that it becomes less accurate over long periods of use. Because the crossovers are getting a powered signal, they heat up. Once they heat to a certain point, they react differently, changing the monitor's sound. Although there are some excellent non-powered monitors, self-powered monitors are conceptually superior, especially for home use. Building a traditional monitor system that's custom designed, using non-powered monitors along with a line-level, external 3- or 4-way crossover and outboard power amplifiers, has great potential for accurate, pristine sound. However, this approach is pretty expensive for most home users.

Volume

If your control room is acoustically accurate, monitor at 85 to 90 dB SPL. This is the most accurate range for the human ear across the frequency spectrum. To verify this mixing volume without getting into high-budget acoustical measurement gear, buy a simple and inexpensive handheld decibel meter. Most of these instruments offer A- and C-weighting along with slow (average) and fast (peak) attack times.

C-weighting is optimized for a full-bandwidth source at levels exceeding 85 dB. A-weighting filters out the high and low frequencies and is optimized for lower volumes. The A-weighted scale more closely reflects perceived volume, whereas the C-weighted scale measures amount of energy (amplitude), which doesn't equate to perceived volume at all volume levels and frequency content.

Monitor levels of 85 to 90 dB SPL become unacceptable when the acoustical space is poorly controlled. The less acoustic integrity a room has, the softer you should monitor. At lower volume levels, room acoustics are less detrimental to the sound coming from the monitors. However, even when monitoring at low SPL, there remains value in checking your music at a louder level just to make sure there isn't a glaring flaw, especially in the lowest and highest frequencies.

DIGITAL VERSUS ANALOG

As digital technology matures, there is some likelihood that analog devices will fade into the sunset. As a guy who really appreciates the advantage of the analog sound and who enjoys the classic activity of razorblade editing, it almost hurts to predict the demise of the format; however, the fact that there is a demand for increasingly excellent digital audio systems has thus far compelled some very dramatic increases in digital sound quality.

Should You Use a Digital or an Analog Source for Mastering?

Unless you're producing vinyl records, at some point the final product to be submitted for replication will end up in a digital format. That doesn't necessarily mean the entire source chain must be digital. Analog is still a preferred audio format because of its silky-smooth warmth, and many producers print the final mixes to half-inch analog tape. When I mix, I print all audio simultaneously to multiple digital formats and to half-inch analog tape running at 30 ips. When mastering, I listen to each format to evaluate its emotional impact. Most of the time, the analog mixes just sound better.

The sonic qualities of the analog format transfer well to the final digital master. The sound of the tubes and tape is much smoother and warmer than the sound of the solid-state and digital circuitry, especially when they reach the point of oversaturation.

It's the engineer's responsibility to know the sonic character of each tool available. If you know the personality of the tools at hand, you'll be better equipped to achieve the best results possible. Your choices will be informed, educated, and respected.

MASTERING TO ERROR-CORRECTING RECORDERS

True random-access media, such as hard disks, optical cartridges, and so on, provide better and more accurate data transfer than sequential digital media, such as DAT and CD recorders. which use an error-correction scheme to fix occasional chunks of bad data. These corrections represent deviations from the actual data and, through multiple generations, they accumulate in a destructive way. Although each correction might not be audible, it is inaccurate. It could manifest as a problem somewhere in the chain from your original master to the final product, especially if error correction is involved at several stages throughout production.

These errors explain the generation-loss phenomenon of DAT and CD recorders. In the early days of digital recordings, we were told that the digital copies were so exact they could be called clones. But error correction does not create exact clones! Listen to Audio Example 10-1. It demonstrates multiple-generation DAT copies of a digital master. Listen to the sonic character of the music as the generations increase. Listen for definition changes, image shifts, EQ discrepancies, and general changes in impact.

.... Audio Example 10-1

Comparison of First- to Sixth-Generation DAT

Errors

It's not practical to expect error-free digital recordings. There's always a chance of imperfections in the media or momentary noise interference with the flow of data. An environment with an ideal signal-to-noise ratio doesn't eliminate the chance of errors. Although it might minimize the chance of errors, it offers no guarantee that they won't happen. Error-correction schemes offer a way to overcome error problems, often in a way that restores the data to its original form. However, certain repairs are merely approximations of the original data. These schemes explain the change in audio quality associated with multiple digital copies, especially in the sequential digital recording media, such as DAT.

In the digital domain, two types of data errors occur frequently: bit errors and burst errors. Occasional noise impulses cause bit inaccuracies. These bit errors are more or less audible, depending on where the error occurs within the word. Errors in the least significant bit (LSB) will probably be masked, especially in louder passages. On the other hand, errors in the most significant bit (MSB) can cause a loud and irritating transient click or pop.

Tape dropouts or other media imperfections, such as scratches on a disk, can cause errors in digital data flow called burst errors. Burst errors, like bit errors, are potentially devastating to the conversion of data to audio, especially considering that they represent larger areas of data confusion.

Data Protection

Given that errors are certain to occur, a system called interleaving is commonly used to minimize the risk of losing large amounts of data. Interleaving data is similar in concept to diversifying investments. If you spread your money between several investments, there's little chance you'll lose it all. Similarly, interleaving spreads the digital word out over a noncontiguous section of a storage medium. That way, if a bit or burst error corrupts data, it probably won't corrupt an entire word or group of words. The damage will only affect part of the word, and the likelihood is great that correction schemes will sufficiently repair any losses.

Interleaving happens at both ends of the digital recording process. From A/D, converter data is interleaved as it stores on the media. Just before the data is returned to an analog form, the interleaved data is reconstructed to its original form. This clever scheme provides a system that is completely faithful to the original data, while spreading the risk of damaged or lost data.

Other correction schemes, such as parity, redundancy, concealment, interpolation, and muting, along with interleaving, act to help ensure the most accurate data storage and recovery process for the selected media.

DIGITAL MODELING

Antares has developed several innovative products. Their microphone modeling systems let users dial up the vintage microphone of their choice. Simply plug any mic into the input, tell the processor what type of mic you've plugged in, and select the mic sound you'd like to hear from the device output. Microphones are popular tools, but they're very expensive—especially the classic vintage models. With a microphone modeler, more recordists have access to the warmth, beauty, and smoothness provided by the most sought-after microphones.

In addition, Antares and other manufacturers are continually coming up with digital models of classic tube gear, new high-tech equipment, and even the sound of analog tape. For those who have actively recorded and produced music throughout the development of the digital era, there is a certain irony to spending hundreds of dollars on a plug-in to recreate the sounds of the mid-1900s.

CABLING CONSIDERATIONS

Cable makes a difference in audio quality. Some of the differences are minor—some are major. If you're spending valuable hours producing and recording music, don't shortchange your creative efforts by using poor-quality cables.

Some Cable Theory

An in-depth study of cable theory involves a lot of math, quantification of miniscule timing inconsistencies, and a pretty good grasp of quantum theory. However, basic understanding of a few concepts provides the foundation for good choices in cabling.

A cable recognizes a signal as voltage (electrical current). Small voltages travel down interconnecting cables (line level, instrument, data), and relatively large voltages (currents) travel down speaker cables. A magnetic field is created in and around a conductor as it passes electrical current. Any materials that optimize the accuracy of this conductance help the accuracy of the transfer process. Any design that takes into consideration the full bandwidth of audio signal relative to frequency, time, and content becomes complex—more complex than simply connecting a copper wire between the output and input.

Once a few manufacturers addressed the effect of cable on sound, it became apparent to those who truly cared about the quality of their audio work that cable design might actually make a difference. Most inexpensive cables consist of a conductor that's made of copper strands and a braided shield to help diffuse interference. Not much consideration is given to bandwidth relative to frequency-specific capacitance and potential frequency-specific delay considerations.

According to Monster Cable, two main considerations must be addressed in cable design—balance of amplitude across the full audio bandwidth and the time delays as different frequencies are transmitted throughout the cable length.

- Balance of amplitude. Monster addresses this with their Amplitude Balanced Multiple Gauged Conductors. Because there are different depths of penetration into the conductor material by various frequency ranges, certain conductor sizes more accurately transmit specific frequencies. It's implied that optimal conductance is accomplished by conductors that match the bandwidth penetration depth. With the frequency range divided among multiple types and sizes of wire, each frequency is carried in an optimized way.
- Timing considerations. High frequencies travel at a higher rate than low frequencies throughout the length of a conductor (wire). Low frequencies can't be sped up, but high frequencies can be slowed down by winding the high-frequency conductors to create inductance at those frequencies. When the windings cause the correct inductance at the specified frequency bands, all frequencies arrive at their destinations in accurate and precise timing and phase relation. This corrected phase relationship restores the soundstage dimensionality, imaging, and depth. When the frequencies arrive out of phase, they exhibit time-domain distortions of phase coherence and transient clarity.

Some people don't believe there is anything to this claim. I recommend you do your own comparison—listen for yourself. All the major cable manufacturers vary slightly in their opinions on how best to handle audio transmission through a cable. However, it is agreed that cabling is a major consideration. As end users, it's our responsibility to listen to what they to say. It's our job to listen to the difference cable makes and determine the most appropriate cabling choices for our own situation. Not everyone can afford to outfit their entire system with the most expensive cable on the market—I realize that some have trouble justifying even one expensive cable. But the more serious your intent with regard to excellent audio, the more you should consider upgrading. Upgrade the cabling in your main monitoring and mixing areas. Procuring a couple of very high-quality cables to connect your mixer to your powered monitors is an excellent place to start. If you use a power amplifier, get the best cables you can afford from your mixer to the power amp and from the power amp to the speakers. It'll make a difference in what you hear, and therefore on all your EQ, panning, effects, and levels.

Do Cables Really Sound Different?

If a narrow-bandwidth signal comprised of mid frequencies and few transients is compared on two vastly different cables, the audible differences might be minimal. However, when full-bandwidth audio, rich in transient content, dimensionality, and depth, is compared between a marginal and an excellent cable, there will typically be a dramatic and noticeable difference in sound quality. The difference between the sound of a poorly designed and a brilliantly designed cable is extreme in most cases.

Listen for yourself. Most pro audio dealers are happy to show off their higher-quality audio equipment. When comparing gear, it's usually best to use high-quality audio recordings that receive industry praise for their sonic and musical excellence—after all, that's the standard you are trying to meet or beat. Listen to great recordings that you're familiar with. Patch them through the equipment and cables you're trying out.

Young recordists are usually happy to get a system connected any way it will work. To dwell on whether the cable is making any difference somehow falls near the bottom of the list of priorities. However, once the rest of the details fall into place and there's a little space for further optimizing, cable comparison might come to mind. In the meantime, they wonder why they can't quite get the acoustic guitar to sound full with smooth transients. They wonder why their mixes sound a little thick when they're played back on a better system, and they wonder why their vocal sound never seems as clear as their favorite recordings. They save a few dollars on cable while making sure their mixer and effects are the newest and coolest on the block.

In reality, you'd be better off building a system out of fewer components connected with excellent cable. There are several very good cable manufacturers. Check with your local dealer to find out who's making great cable. It's not cheap, but it affects everything you do: how you mix, how you track, which effects you choose, and how you apply equalization, just to mention a few. If the cables that connect your mixer to your powered monitors are marginal in quality, you'll base every decision concerning the sound of your music on a false premise.

Listen to Audio Example 10-2. The acoustic guitar is first miked and recorded through some common-quality cable. Then it's recorded through a microphone with some very high-quality Monster Cable. Notice the difference in transient sounds, depth, and transparency.

························· Audio Example 10-2
Mic on Acoustic Guitar Using Common Mic Cable and then Monster Studio Pro 1000 Cable

Audio Example 10-3 demonstrates the difference in vocal sound using marginal mic cable first, then a high-quality mic cable from Monster Cable. Notice the difference in transient sounds, depth, and transparency.

························· Audio Example 10-3
Vocal Using Common Mic Cable and then Monster Studio Pro 1000 Cable

The previous examples demonstrate the difference cable choice makes on individual instrument tracks. These differences are magnified in the mastering process when the entire mix is conducted from the source to the final replication master. In mastering, wherever signal passes through cable, get the best possible cable for the job.

Note: The influence of cable on sound quality is highly disputed by many. With ardent fervor, many proclaim the idiocy of suggesting that one cable "sounds" better than another. This contingent contends that there is no way that Monster or Mogami or any other high-profile and touted cable will sound better than an inexpensive modest cable designed for the same application—and they can get pretty heated and demeaning in the expression of their opinion. Here's my two cents on this issue: I believe I can hear a difference between some cables, and I'm willing to invest in anything that I think gives me a competitive edge in the business of audio creation and production. I recommend that you listen for yourself. That's why I include Audio Examples in my books. The audio comparisons in this chapter speak for themselves—listen to them. If you don't think there is any difference between the sound of the high-priced cable and the more pedestrian version, that's fine—at least you've listened and made up your own mind.

Digital-Interconnect Cables

Digital-interconnect cables also have an effect on the sound quality of digital masters and clones. Listen to Audio Examples 10-4 through 10-8. In each example a different cable and format configuration is demonstrated.

Listen specifically to all frequency ranges as well as transients. Also, consider the "feel" of the recording. Often the factor that makes one setup sound better than another is difficult to explain, but it's easy to feel. The following examples use exactly the same program material, as well as the identical transfer process as the included CD.

The differences you hear on your setup depend greatly on the quality and accuracy of your monitoring system, as well as your insight and perception. Once you understand and experience subtle sonic differences, you'll realize the powerful impact they hold for your musical expression. Constantly compare and analyze the details of your music. It will result in much more competitive quality. You'll realize more satisfaction and you'll probably get more work.

Audio Example 10-4
AES/EBU to DAT Using Common Cable and then SP1000 AES Silver Digital Monster Cable

Audio Example 10-5
S/PDIF to DAT Using Common RCA Cables and then M1000 D Silver Digital Monster Cable

Audio Example 10-6
Analog Out to DAT Using Common XLR Cables and then Prolink Studio Pro 1000 XLR Monster Cables

Audio Example 10-7
ADAT Light Pipe into Digital Performer Using Common Optical Cable, Bounced to Disk

Waveform Differences between Cable

In both of these sets of waves, the top wave was captured digitally through S/PDIF using M1000 D Silver Monster Cable and the bottom wave was captured using a common RCA cable. In case there's a doubt about whether the cable really matters in an audio environment, these comparisons speak very graphically that they do. If the transfers were identical in data, they'd look identical.

Monster M1000 D Digital Coaxial Cable

Common RCA Cable

Monster M1000 D Digital Coaxial Cable

Common RCA Cable

· Audio Example 10-8
ADAT Light Pipe into Digital Performer Using Monster Cable's Interlink Digital Light Speed 100 Optical Cable, Bounced to Disk

If you can't hear much difference in some of these comparisons, try listening on different systems. Try auditioning several different monitors, power amps, or mixers with your own system. Keep in mind that there is a substantial cost difference between cables. It's entirely possible to spend more on the cable connecting two devices than you spent on either device, or maybe both devices. Cable prices vary greatly. With a budget in mind, choose first to connect your basic components with the best cable possible.

Cable differences are often so extreme that they can be seen in the onscreen waveforms. The previous illustration shows two identical waveforms—one recorded through a common RCA cable into a digital S/PDIF input and the other through an M1000 D Silver Monster Cable.

ASSEMBLING THE ALBUM

There is an art to assembling an album so that it draws the listener through all the songs. When all songs have been placed in an artful order:
- The album is easy to listen to as a complete work.
- Each song leads gracefully into the next.
- Contrasts in texture, tempo, and lyrical content hold the listener's interest.
- All material plays to the same audience, so your intended audience can relate to everything on the album—there aren't a couple tunes that seem out of place.

A good mastering engineer thinks of the flow of an album. Spacing between songs might be adjusted to hold interest or contrast textures. Throughout the course of an album, the level of the songs might increase to help hold attention, or the limiting might increase to make the songs seem progressively louder. This way, the momentum of the songs seems to increase slightly, although the level of each song is still optimized. As the mastering engineer you must listen for perceived volume; don't merely look at signal levels. At the identical amplitude, a simple production consisting of minimal or no instrumentation and one voice sounds much louder than a full production. The mastering engineer must compensate for these variations in musical density.

Spacing is easily adjusted during mastering, but it's often best to listen to the entire album several times to determine whether the spacing flows well with a natural momentum. Therefore, spacing between songs is often best determined prior to the actual mastering session.

EQUALIZING

Equalization is an important part of the mastering process. Each song must sound compatible with the progression of the album. If one or two songs are deficient in low frequencies, or if a song or two lacks high end, they'll stand out over the course of album play. Each song has to sound like it belongs in the kettle with the rest of them.

Variations in EQ are common from song to song, especially when a project is completed over the course of several months. Equipment changes, tastes change, and skill levels change throughout the progression of any album. Try to mix all songs on the same monitors and in the same studio; it will make life easier during mastering. Once, a studio owner changed the weighting of the woofers without telling me just before I mixed the final song of an album. When the low-frequency response changes dramatically, the resulting effect of the mix is very graphic. Once you get into the mastering studio, it's obvious that something went suddenly astray. The song I mixed on the woofer-altered speakers sounded like it had been mixed on a different planet compared to the other 10 songs on the album. Fortunately, since the deficiency was global, the mastering engineer was able to pump a substantial amount of low-frequency boost into the song. In the final product, it flowed very nicely with the other songs. You'd never know there was any problem with the mix.

Find a specific recording that you think sounds great. A group held in high esteem by the recording industry provides a strong example to compare your mixes to in each session. If you reference each mix to the same recording, you'll have a good chance of creating mixes that flow well together. When referencing mixes to confirm your mix integrity, listen especially to the low frequencies and very high frequencies. Listen to how transparent the mix sounds in the midrange.

Air

Most of my favorite albums have excellent and controlled high-frequency content. The frequencies around 18 to 20 kHz are subtle, yet they add greatly to the feel of the mix. Inclusion of this frequency range, often referred to as "air," gives a mix song an open feeling—a perception that the sound isn't closed in.

Highs

All frequencies are important when mastering, but without solid, controlled high frequencies, any song can sound dull and lifeless. Too many highs create a brittle and harsh sound, especially when they are added by an equalizer. Excellent recording and mixing technique honors the transient component of sound—a mix that contains many natural transients has more impact and clarity than a mix that has been heavily compressed or limited with no regard for maintaining transients.

Mids

We often concentrate so much on high and low frequencies that we forget the importance of mid frequencies. A mix with controlled and balanced mids is typically very warm, smooth, and easy to listen to. This is also the frequency range that's capable of placing a sonic cloud over any mix when in improper balance.

De-Essing

Often in the tracking and mixing process, extreme compression techniques over-exaggerate vocal sibilance. When this happens, a de-esser is necessary to bring the sibilant sound back under control. A de-esser is simply a very fast, frequency-specific compressor that can sweep the high-frequency range to locate problem sibilant sources. The de-esser must be set carefully to only bring under control the exact frequencies causing the problem, or it will rob the music of life.

Lows

Low frequencies often provide the greatest challenge. They contain the most energy of any frequencies and, when too powerful, they can produce an artificially hot mix level, which results in a quiet-sounding track. A good mastering engineer crafts and molds the low frequencies to create a master that is powerful yet controlled for optimum impact.

.... **Audio Example 10-9**
Reference Mix (No EQ)

.... **Audio Example 10-10**
Air Increased and then Decreased at 18 kHz

Chapter 10 .... MASTERING

> **Audio Example 10-11**
> Highs Increased and then Decreased at 5 kHz

> **Audio Example 10-12**
> Mids Increased and then Decreased at 400 Hz

> **Audio Example 10-13**
> Lows Increased and then Decreased at 60 Hz

Software Versus Hardware Equalizers

Many engineers are very attuned to their analog equipment and only prefer to use their hardware. This is an excellent approach when every part of the signal path is meticulously designed and crafted. Keep in mind that the quality of your audio depends on the integrity of the least common denominator. High-quality analog equipment is typically very complicated to set up and expensive to maintain properly so most home users are better off using some of the many excellent software processors, which are readily available in today's marketplace.

Many excellent software packages are available for both Mac and PC platforms. Refer to *Recording Software & Plug-Ins* from the *Hal Leonard Recording Method* for an excellent reference on computer-based plug-in processors.

NOISE REDUCTION

The mastering engineer must listen critically to the entirety of the recording and all of its characteristics. If inherent noise is an issue, it must be addressed in the best way possible. Noises, including hiss, clicks, pops, and so on, can be minimized or eliminated through the use of noise reduction software plug-ins like those available from Waves and iZotope.

Clicks in the mixed master can be caused by a number or reasons, such as non-zero cross-point edits, lip smacks, and so on. Some of these noises can be automatically eliminated with software, but sometimes it's necessary to zoom in on the waveform in the DAW and use the pencil tool to redraw the portion of the waveform containing the click.

Noise Reduction Plug-Ins

Software manufacturers such as Waves and iZotope provide noise reduction software that assist the engineer in removing several types of noises. The valuable tools have the capacity to "learn" the noise and create an algorithm to eliminate it—very handy, indeed!

The Waves X-Noise plug-in (below) has learned the noise component of the track and very effectively eliminates that noise from the recording during playback.

REAL-TIME ANALYZER (RTA)

Some engineers like to mix while referencing a real-time analyzer (RTA). This tool displays the level of specific frequencies across the audible spectrum. I've seen engineers who couldn't use the restroom without consulting their three-dimensional RTA. To top it off, their mixes didn't always sound that good. If you use a tool such as a real-time analyzer, consider that it is just a simple tool designed to help. The true test is in the listening. A song can look mighty fine on the analyzer yet sound like garbage, or it might look bad on the analyzer and sound great. There's always the possibility it will look good and sound good. I love it when that happens!

The RTA divides the audible frequency spectrum into regions—typically 31 regions, correlating to the 31 bands on a 1/3-octave graphic equalizer. Each region is represented by a series of LEDs, which indicate the region's energy level in the same manner as the audio level meter on your mixer or recorder. A good mix is typically flat across the spectrum, with a little roll-off at the very top and bottom of the frequency spectrum.

The RTA receives its signal in one of two ways:
- Through a calibrated microphone
- Through a direct line input

······················· Video Example 10-1
Noise Reduction, Metering, and the RTA

Acoustical RTA Measurements

Use the microphone when checking the frequency integrity of your monitoring environment. If you set the microphone at the same position where you monitor the mix, and then play pink noise through the system (with all frequencies at an equal level), you should see each band on the RTA at the same level. If you see an abundance or a lack of certain frequency bands, you have a couple of options:
- Make changes in the mixing environment, which will affect the acoustic character. Physical construction isn't always the easiest route to go, but in the end it's often the best solution. If you tune your studio so it's accurate, you'll be able to trust that your work will transfer favorably to the rest of the world.
- Hire an acoustics consultant. It could be the best money you spend on your studio.

If your acoustical problems are insurmountable, try inserting a 31-band graphic equalizer between the output of your mixer or computer and the inputs of your monitor system. A 1/3-octave graphic EQ (31-band) correlates directly to the bands on a real-time analyzer. If you have a predominance of energy at 500 Hz, simply turn that frequency range down on the RTA until it registers flat when the calibrated microphone hears pink noise through your monitors at the mastering engineer's position. This way, it's possible to get a room to register properly on the RTA, but it's not always preferable. Simple equalization is accomplished through filters and phase-altering circuitry. These circuits have the potential of causing more problems in your listening environment than they're fixing. The importance

Seeing is Believing

Music is really all about what you hear and how that experience makes you feel. It's about emotion and passion and power and control. A well-produced musical work connects with the listener on many levels. But it's also pretty instructive to see what you're hearing. The audio waveform or an RTA readout gives our mind a picture of what our ears are hearing, which is instructive when we build a mix and question certain of its aspects.

The waveform to the right is "Gaslighting Abbie" from Steely Dan's *Two Against Nature* album. This is an amazing example of the power of space in an arrangement. You can see it *and* you can hear it. Listen to this production and look at this waveform.

This waveform (right) is "Beat, Broken, and Scarred" from Metallica's *Death Magnet* album. Metallic has become known for taking mastering levels to the limit. This song has the exact same peak levels as the Steely Dan song above.

of this connection dictates the use of very solid and sonically transparent EQ. In other words, it's not cheap.

Electronic Evaluation of Frequency Content

A real-time analyzer also receives a line-level input. Many mix and mastering engineers prefer to connect a send of the source to an RTA to evaluate frequency content across the audible spectrum. This tool helps quantify what you hear. Most commercial mixes contain a fairly even balance of frequencies throughout the duration of the song, with a slight roll-off around 20 kHz and about 60 Hz. With the advent of higher-quality consumer audio equipment, the highest and lowest frequencies have become more and more practical to include in a mix. As a mastering engineer, it can be comforting to actually see that the frequency content of the final master is consistent across the spectrum and that there are no obviously glaring peaks or dips in the curve. However, some of the very best mastering engineers never use an RTA; they rely on their ears.

LEVELS

During the mastering process, mix levels are a primary concern. Optimizing levels is important during the mixdown process, but mastering is the place where the final adjustments are made with regard to the level, flow, and momentum of the entire album.

It's technically gratifying when each song on an album reaches maximum level at least once. However, some songs just sound louder when they are set to maximum levels than others. The ideal in the mastering process is to keep the levels maximized while creating a complete work that sounds great in its entirety.

Normalize

Normalizing is the easy way to move all the levels up to the point where the peak(s) hit maximum level. Conceptually, this helps ensure that song levels are as hot as they possibly can be and that the full word is being used (the maximum number of bits). However, it should not be an automatic move to normalize every song on an album.

Often without thinking, young recordists normalize each song. I don't see that happen when I sit with some of the best mastering engineers in the business. What I do see is careful evaluation of the song, the sound, the style, the content, the character, and so on. Careful consideration must be given to the intent of the artist and to the music's audience. A plan should be developed for the impact of the album as a whole.

Normalizing isn't necessarily a bad thing to do, but it shouldn't be automatic. There are other means to create the proper levels in a more pristine and musically desirable way, one of which is limiting—a key toll in the mastering engineer's kit.

Real Versus Apparent Levels

A song's level seems blatant, right? Either it's maximized or it's not. In reality, it's not that simple. Frequency content, instrumentation, and orchestration all play parts in how loud a song sounds. If your album contains a wide range of instru-

Differences in Apparent Volume

There can be a distinct difference in the apparent volume between two audio recordings that achieve the same peak levels. So, are all "louds" the same? No. Just because two signals register the same on a PPM or even on a VU meter, it doesn't mean that they sound like they're the same volume. Remember, according to the Fletcher-Munson curve of equal loudness, the human ear hears best between about 1 and 4 kHz, especially at quieter volumes. Also, as noted previously—and also as quantified by Fletcher and Munson—it takes much more low-frequency energy for the human ear to perceive a specified loudness relative to our most sensitive range between 1 and 4 kHz.

We must also consider transients. The human ear tends to interpret transients as clarity and intelligibility more than volume, so a mix with substantial transient content that reaches 0 dBFS might sound very clean and clear without being perceived as loud. It is this principle that explains the effectiveness of the peak limiter at increasing apparent volume—it decreases the transient peaks by a user-set amount, which allows the entire mix to be turned up by that same amount in order to reachieve the initial playback level. A multiband peak limiter can control transients while also rebalancing the low, low mid, mid, and high bands

Here are some factors that affect volume—assuming that each mix achieves 0dBFS—listed in order from quietest to loudest:

1. A boomy-sounding mix that contains primarily low frequencies and is deficient in mids and highs (no peak limiting).

2. A bass-heavy mix that has balanced but minimized high- and mid-frequency bands (no peak limiting).

3. A well-balanced mix (no peak limiting).

4. A mix that is deficient in low frequencies and strong in mid and high frequencies (no peak limiter).

5. A bass-heavy mix through a peak limiter set to increase gain relative to the amount of peak reduction.

6. A well-balanced mix through a multiband peak limiter set to increase gain relative to the amount of overall peak reduction across all four bands—typically three, four, or five bands.

7. A mix that is deficient in low frequencies through a peak limiter.

8. A mix that it distorted and comprised primarily of the band from 1 kHz to 4 kHz. By modern standards, a mix like this would sound terrible, but it would be very loud, plus the distortion would quickly cause ear fatigue.

mentation, from full band with strings and horns to voice and guitar or even just voice, you'll need to evaluate the volume of each song in relation to the others. You won't be able to count on normalizing every track, that's for sure.

The fewer instruments involved in the mix, the louder it'll seem at maximum levels. Have you ever noticed how full and punchy basic tracks sound before all the synth and filler parts have been added? It seems as if the song sounds softer and softer as you put more and more into it.

Tasteful limiting and compression can help even out the levels, but simply using your ears to find the levels that flow best from song to song is also a good

Metering Peaks Versus Assessing Apparent Volume

The Dorrough Model 40—in hardware or software format—simultaneously displays peak and average levels, making it easy to keep track of apparent loudness (average levels) relative to peak signal levels. The leading (right) lights on each meter indicate peak levels while the block level that follows each peak indicates the average level.

When mastered well, each genre or style tends to exhibit a predictable and characteristic difference between the peak and average level. Use a meter like this to assess a successful and highly-respected production. Note the difference between it's peak and average signal level and then work with your song to find the settings that produce similar results. It's usually possible to find a good balance of compression, limiting, and peak limiting to approximate the reference. Once you've achieved this, and you like the sound and feel of the mastered track, you can be more confident that your mastered track will have a similar level, presence, and punch when compared to other songs in the same genre.

plan. If you have level questions throughout the album, be sure to listen to the entire album on several different systems. What might seem like the perfect relationship between tracks in your studio might seem distracting and inconsistent in your car. It pays to check the level relationship in as many separate environments as possible. One value of an experienced mastering engineer is the accuracy with which these adjustments are made.

The Highpass Filter

It's important to use a high-pass filter to eliminate the frequencies below 20 Hz. In most listening environments, this extremely low band is inaudible, but that doesn't mean that it doesn't contain information. It's best to ensure that these lows are cleaned up because they contain a large amount of energy and can adversely effect the mastered recordings.

IMAGE ENHANCEMENT AND REVERBERATION

Over the years there have been several devices that increase the apparent width of the stereo image, taking the left and right pan placements and seeming to move them farther apart. This type of tool can be an effective mastering tool but be careful not to overuse it because it sometimes adds an unnatural and artificial feel to the end result. Its best to avoid using stereo image enhancers during mixdown, leaving such treatments for the mastering engineer to add tastefully and sparingly. If the enhancer is used during mixdown, it can affect the engineer's stereo placement, which threatens to negate the effect of the plug-in or device.

There are several software plug-ins and a few hardware devices that enhance that enhance the stereo image. They all make the image sound bigger and wider, but beware that anytime the entire mix is run through any software plug-in or hardware device, the utmost care must be taken to ensure proper gain structure and implementation. It's also very important that the output of the enhancer faithfully represents the frequency and transient content of the original signal.

On rare occasions, it's appropriate to add reverberation during mastering. As a rule, the application of reverb should occur during the mixdown process—in fact, compression and peak limiting during mastering tend to magnify the reverb that is part of the mixed master. Adding reverberation to the entire mix effectively moves the mix farther away from the listener, which is rarely appropriate; however, a minimum amount of the perfect reverb can warm up the sound a bit and might be the right choice for some mixes.

·························· **Video Example 10-2**
Widening the Stereo Image

Stereo Image Enhancement

Stereo enhancers widen the stereo image. Plug-ins such as iZotope's Ozone 5 include a suite of effects including spacial and image enhancers. Be careful when applying image enhancers because overuse can result in an artificial sound that lacks realism and warmth.

LIMITING: HOW TO SOUND LOUD

Most mastering engineers use some degree of peak limiting to help control sporadic peaks and to help keep the overall level of the album as high as possible within the constraints of taste and style. Keep in mind that if your peak limiter registers 6 dB of limiting sometime during the mix, you can boost the level of the entire mix by 6 dB to reattain maximum levels. Therefore, your song will sound 6 dB louder. That's an amazing difference in volume.

Typically, the best mastering results are accomplished using a multiband limiter. Dividing the frequency range into two or more separate ranges that are limited independently produces the most punchy and consistent sound. However, as the individual bands limit, they change in their relative levels to each other. When highs, mids, and lows are limited separately, there is the potential for adverse impact on the sound you toiled over. It's a good idea to use limiting in moderation. The best plan is to mix with mastering in mind. If you create your mix so it maintains constant levels, and if you're very deliberate and precise in the development of your sound, there will be less need for limiting. The mastering process might include slight peak limiting, which is used primarily to keep a lid on the level to protect against levels above digital maximum. This way, more integrity and control lie in your hands from the onset of the project through its completion and duplication.

Overuse of limiting creates a sound that is thin and lacking in life. When the entire mix stays at maximum level throughout the song, there's no release. Transparency, contrast, and depth are lost. Even the best multiband limiters lose punch when they're pushed too hard.

Some mastering engineers never use multiband limiting because they want to remain very true to the original mix. This is especially true in jazz, folk, and other genres that are characterized by a wide dynamic range and expressive texture and level changes. In these cases, careful use of a high-quality single-band compressor/limiter helps control the overall level while maintaining much of the originally intended life and musical power. When applied to music that is more open and dynamic, aggressive multiband limiting will almost always change the balance between instruments and voices in a way that is destructive. A solo voice or instrument that is well-balanced in the original mix might get buried after severe or poorly adjusted multiband limiting is applied—extreme changes in the relative levels between bands effectively changes the balance between mix components.

How Hot Is Hot Enough?

Throughout the course of each album, levels should reach just below 0 dBFS several times. Some recordists like to leave a decibel or two of headroom to avoid overdriving the electronics of older CD players but most modern mastering engineers limit peak levels to somewhere between -0.5 and -0.1 dBFS. That's not what I've historically seen in the real world, though. It has been common to see radical amounts of compression and peak limiting with everything pushed to the max. Everyone has gotten used to having hottest mix on the planet with some mastering engineers recommending pushing the digital levels over maximum level. Fortunately, there is a trend away from such radical limiting and compression.

The aggressive approach isn't appropriate to all styles. It's inappropriate for most jazz, classical, bluegrass, gospel, and country-western albums. Your understanding of the style you're working with should guide your decisions in mastering.

Listen to Audio Examples 10-14 through 10-17. The same mix is played with three different limiting levels. The first is normal as mixed. The second demonstrates 3 dB of limiting, and the third and fourth demonstrate 6 dB and 9 dB of gain reduction. Remember that once the gain is reduced on the limited portions, the levels are brought back to optimum, where the strongest section peaks at zero on the digital meter.

............................Audio Example 10-14
Normal Mix

............................Audio Example 10-15
3-dB Louder Waves L3 Multimaximizer

............................Audio Example 10-16
6-dB Louder Waves L3 Multimaximizer

............................Audio Example 10-17
9-dB Louder Waves L3 Multimaximizer

Software Versus Hardware Limiting

I use an excellent hardware multiband limiter patched between the digital mixer output and my CD recorder input. I use this primarily for printing reference mixes for the artist and me to evaluate outside the studio. I like its sound, but I've never used it to create the final master for replication. I use it because I can run a quick copy of the mix straight off the interface output, in real-time, and while everyone listens through the production one last time at the end of the session. This is the simplest way I've found to hand off a reference CD. It doesn't require any bouncing (best accomplished in real-time in some DAWs), importing, or burning.

Software applications designed for mastering are very trustworthy and typically more quantifiable than most hardware limiters. Again, there are excellent renditions of both hardware and software mastering tools, but most of what creates great masters are the subjective, objective, and creative musical decisions made by the mastering engineer.

DE-ESSING

De-essing is required when the vocals contain exaggerated sibilance. When vocals are over-compressed with an attack time that's too long, the sibilant sounds shoot through uncompressed while the rest of the vocal sound is compressed. This results in an "s," "t," "ch," and "sh" sounds that are artificially loud. Exaggerated sibilant sounds are also dependent on the vocalist's diction and enunciation.

A de-esser is a frequency-specifc compressor that can be set to reduce the exaggerated sibilance that results from poor compression technique. It is ideal to de-ess the vocal tracks during mixdown so this is not an issue during mastering, but that doesn't always happen. These exaggerated sibilant sounds are intrusive to the overall mix quality and they sound amateurish. A good mix engineer will address any need for de-essing prior to mastering, so often the problem will be solved by the time the project gets to mastering, but sometimes the mixed master (mastering engineers often call this the "pre-master") contains these harsh sounds that must be addressed.

The de-esser must be carefully set so that, as much as possible, it only affects the sibilant vocal sounds. Run the track through an RTA to help locate the problem frequency and then match that frequency with the de-esser—the exact frequency selected often requires fine-tuning while listening to the track. Set the controls for the least amount of intrusion on the overall mix. The threshold setting is crucial and must be adjusted so only the vocal sibilance triggers compression. It's important to note that de-essing is a momentary process that turns the offending frequency down very quickly once it exceeds the user-set threshold and then releases it very quickly once the signal moves back under the threshold.

Video Example 10-3
Using the De-Esser

Types of De-Essers

The de-esser can be set to reduce gain in a few different ways:

- Broadband. The entire track can be turned down when the sibilance exceeds the threshold—this is not recommended for mastering.

- Focused frequency. A curve centered on the offending frequency is turned down when the sibilance exceeds the threshold—this is recommended for mastering.

- Shelving. A shelf above the set de-essing frequency is turned down when the sibilance exceeds the threshold—this is not usually recommended for mastering.

Mixing & Mastering .... by BILL GIBSON

THE CD-MASTERING ENVIRONMENT

There's more to preparing a CD master than simply digitally recording and spacing 10 or so songs in the correct order. The encoding format must be correct for the intended CD usage. Codes need to be correct, verified, and confirmed. Protocol must be followed to ensure proper duplication and replication.

To effectively operate in a CD-mastering environment, make yourself familiar with its language. Absorb the specialized terminology that pertains to mastering alone. Be sure you know what the replication facility expects to ensure the best possible outcome for your music.

Write Modes

There are two basic modes used to write an audio CD.

- Track-at-once mode. This mode writes one track at a time. The laser is turned off and put to rest after each track, after the lead-in, and before the lead-out. This system lets the user record song after song in different sessions and at different times. The material doesn't need to be recorded all at once in track-at-once mode. When the laser is turned off, small areas are left unrecorded on the CD media. These unrecorded sectors, called runout sectors, are perceived as corrupted by the player. While many CD players are able to skip over the corrupted areas, CD readers at the duplication facility are likely to view them as errors. Track-at-once offers the advantage of letting the user write more audio data to the CD in separate sessions until the CD is full. This mode is best left for less-critical projects, such as quick references, compilations, or archiving mixes. Track-at-once CDs do not meet Red Book standard.

- Disc-at-once mode. This mode writes the entire disc, including the table of contents, lead-in, audio data, and lead-out, in one continuous pass. The laser is never turned off and there are no unwritten (or runout) sectors. This mode is the professional standard for the creation of a CD master. Disc-at-once mode conforms to Red Book standard.

Red Book

Sony and Philips defined the Red Book standard (in the form of an actual red book) for playback of digital audio CDs (CD-DA). They also defined various formats for audio, video, image, and data storage. Each standard was released in a colored binder, hence the terms Red Book, Orange Book, and so on.

The Red Book standard defines the proper format for an audio CD to play back on a CD player, and it defines the format for a CD player to play back a CD. Any Red Book–compatible CD can play back on a commercial audio CD player.

The Red Book standard defines the number of digital audio tracks on the CD as well as the type of error correction used to guard against minor data loss. The standard calls for up to 74 minutes of digital audio, transferable at the rate of 150 KB per second.

Red Book standard requires certain specifications be met.

- Each track must be at least four seconds in length.
- All track numbers and index times must be unique and in ascending order.
- There must be a minimum Index 0 gap length of four seconds.
- The maximum number of tracks is 99.
- Index 0 must always be at zero seconds.
- Index 0 of the first track must be between two and three seconds in length. In other words, Index 1 must start between two and three seconds after Index 0.
- The disc must be finished. In disc-at-once mode, the data is written from beginning to end without stopping; the laser isn't turned off during the write process. The table of contents, lead-in, audio data, and lead-out are written continuously and in order.

Each CD track typically contains one song. Tracks are divided into 2,352 byte sectors that are 1/75 of a second long.

If a disc is scratched or dirty, Red Book standard specifies an error-detection code and an error-correction code (EDC and ECC) so the player can recreate the music according to code.

Most commercially produced CDs conform completely to the Red Book standard, which is also called the Compact Disc Digital Audio Standard. A disc conforming to the Red Book standard usually says "Audio CD" under the Disc logo.

Scarlet Book

The Scarlet Book contains the standard for Super Audio CD (DSD) format. Scarlet Book specifications include the option for three different disc formats:

single-layer DSD, dual-layer DSD, and a dual-layer hybrid, which also contains a standard Red Book CD layer that is functional on a standard CD player.

Yellow Book

The Yellow Book contains the standard for CD-ROM. When a disc conforms to Yellow Book standards, it typically says "Data Storage" under the Disc logo.

The Yellow Book standard emphasizes accuracy for data storage. Whereas an audio CD operates peacefully within an error-correction scheme, errors in data storage easily render a file or application useless. Error-free schemes are essential for storage of computer data.

The Yellow Book augments Red Book protocol by adding two different types of tracks: CD-ROM mode 1 for computer data and CD-ROM mode 2 for compressed audio and video data.

Green Book

The Green Book is the standard format for CD-I (CD-Interactive). This standard was designed for multimedia applications that play in real time, combining sound, images, animation, and video. The CD-I format and the playback unit associated with it were designed to use an inexpensive computer and audio disc player along with an ordinary NTSC television as a monitor.

Orange Book, Parts I and II

The Orange Book standard defines the format for write-once CDs (CD-WO) of both audio and CD-ROM data. The Orange Book specifications are designed so that a Red Book–compatible CD can be created on a write-once disc.

Part I of the Orange Book specifies the standards for magneto-optical systems that use rewritable media (CD-MO).

Part II of the Orange Book standard defines the CD-Write-Once specification (CD-WO). The standard divides the disc into discrete areas, each for a specific function. The Program Calibration area is used for a test run to calibrate the recording laser. The Program Memory area is used to record track numbers along with their stopping and starting points. The Lead-In area is left free to write the disc's table of contents after all data is completely recorded. The Program area is where the actual data is written, and the Lead-Out area is placed at the end of the disc to let the player know when to stop reading.

White Book
The White Book standard represents the fourth major extension of the Red Book standard. It is a medium-specific standard allowing for 74 minutes of video and audio on a compact disc in MPEG format. The Sony/Philips Video-CD is White Book compliant.

Blue Book/CD-Extra
The Blue Book/CD-Extra standard stores Red Book audio in the first portion of the disc and Yellow Book data in the second, completely separate, section. Because an audio CD player is a single-session machine, it only recognizes the audio session, since it is first on the disc. CD-ROM drives are typically multi-session devices, so they see both the audio and data sessions.

CD-Extra, originally known as CD-Plus, solves many of the problems originally encountered with enhanced CDs.

PQ Subcodes
All audio CDs have eight channels of subcode information interleaved with the audio data. These subcodes serve various functions depending on the actual digital information being stored. Some codes apply specifically to audio, some to video and graphics, and others to MIDI data. The subcode channels are identified by the letters P, Q, R, S, T, U, V, and W. Channels R through W are used to store video information on CD+G discs or MIDI information on CD+MIDI discs.

Audio CDs use only the P and Q subcodes. The information on the P channel tells the CD player when the tracks are playing and when they aren't. The Q channel contains much more information, including copy protection and emphasis information, track and disc running times, disc catalog codes, and track ISRC codes.

ISRC Code
The International Standard Recording Code (ISRC) uniquely defines each specific track on the CD with the country of origin, information about the song's registrant (a code is assigned by the RIAA to the mastering engineer), the year of production, and a unique designation number that represents the track. The ISRC can be written directly into the CD's Q subcode channel. Each track on the CD can have its own unique ISRC information. The ISRC code is entered during

mastering in a standard format: Country Code-Agent Code-Year-Designation Number. For example, for a mastering engineer with an RIAA-assigned agent code of WAG, mastering his or her 425th song in 2012, the ISRC code could be US-WAG-12-00425.

The actual number assignment doesn't have to be sequential from the beginning of the year, but many mastering engineers use this system because it is easy to track—an identifying number can be used only once during each calendar year. To become an agent and receive your own ISRC code, apply to the RIAA. There is a one time fee of $75.00 to register.

Emphasis

The emphasis flag in the Q subcode alerts the CD player to activate the de-emphasis circuitry in its analog output. Early CD players had poor-quality digital-to-analog converters, so CDs were recorded with a pre-emphasis, high-frequency boost. Emphasized CDs must be played back through an analog de-emphasis circuit to ensure accurate EQ.

Converters have improved dramatically over the years, and emphasis is no longer necessary; it's rarely, if ever, used. However, when source material is used that was originally emphasized, it must be de-emphasized in playback.

SCMS

The Serial Copy Management System (SCMS) resides in the Q subcode. It allows the audio to be digitally recorded once but prevents second-generation digital copies. When the SCMS flag is present, it is encoded in the data stream when a digital copy is made. If the SCMS or Copy Prohibit codes are inactive, unlimited copies can be made from the source. Whenever you are distributing your material on CD for review, select SCMS or Copy Prohibit to help defend against piracy. However, note that these schemes don't offer much protection because it's child's play for an adept tech-head to break the copy-protection scheme.

Track Number

Each song or contiguous audio segment on a CD is called a track. There can be up to 99 tracks on each CD, numbered from 1 to 99, always in consecutive, sequential order. A CD can start with any track number from 1 to 99, allowing for continuous numbering of tracks in multiple CD sets.

Indexes

Each track on a CD can contain up to 100 marked locations, called indexes, within each track. The indexes, numbered from 0 to 99, are always in consecutive, sequential order. All tracks contain at least one index. Index 1 defines the start of the track. If there is a gap of silence after the previous audio ends and before the actual audio data begins, it's labeled as index number 0. All other index points are optional and user-definable.

There are two types of indexes: absolute and relative. Absolute indexes calculate and display all times relative to the beginning of the CD. Relative indexes calculate and display all times relative to the beginning of the individual track that they're indexing.

Noise Shaping

Noise shaping is an option sometimes present in the dithering process. Previously, I discussed the value of dither when very low-level signals are present. Noise shaping uses digital filters to remove noise that falls in the middle of the audible spectrum, typically around 4 kHz—the human ear's most sensitive range. Because noise is actually important in the control of quantization errors it isn't completely removed through noise shaping, but is instead shifted to a range that is harder to hear. Noise shaping lessens our perception of the noise essential to the dithering process.

Image Files

When it's time to create your CD master, it's usually preferable to create an image file from which the actual CD master will be made. Any good CD-mastering software provides a means of creating an image file. When an image file is created, all the songs and segments are copied to a contiguous section of one of your drives. When you create a CD from files that are scattered all over your drives, there's opportunity for inaccuracies and errors to creep into the data flow. However, an image file is an accurate and continuous copy of all data. When the CD master is created from an image file the data flows smoothly and freely onto the disc. The transfer can take place with greater accuracy and at faster speeds. When printing from an image file, it's better to print the master at faster speeds because the data will be backed up and bogged down at slower speeds.

The image file was originally used to facilitate the use of slower CD burners, but it offers a way to make smooth and accurate data transfers and provides a means for trustworthy archives of all audio data in a project.

Dither

At especially low signal levels, the digital recording system performs very poorly. In a 16-bit system, a low-level signal (around 10 percent of maximum level) uses just under two bits to record whatever audio signal is present. These low-level signals are common during the fade out of a commercial song and during classical recordings: symphony, choir, string quartet, etc.

Dither is simply white noise added to the program source at very low levels (typically half of the least significant bit). Though it seems ironic to add noise to an otherwise noiseless system, the inaccuracies and waveform distortions of these low-level signals must be addressed.

Dithering provides a means to more accurate recording at low levels. Noise combines with the signal in a way that increases the overall amplitude, therefore realizing greater accuracy through increased bits. In fact, dither enables the encoding of amplitudes smaller than the LSB.

Dither combines with the outgoing digital signal for linearity of audio playback. Although it uses noise as an active part of the process, dithering is worthwhile considering the improvement it gives us in accuracy and linearity.

Dither is typically selected as a function at the input to the A/D converter or on its output. The correlation between error and signal can be removed through the addition of dither prior to the A/D converter. Therefore, the effects of quantization error are randomized. Dither doesn't simply mask the artifacts; it removes them.

Dithering is typically left for the final stage of production and is reserved for producing mastered recordings at lower bit depths than the original. For example, it is recommended that the mix engineer provide 24-bit digital audio files to the mastering engineer; since standard Red Book CD audio specifies 16-bit audio, the mastered audio should include dither when rendering down to 16-bit audio from 24-bit audio. Dither should not be used at other stages of the tracking and

Dither

Dither is simply white noise added to the program source at very low levels (typically half the least significant bit). Though it seems ironic to add noise to an otherwise noiseless system, the inaccuracies and waveform distortions of these low-level signals must be addressed.

Success is achieved through the combination of the lowest-level bit with specific noise. The noise fuses with low-level digital signal in a way that results in noise blocks rather then stair steps (the simple 1,0,1,0 ... sequence in the digital realm translates to a square wave in the analog domain, so it is necessary that it is smoothed and masked). When these blocks are converted to analog, the result is the average of the level across the time axis. The average closely approximates a smooth waveform. This is far different from what would have been a very inaccurate and grainy-sounding facsimile of the original waveform. Dither, though introducing noise, provides a means to more accurate and pleasing audio at low digital levels.

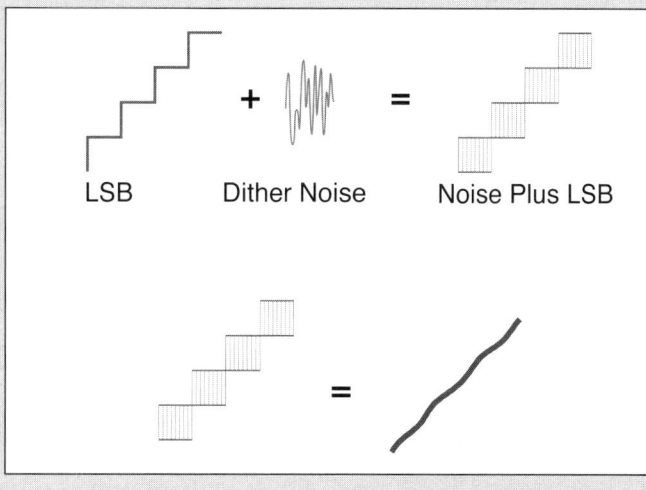

When converted and averaged over time, the combined dither low-level bit blocks closely approximate a smoothly rising analog signal.

mixdown process. Use of dither too early in the recording process promises only to add unnecessary noise to a recording.

It's interesting to note that, frequently, preamp noise or other resident noise in the recording chain is sufficient to perform the same function as dithering. Also, files that remain in an HD format such as 96 kHz/24-bit do not require dithering because the least significant bit is sufficiently far below an audible level.

A SYSTEMATIC APPROACH TO THE MASTERING PROCESS

In *Desktop Mastering* by Steve Turnidge, published by Hal Leonard Books, the author recommends an eight-step process for mastering. It is a prescription for a thorough and efficient mastering workflow:

1. Low-end frequency control
2. Noise reduction
3. Stereo enhancement
4. Reverberation
5. De-essing
6. Multiband compression, expansion, and equalization
7. Look-ahead limiting, quantization, noise shaping, and dither
8. Visual analysis

SUMMARY

Mastering is a key part of the recording process. It is an art that requires a lot of decision-making, and it's always best if those decisions are made according to some serious experience and an accurate listening environment. Take the information and suggestions contained in this book and practice mastering. Master a song, and then listen to it everywhere you can. Make notes on anything you hear that could make the song sound better. Then go back and remaster to see whether you can beat your first try. If you have some friends who would enjoy helping with the process, test your mastering out on them. Either master their music or have them critically evaluate yours.

This is an art that greatly benefits from a sonically accurate room and from meticulous electronic installation of very good gear. Wire matters. Power matters. Experience matters. Musical taste matters. The more you master music, the more you have to offer in the process.

Learn to be a musical chameleon. Don't hang on one style. Learn what they all sound like and adjust your approach accordingly. Although you'll develop some go-to settings and signal chains, it's best to listen to each song with a fresh perspective, being open to the exact techniques that will help each piece of music sound best and that will build an entire album that is cohesive and compelling.

Jazz is obviously different from hip-hop, just like western is different from metal. The more musically informed you become, the better job you'll do on a wider range of projects. Do your homework; learn what's expected from each genre and style; and practice, practice, practice!

CHAPTER TEST

1. Mastering entails many _____ combined with many _____.
   a. years of practice, meters and gauges
   b. technical decisions, subjective choices
   c. people working together, lucky guesses
   d. All of the above

2. The mastering engineer listens for consistent _____ from song to song.
   a. equalization
   b. levels
   c. tonality
   d. All of the above
   e. Both a and b

3. Mastering engineers can pinpoint specific instruments and EQ them separately from the rest of the mix.
   a. True
   b. False

4. _____ and _____ are commonly used during mastering.
   a. Limiting, compression
   b. Reverberation, ambience
   c. Delay, ringing out
   d. Dynamics, effects

5. If the mastering engineer sets the limiter for 6 dB of gain reduction, then the net gain in level can be as much as 12 dB.
   a. True
   b. False

6. A good mastering engineer creates a flow where the songs actually _____ in level throughout the album.
   a. increase radically
   b. decrease slightly
   c. increase and then decrease slightly
   d. increase slightly

7. There should be _____ considerations that drive the decisions on spacing between songs during mastering.
   a. continuity
   b. flow
   c. managerial
   d. legal
   e. Both a and b

8. If a very slow song follows a very fast song, it's typically a good idea to leave a little _____ after the slow song.
   a. more space
   b. less space
   c. more fade
   d. less fade

9. The biggest advantage to hiring an experienced mastering engineer is:
   a. cost
   b. nothing
   c. competitive edge
   d. sonic purity

10. One of the essential factors in successful mastering is:
    a. a strong manager
    b. a finely tuned, finely designed listening environment
    c. a great guitar part
    d. a rock-solid drum part

Chapter 10 .... MASTERING

11. Be sure that your monitor environment is _____.
    a. trustworthy
    b. dependable
    c. clean
    d. smoke-free
    e. Both a and b

12. Non-powered monitors tend to become _____ accurate over long periods of use.
    a. less
    b. more
    c. pretty
    d. very

13. If your control room is acoustically accurate, monitor at _____.
    a. 65 to 75 dB SPL
    b. 0 VU
    c. 95 to 105 dB SPL
    d. 85 to 90 dB SPL

14. _____ is optimized for a full-bandwidth source at levels exceeding 85 dB.
    a. C-weighting
    b. B-weighting
    c. A-weighting
    d. D-weighting

15. A(n)_____ scale more closely reflects perceived volume.
    a. C-weighted
    b. B-weighted
    c. A-weighted
    d. D-weighted

16. In mastering, _____ is a frequently preferred audio format because of its silky-smooth warmth.
    a. digital
    b. analog
    c. vinyl
    d. cassette

17. LSB stands for:
    a. last sibilance band
    b. least significant bit
    c. least significant band
    d. lazy stinking bandmember

18. Because digital audio is data and not imprinted magnetism, digital-interconnect cables have no effect on the sound quality of digital masters and clones.
    a. True
    b. False

19. The frequencies around 18 to 20 kHz are often referred to as _____, and they add greatly to the feel of the mix.
    a. highs
    b. sizzle
    c. air
    d. sweetness

20. Some engineers like to master while referencing:
    a. an old Elvis record
    b. a real-time analyzer
    c. a compressor
    d. the tango

Test answers are on page 299

Index

Symbols
0 dBFS 241, 242, 275
0 VU 31, 32, 35, 242
1/3-octave graphic equalizer 267
+4 dBm 26
-10 dBV 26
16-bit 34, 78, 94, 123, 187, 284
24-bit 78, 123, 187, 284
31-band graphic EQ 43, 67, 267

A
AAC 57, 243
absolute index 283
absorption 58, 60
acoustic guitar 103, 141, 143, 146, 157, 198, 210, 258, 259
acoustics 58, 60, 251
　accumulations 60
　ambience 84
　considerations 250
　dimensions 58
　environment 57
　interaction 53, 58
Acoustic Sciences Corporation 59, 60
AES/EBU 22
AIFF 92, 243
air 263
AKG 216
album 242
　master 225
　version 227
Alesis ADAT 220
alignment 29, 33
ambience 232
ambient chamber 139
Ampex ATR-100 21
amplitude 79
analog 20, 180, 221
　2-track 32
　domain 227
　equipment 10, 15
　tape speed 45
analyzer 43
Antares 150, 256
　Mic Modeler 214
Aphex Dominator 43
API 221
Apogee 13
apparent loudness 77
Apple Lossless 243
arrangement 74, 118, 157, 216

audible spectrum 210, 267, 283
audio image 116
audio post production 94
Audio-Technica 214
　4047 215
Auratones 54, 62
auto latch 167
automation 5, 10, 148, 163, 165, 166, 167, 176, 183, 184
　absolute mode 167
　auto read 167
　auto touch 167
　computer-assisted 10
　dynamic 166
　moving-fader 164, 170
　pan 169
　snapshot 166
　Total Recall 165
　VCA-based 163, 167
auto-save 173
Auto-Tune 150, 155
aux bus 153
Avalon 203, 214
Avantones 54
average level 187
A-weighting 253
axial standing wave 59

B
backing vocals 93, 154, 205
balance 82, 219, 225
bandwidth 133, 136, 182, 204, 258
basic tracks 156
bass 74, 112, 132, 154
　sound 140
bass frequencies 140
bass guitar 79, 131, 212
Beatles 144
believability 73
bias 18, 33
Big Ben 13
bit errors 255
Black Flag 194
blend 89, 99, 152, 197
　vocal 207
blues singer 151
Blu-ray 184
BMS Chase 8
bounce 184, 186, 220
bounce to disk 11, 15, 39, 220
broadband spectrum 131

building the arrangement 79
burst errors 255

C
cable 257, 258
　speaker 256
　sync 13
　theory 256
calibrate 33
calibrated microphone 67
calibration tape 32
cassette 226, 238
CCD 8
CD 22, 184, 226, 238
　burner 284
　master 283
　mastering 278
　media 278
　write-once 280
CD/DVD Media 36
CD/DVD recorder 186
CD-MO 280
CD-Plus 281
CD-R 91
CD±R 37
CD-R media 37
CD-ROM 37, 281
　mode 1 280
　mode 2 280
CD-RW 37
CD standard
　Green Book 280
　Orange Book 280
　Red Book 278
　Scarlet Book 279
　White Book 281
　Yellow Book 280
center position 124
center surround channel 218
chord comping 156
chorus 90, 143
chromatic 151
cleaning and demagnetizing 30
cleaning solution 29
cleaning tape 26
client-artist relationship 94
clock source 13
clone 254
codec 243
combining EQ 79, 130
combining sounds 119
commercial music 247

comp 157, 158
Compact Disc Digital Audio Standard 279
comparison 69
compression 85, 86, 89, 90, 141, 152, 155, 183, 202, 275
  attack time 90, 142, 152, 202
  extreme 152
  ratio 142, 202
  release time 90, 142, 152
  threshold 142, 152, 277
compressor 88, 147, 152, 203
  stereo 89, 155
  Universal Audio 1176 203, 212
computer-based recorder 26
computer system 163, 191
concealment 256
conceptualizing 1
concert hall 103
condenser 84, 108
conductance 257
conductor 257
congas 140
console 165
Content Creator Data Collection Tool 8
contrast 77
controller data 170
controlling dynamics 79
control room 54, 60, 210, 250
  design 53
control surface 181
converters 178
counter 26
country music 86
cowbell 113
creative boundaries 129
creative freedom 75
crossed bidirectional configuration 107
crossfade tool 235
crossover 252
  circuitry 50
cross-reference 68, 83, 93
Cubase 178
C-weighting 253
cyanine dye 37
cylinder 226
cymbals 137, 138, 140, 161

D

dance mix 227
DAT 34, 185, 254
data 184
  audio 92
  compression 57
  loss 36
  storage 279
  transfer 23
DAW 6, 10, 17, 21, 67, 91, 145, 148, 167, 168, 173, 176, 181, 184, 186, 206, 220, 226, 236, 265
dBFS 187
dbx 20, 26, 203, 215
DCA 89
Death Cab for Cutie 144
decibel 247, 275
  meter 253
decode 26
de-esser 264, 276
delay 43, 82, 99, 114, 120, 121, 144, 156, 208, 213, 215
  slapback 144, 153, 205, 215
  stereo 153
delivery standard 226
demagnetizer 27
depth and sound quality 118
Desktop Mastering 286
Diana Krall 194
diatonic 151
diffusion 60
digital 180
  audio network 24
  audio workstation 178
  clock 13
  console 167
  delay 43, 120, 123
  domain 40, 227
  editing 235
  equalizer 182
  format 22, 226
  format converter 22
  interconnect cables 260
  levels 78
  master 227, 240
  meter 34
  mixer 87, 165, 170, 178, 184
  modeling 256
  network 13
  recordings 255
  technology 253
  workstation 239
Digital Performer 178
dimension 216
dimensional ratios 58
directionality 100
directional realism 100
disc-at-once mode 279
disc longevity 37
disco smile 211
distortion 48, 144
Distressor 203
dither 284
  noise shaping 283
Dolby 20, 25
  AC-3 243
  B 25
  C 25
  Digital 222
  SR 25
doubling 143, 214
download 226
downmix 222
  automatic 222
Drawmer 203
drum machine 39, 137, 139, 140
drums 74, 116, 139, 154, 160, 213
  live 136
  overhead mics 89, 137
drum sound 196, 214
drum track 89, 134
dry 119, 124, 214
DSD 279
DTS 221, 243
dubbing machine 35
dubs 42
duplicate 226
duplication 247, 274
  facility 42
DVD 22, 184
DVD-Audio 185, 222, 226
DVD±R 37, 184
dye
  phthalocyanine 46
dynamic expression 134
dynamic range 20, 43, 77, 88, 147, 186, 220
dynamics 194, 221
dynamics processor 89

E

ear fatigue 48
East Coast sound 86

edgy sound 81, 132, 207, 210
edit
  30-degree 230
  45-degree 230
  90-degree 230
  bin 233
  button 231
  decision list 165
  placements 233
  point 231, 233, 235
  razorblade 228, 230
edit-capable mix recorder 228
edited master 35
EDL 165
effects 43, 83, 124, 129, 143, 221
  parameters 165
  processor 141, 176, 180
  stereo chorus 125, 128
egg cartons 58
electric bass guitar 89
electric guitar 79, 143, 144, 145, 197, 212
electronic crossover 50
emotional performance 149
emotional power 150
Empirical Labs 203
  Distressor 213
EMT plate 215
encode 26
engineer 116
  tracking 225
enhancer 43
equalization 29, 81, 132, 166, 197, 203, 206, 214, 221, 247, 254, 263
Eric Clapton 212
error correction 254, 256
error rate 36, 240
Ethernet 221
Euphonix 170
exciter 153
expander 152, 183
experimentation 118

F
fade out 158, 185, 187
fader 166
Faith Ecklund 197
Faith Hill 215
far-field monitors 83, 140
fast-forward 38
fast-rewind 38

Fender 197
fidelity 77
fills 158
film and video 116
filter 219
finalize 186
final mixdown 40, 90, 103
  versions 90
FLAC 243
flanger 125, 128, 143
flat room response 68
flow 83
flutter echo 60
flux 32
fluxivity 32
foam 58
focal point 74, 75, 83, 147, 158
focus 83
Focusrite 203
Focusrite Red series 203
Foley 94
Free Lossless Audio Codec 243
frequency 182
  band 131
  content 53
  range 129, 147, 252
  response 47, 251
  spectrum 201
full-range system 159
Full Scale 187

G
gain 142
  reduction 152, 202, 275
  structure 272
  trim 179
gate
  range 152
gating 136, 183
generation 185
  loss 254
generator 30
gigabit Ethernet 221
Glimpse 197
global panorama 99
gospel 87
graphic EQ 43
grease pencil 229, 230
guitar 86, 112, 119, 120, 132, 144, 157, 172, 176, 197, 214

H
Haas effect 123
hard drive 22, 26, 184, 254
hardware 265
harsh timbre 81
HD format 285
head gap 229
headphones 57, 82, 193
  leakage 180
head position 33
headroom 34, 275
heads 27
hi-fi 238
high-frequency ringing 58
high-pass filter 136, 143, 147, 204, 207, 272
highs 138, 274
hiss 238
home hi-fi stereo 91
home theater 56
home user 252
honky 210
humidity 38
Husky Huskolds 202

I
idlers 27
image 113
  vocal 204
  widen 125
image files 283
imbalance 113
impedance 26
inaccurate mixing space 57
Incubus 144
indexes 248, 279, 283
input levels 33
input meters 33
inserts 179
instrumental solo 80, 159
intelligibility 199, 204, 207
interface
  video 165
interleaving 255
internal calibration level adjustments 33
International Standard Recording Code 281
International Telecommunications Union 65
interpolation 256
intimacy 88

intonation 149, 155, 205
intro 90, 158
iPod 57
ips 22, 45
isopropyl alcohol 29
ISRC 281
ITU 65
iTunes 186
iZotope 265

J
Jamie Dieveney 198
jitter 13
Juno 106 146
Jupiter 8 146

K
karaoke 93
keyboard 120, 145, 156, 157
kick drum 131, 132, 135, 137, 160, 213, 214
Kodak 37

L
laptop computer 80, 193
large hall sound 118
layering 119
LCRS surround 65
lead vocal 74, 88, 89, 94, 119, 147, 152, 154, 159, 199, 201, 202, 204, 214
leakage 136, 180
least significant bit 255
LED 43, 267
Les Paul 145, 213
level 35
  control 205
    digital recorder 34
    setting 40
levels
  blending 79
LFE 218, 219
LFO 213
Library of Congress 8
light pipe 261
limiter 86, 88, 183, 209, 275
  multiband 274
  peak 274
Line 6 197
linearity 284
listening environment 56, 250, 251
listening experience 218

live performance 73
localization 100, 113
locate point 181
London 87
lossless 243
lossy compression 243
low frequencies 81
  accumulation 80
low-frequency band 132
Low Frequency Effects 218
low-frequency response 54
lows 138
LSB 255, 284
lyric 77, 189
  sheet 5
lyrical intensity 200

M
Mac 174
magnetic
  strength 32
  tape 36
  tape recorder 29
magnetism 29
main mix bus 69
maintenance technician 29
major scale 151
Manley 203, 214
marimba 118
markers 181
Marshall 197
masking artifacts 284
master
  analog 237
  recording 225, 228
  reel 42
mastering 88, 225, 247, 251, 286
  engineer 86, 219, 221, 237, 238, 247, 248, 249, 262, 265, 269
  environment 278
  post 249
  process 77, 269
  session 239
  software 249
master mix 94, 242
  level 140
Matchless 197
maximum level 34
MDM 220
mechanical adjustment 42
media imperfections 255
melody 206
Melodyne 155

M&E mix 94
Mesa 197
  Triple Rectifier 213
metadata 7
Metallica 144
meters
  output 32
microphone
  choice 153
  omnidirectional 140
  technique 102, 141
microphones
  tom 161
microphonic tube 214
mic technique
  MS (mid-side) 104, 107, 108
  spaced omni pair 106
  stereo 104
  X-Y configuration 104, 107
MIDI 10, 170, 176, 180
  automated mutes 136
  controllable parameter 40
  data 164
  interface 40, 41
  parameters 145
  sequence 39
  time code 165
midrange 81, 138, 264, 274
Minor Threat 194
mix
  analog 226
  editor 171
  image 54
  ingredient 146, 176
  level 77, 79, 88, 131, 132, 186, 211
  pop 202
  position 54
  procedure 179
  processor 165
  rough 90
  sheet 10
  stereo 82, 208
  TV 93
  two dimensional 82
MixCube 55
mixdown 1, 5, 17, 31, 40, 43, 52, 68, 73, 83, 87, 88, 89, 90, 119, 125, 129, 133, 134, 141, 142, 145, 147, 150, 153, 172, 199, 212, 214, 220, 225, 247, 276
  accuracy 54

automation 170, 182
data 165
density 193
engineer 53, 57, 75, 77, 86, 132, 156, 211, 225
environment 47, 58, 126
format 219, 237
machine 32, 90
parameters 158
recorder 11, 24, 33, 34, 35
technique 68, 71, 264
techniques 193
versions 90, 91, 93
  master mix 92
  TV mix 92
  vocals down 92
  vocals up 92
mixdown machine
  analog 34
mixed master 35
mixer 179
  analog 163
  format 220
  line 221
  output 34
  status 172
mixing 42, 88, 251
  in the box 10
  lead vocal 204
  panorama 83
  skills 91
Mogami 259
momentum 77, 82
monitor
  powered 50
  switcher 56
monitors 57, 99, 103, 124, 126, 128, 135, 253
  choice 47
  environment 252
  far-field 48, 53, 54
  inexpensive 50
  large 80
  mid-field 48
  near-field 47, 48, 53, 56, 62, 83, 103, 126, 140
  non-powered 252
  radio-like 83
  self-powered 252
  small 54, 80
  studio 39, 50, 139
mono 82, 104, 110, 114, 120, 123, 125, 143, 208

Monster Cable 257
most significant bit 255
motion 83
MP3 57, 226, 243
MPEG 281
MSB 255
MTC 165
multi-effects processor 42
multitrack 17, 24, 40, 165, 220, 236
  analog 24, 32, 40, 91
  master 25, 225
  recorder 33, 167
musical
  arrangement 90
  arranger 156
  feel 74
  flow 73
music merchandiser 52
mute 76, 163, 166, 180, 191, 256

N
nanoWeber 32
Nashville sound 86
natural acoustic sound 100
Nelly 213
Nelly Furtado 214
network 221
Neumann
  U47 214, 215
  U67 213, 215
  U87 215
Neve 203, 212, 221
noise 43, 76, 220
  floor 152
  reduction 26
Norah Jones 194, 200, 202
normalize 269, 271
NTSC 280

O
OBX 146
octave 135
onscreen faders 170
operating level 26, 240
operating system 174
operational procedures 172
optical
  cable 261
  format 22
optical cartridge 184, 254
orchestration 157

oscillator 30, 31, 33, 35
OS X 221
Otari 21
outboard equipment 42, 180
overdrive 145
overloads 187
oversaturation 254

P
pad 119, 132, 156
pan 40, 73, 76, 111, 113, 116, 118, 120, 124, 129, 138, 166, 169, 176, 194, 197, 208, 225
  cymbals 139
  placement 103
  position 57, 84, 119
P and Q subcodes 281
parallel surfaces 59
parametric equalizer 43, 133, 135
parity 256
passive crossover 50
patch bay 179
peaks 79, 187, 248
percussion 74, 82, 106, 113, 138, 140, 198, 210
percussion parts 140
phase 122, 153, 257
  shifter 125, 128, 143
Philips 278
phthalocyanine dye 37, 46
piano 146, 186
pink-noise generator 67
pitch 150
  control 152
  manipulation 149
playback 95
  alignment 32
  electronics 240
  equalization 35
  head 231
  levels 18, 32
  machine 240
plug-in 177, 178, 265
  tuning 150, 151, 155
portable acoustic control 59
predelay 116, 118, 205
pre-master 276
Primacoustic 59, 60
processing
  power 178
  signal 43, 81
processor
  settings 171

producer 129, 225
production experience 74
Prophet 5 146
Pro Tools 178
proximity 48
PRS 213
psychoacoustic 114
punching in 167

Q
Quadraphonic 65
quantization error 284

R
radio frequency interference 26
Rancid 194
razorblade 227, 232, 233, 235
  demagnetized 229
RCA
  cable 262
  connections 23
realism 84, 117
real-time analyzer 43, 67, 268
reamping 104, 139
recordable media 36
record alignment 33
record equalization 33
recorder
  analog 18, 26, 27, 29, 33, 211
record head 20, 231
recording
  device 181
  environment 60
  hardware 12
  process 87
record levels 33
redundancy 256
reel-to-reel 29, 238
reference fluxivity 32
reference levels 32
reference mix 221
reference tones 31, 32, 33, 35, 242
  1-kHz 31, 35, 42
  10-kHz 32, 42
  100-Hz 32, 42
  analog recorder 30
  digital recorder 32
reflection 58, 200, 216
  characteristic 58
  problems 60
relative index 283
remix 227

replication 226, 253, 259
reproducer calibration tape 32
resolution 192
reverberation 43, 80, 99, 104, 114, 138, 144, 154, 204, 216, 272
  hall 120
  mono 114
  plate 138
  room 117
  stereo 114
RFI 26
rhythmic
  drive 147
  feel 195
  offbeats 233
rhythm section 88
RIAA 281
Rock Band 94
rock genre 144
room ambience 102
room mics 89
room sound 84
rotating head 26
routing 165
RTA 67, 266, 267
rubbing alcohol 29

S
SACD 185, 226
sample 22
  rate 185, 187
sample rate 94
SATB 206
Save As 173
SCMS 282
sel-sync 24
sequencing 39, 238
sequential digital recording mediums 255
Serial Copy Management System 282
session 156
shaping sound 117
Shure SM58 212
sibilance 152, 276
signal
  degradation 50
  level 187
  line-level 50
  path 50, 151
signal-to-noise ratio 20, 22, 255
simul-sync 24

sine wave 31, 32
slip tool 235
SMPTE 148, 165, 237, 240
  generator 40
  reader 41
  striping 40
  track 40
snapshot 5, 42, 171, 172
snare drum 114, 132, 136, 137, 138, 160, 215
solid-state 254
Solid State Logic 221
solo 93
solo licks 157, 158
solos 73
sonic character 84, 130, 254
sonic personality 145
sonic signature 195
Sony 216, 278
Sony Music Group 8
Sony/Philips Video-CD 281
sound
  module 4
  quality 118, 123, 220
  reinforcement 212
soundfield 120
soundscape 83, 89, 110, 116
sound shaping techniques 138
spacing 237, 248, 262
S/PDIF 22, 23, 262
special effects 183
specifications 42, 46
spectrum analyzer 43
splicing block 230, 234
splicing tape 229, 234
SSL 165, 204, 212
static charge 30
mute 169
Steely Dan 214
stems 94
stereo 53, 83, 99, 100, 112, 114, 123, 125, 143, 144, 218
  bus 33
  master 35
  meters 138
  mix bus 24, 33
  system 101
  width and fullness 123
stereo image 99, 103, 111, 112, 113, 114, 116, 118, 120, 122, 123, 126, 128, 272
Steve Turnidge 286
storage device 184

storage media 36
Stratocaster 145, 213
string pad 82
structure 74
Studer 20, 21
Studio One 178
style 129
sub-bass 54, 211
subcodes 248, 281
subgroup 5, 165
submix 94, 215
subwoofer 54, 56, 62, 66, 218, 219
summing to mono 121
Summit Audio 203
Super Audio CD 279
supply reel 27
surround 24, 53, 83, 99, 100, 144, 208, 216, 220, 221, 225
  5.1 63, 67, 100, 218, 242
  7.1 67, 100, 218
  7.2 64
  mix 10
  rear channels 218, 219
  track-assignment standards 221
S-VHS 220
sweet spot 53, 135
Switchfoot 202
symphony 186
sync 220
  master 13, 15
  sample-accurate 24
synchronize 236
synth 146, 208, 271
  effects 146
  pad 131
system interface 170

T
tails out 38
Taiyo Yuden 37
take-up reel 228
tape
  analog 17, 21, 185, 220, 227, 229, 235, 237, 240, 253
  cassette 29
  damage 38
  dropouts 255
  edges 234
  formulations 36
  guides 27
  noise 152, 220
  path 27

shuttling 38
speed 22, 45
storage 37
tension 233
tape speed
  7-1/2 ips 231
  15 ips 22, 231
  30 ips 22, 231
Tascam DA-88 220
T-DIF 22
TDK 37
technical support 179
techno-dance 87
Telecaster 145
Teletronix LA-2A 203
tempo map 236
textural contrast 154
texture change 77
three-dimensional audio 114, 125, 128
tight room sound 118
timbre 119, 159
time code 26, 39, 40, 165, 166, 167, 181
Toast 186
toms 89, 136, 138
tonal character 107, 124
tonality 141
tonal response 58
total harmonic distortion 49
track 282
track-at-once mode 278
tracking 84, 88, 152, 156, 251
track list 3
track number 239, 279, 282
track sheet 3
trade magazines 126
trance 87
transient 48, 52, 123, 137, 161, 232, 258, 264, 272
trax 93
triangle 113
Trident 221
trim 4, 168
  input 5
tube sound 214, 215
Tubetech 203
Tube Trap 60, 251
tuning 144, 151

U
U2 200
understandability 206
undo 173
unity 168
Universal Music Group 8
Unix OS 174, 221

V
VCA 89, 164
VHS 26
vinyl 211, 226, 238
virtual instrument 163
visibility and clarity 123
visual image 125, 194
vocal sound 199, 207, 215
vocal track 89, 119, 149, 180, 209, 276
  group 209
  level changes 148
  performance 147
voice 219
voltage-controlled amplifier 164
voltage-controlled motor 164
VU meter 33, 34, 183, 186

W
Walt Disney's Fantasia 63
WAV 92, 243
Waves 265
  L3 Multimaximizer 275
Weber 32
West Coast sound 86
Windows 174
woofer 39, 263

X
XT20 220

Y
YouTube 226

Z
zeroing 42

Test Answers

Chapter 1

1. b
2. c
3. c
4. d
5. a
6. b
7. b
8. e
9. a
10. d
11. b
12. b
13. c
14. a
15. a
16. d
17. b
18. a
19. b
20. e

Chapter 2

1. a
2. d
3. a
4. a
5. b
6. d
7. b
8. a
9. e
10. c
11. e
12. b
13. e
14. a
15. a
16. b
17. b
18. c
19. a
20. b

Chapter 3

1. b
2. a
3. b
4. b
5. c
6. c
7. a
8. a
9. d
10. a
11. b
12. a
13. d
14. c
15. c
16. e
17. a
18. e
19. c
20. b

Chapter 4

1. a
2. d
3. b
4. c
5. e
6. a
7. c
8. d
9. d
10. b
11. b
12. a
13. d
14. c
15. d
16. b
17. a
18. c
19. c
20. e

Chapter 5

1. a
2. c
3. c
4. e
5. c
6. a
7. e
8. a
9. e
10. c
11. d
12. d
13. b
14. a
15. a
16. d
17. e
18. b
19. b
20. e

Chapter 6

1. a
2. c
3. d
4. c
5. a
6. a
7. a
8. a
9. e
10. b
11. a
12. d
13. c
14. a
15. a
16. e
17. b
18. d
19. a
20. b

Chapter 7

1. .... e
2. .... b
3. .... d
4. c
5. .... d
6. .... a
7. .... a
8. .... b
9. .... d
10. ...... a
11. ...... b
12. c
13. ...... b
14. ...... d
15. ...... e
16. ...... a
17. c
18. ...... a
19. ...... d
20. c

Chapter 8

1. .... a
2. .... d
3. .... b
4. .... d
5. .... b
6. c
7. .... b
8. c
9. .... e
10. ...... b
11. ...... a
12. c
13. ...... b
14. ...... e
15. ...... a
16. ...... b
17. ...... a
18. ...... a
19. ...... b
20. ...... e

Chapter 9

1. .... d
2. c
3. .... d
4. .... b
5. .... b
6. .... b
7. .... b
8. .... a
9. c
10. ...... a
11. c
12. ...... e
13. ...... b
14. ...... e
15. ...... a
16. c
17. ...... e
18. ...... a
19. ...... b
20. ...... a

Chapter 10

1. .... b
2. .... e
3. .... b
4. .... a
5. .... b
6. .... d
7. .... e
8. .... a
9. c
10. ...... b
11. ...... e
12. ...... a
13. ...... d
14. ...... a
15. c
16. ...... b
17. ...... b
18. ...... b
19. c
20. ...... b

The Entire Recording Process Explained!

The Hal Leonard Recording Method by Bill Gibson is the first professional multimedia recording method to take readers from the beginning of the signal path to the final master mix.

ALL BOOKS INCLUDE

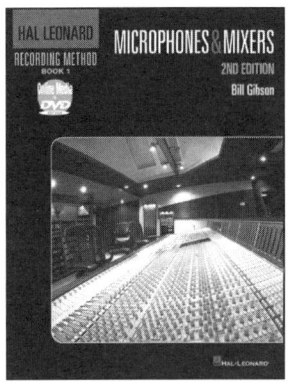

BOOK 1: MICROPHONES & MIXERS – 2ND EDITION
Revised and Updated

Topics include how professional microphones work, which to choose and why (plus accepted techniques for using them), understanding the signal path from mics to mixers and how to operate these critical tools to capture excellent recordings, and explanations of the most up-to-date tools and techniques involved in using dynamics and effects processors.

HL00333253 Book/DVD Pack $39.99
978-1-45840-296-7

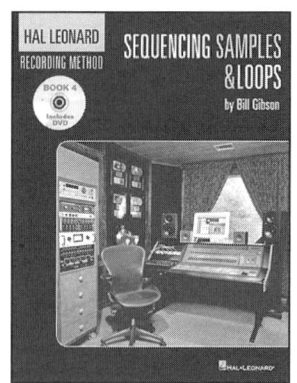

BOOK 4: SEQUENCING SAMPLES & LOOPS

Learn to create amazing music productions using the latest sequencing techniques with samples and pre-recorded loops. With detailed screen shots, illustrations, video and audio examples, and more on the accompanying DVD, you're on your way to rounding out your recording education.

HL00331776 Book/DVD Pack ... $39.95
978-1-42343-051-3

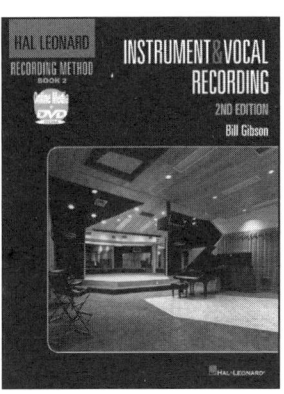

BOOK 2: INSTRUMENT & VOCAL RECORDING – 2ND EDITION
Revised and Updated

This edition addresses new equipment and software concerns that affect the way excellent recordings are made. You'll learn what you need to know about capturing the best vocal and instrument tracks possible, no matter what kind of studio you are working in or what kind of equipment is used.

HL00333250 Book/DVD Pack $39.99
978-1-45840-292-9

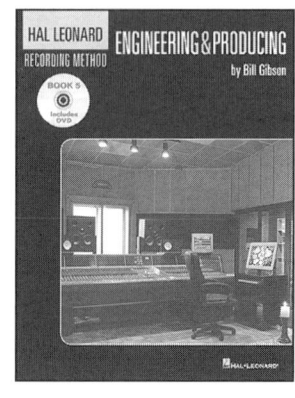

BOOK 5: ENGINEERING & PRODUCING

Learn what it takes to engineer a session like a pro, combining the teaching of the previous books to record excellent tracks ready for the mix. This book also dives into what makes a producer great, how to inspire awesome performances from the musicians you record, tricks for selecting the best tracks from your sessions, and what it takes to be both producer and engineer on the same session.

HL00331777 Book/DVD Pack ... $39.95
978-1-42343-052-0

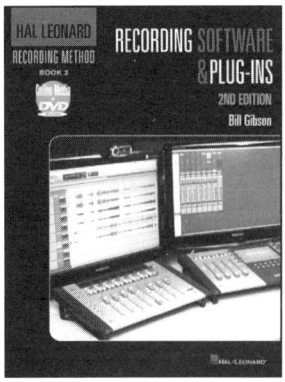

BOOK 3: RECORDING SOFTWARE & PLUG-INS – 2ND EDITION
Revised and Updated

Once you've learned how to use microphones and mixers, and to record instruments and vocals, you'll need to know how recording software programs work and how to choose and optimize your recording system. This book and DVD use detailed illustrations and screen shots, plus audio and video examples, to give you a comprehensive understanding of recording software and plug-ins.

HL00333437 Book/DVD Pack $39.99
978-1-45841-651-3

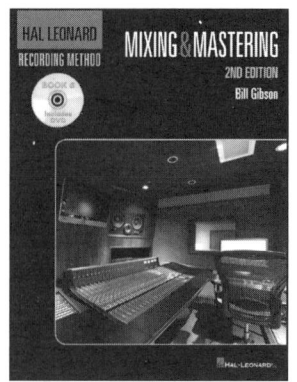

BOOK 6: MIXING & MASTERING – 2ND EDITION
Revised and Updated

This important second edition demonstrates techniques and procedures that result in a polished mix and powerful master recording, using current plug-ins, software, and hardware. You'll then learn how to prepare the mastered recording for CD replication, streaming, or download. Updated illustrations, photographs, and audio and video examples on the accompanying DVD will reinforce your understanding of what you need to mix and master like the pros.

HL00333254 Book/DVD Pack ... $39.99
978-1-45840-297-4

www.halleonardbooks.com